The White Stripe[s] at the legendary Gold Do[...]

The Hamtramck
Blowout

Jack White with
the Go

Jack White performing with
John Hentch of the Hentchmen
at Jacoby's in Detroit, MI., Spring 2002

Release Party for De Stijl

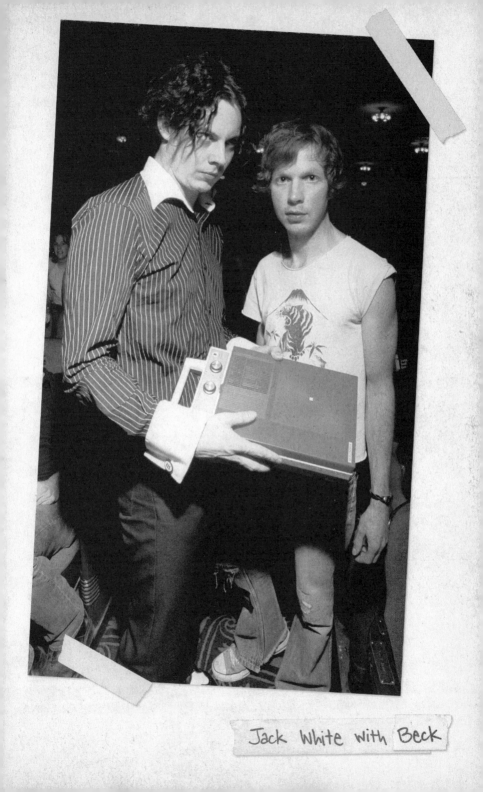

Jack White with Beck

Fell in Love with a Band

Fell in Love with

St. Martin's Griffin ≋ New York

a Band:
The Story of the White Stripes

Chris Handyside

www.stmartins.com

Photos by Doug Coombe
Illustration on page xi by Darin Overholser (www.illustratorguy.com)

Book design by Irene Vallye

Library of Congress Cataloging-in-Publication Data

Handyside, Chris.
    Fell in love with a band : the story of the White Stripes / Chris Handyside.—
1st U.S. ed.
       p. cm.
     ISBN 0-312-33618-7
     EAN 978-0312-33618-9
     1. White Stripes (Musical group) 2. Rock musicians—United States—
Biography. I. Title.

   ML421.W49H36 2004
   782.42166'092'2—dc22

                                                                        2004048697

First Edition: September 2004

10 9 8 7 6 5 4 3 2 1

For Kelly, Nolan, and Elliot

Acknowledgments

Jack and Meg White, Becki Heller, Kim Goldstein, Matt, Lala, Willy, Tom and Linda, Fred and Claudia, Carol Falle, Driveway, Doug Coombe, Sneakers, The Wolf, Arthur Dettweiler, Kevin Twitch, Dave Garant, Alex Pappademas, Metro Times (Smith, Doster, Guyette, Cavalieri, et al.), George Tysh, Des Cooper, John and Tim, and the Dirtbombs.

An Introduction

On an unseasonably warm autumn day in downtown Detroit, I was standing on the corner of Woodward and Fort in the shadow of the three-story Soldiers and Sailors Monument. I was taking a break from work, grabbing a quick smoke, and searching in vain for a light when I was interrupted by a strange figure ducking behind a streetlamp across the street, like a kid blissfully unaware that his hiding spot is a dead giveaway. Jack White's healthy 6'1" frame is not easily hidden by a lamp-post. Grinning, I jogged over to meet him, confident that he'd have a light. He was not wearing red and white and thus passed through downtown Detroit as anonymously as any other underemployed twentysomething.

He asked after my family and I wondered aloud why he'd ventured into the heart of downtown's workaday office bustle. "I'm trying to find my bank," he said, a backpack-size satchel slung over his shoulder.

"What's in the bag?"

"English pounds!" he grinned, trilling the letters with an arch-Dickensian inflection.

That's when it hit me: The White Stripes had just returned, critical and pop culture conquerors, from their much-ballyhooed second tour of the British Isles. The guy whose face could be seen scowling mysteriously from tabloid and music rag covers throughout Britain was standing in the center of the Murder Capital of the U.S. (or whatever other dangerous appellation they want to assign to the city), with a bag full of cash, not exactly sure where he was headed.

Somehow the only comment I could muster was the beyond-obvious question "how'd the tour go?" and the equally insightful "awesome" at his enthusiastic recap. I pointed him in the direction of the bank, a forty-story office building with the institution's name written in ten-foot letters on the side, and he went bounding off down Woodward Avenue, half in the middle of the traffic lane.

Within a year, the White Stripes would capture the imagination of the MTV nation, become the de facto figureheads of the so-called guitar rock revival, sign a record deal that would allow them to never have to work a day job ever again, buoy the tiny downtown Detroit rock scene from which they sprang into the national critical spotlight, and record the album that would propel Jack and Meg uncomfortably into the ranks of celebrity. But for the moment at least, Jack White was happy running through the streets of his hometown like a kid playing hooky.

The White Stripes are the make-good story of the Detroit music scene, the band that all of the still-struggling music fanatics that comprise the community point to when they need inspiration. They're the make-good story for indie rock in the early 2000s—the band that stuck to their independent guns and succeeded. And they are utterly impossible to duplicate. Despite the music industry's best efforts to shoehorn in a "garage rock" movement on the Stripes' coattails and try to make platinum lightning strike twice, Jack and Meg remain sublimely singular.

The definitive history of the White Stripes is impossible to tell. Jack and Meg have designed their little room to include all sorts of false-bottomed drawers, trick bookcases, and secret cubbies hidden in the dark corners of the closet so that it would be nigh-on-impossible to sort through all the stuff to achieve the definitive story. Besides, sorting the White Stripes into neat little piles takes away the mystery that lies at the center of this little band that could. They rightly (at least in part) get credit for bringing back an awareness of guitar-based rock 'n' roll to the pop charts after a ten-year absence. They've also resurrected the good names of—and posthumous interest in—a handful of blues performers so old that they'd slipped into unspoken legend. Jack White even produced a vital, critically adored, major label record with Loretta Lynn (occasioned by an offhand mention in the liner notes to the Stripes' *White Blood Cells*). Pre-Jack, Lynn may have been content to tour casinos and manage her Tennessee tourist attraction-cum-homestead. And without White, the music-loving world may have been content to keep listening to "Coalminer's Daughter," "Rated X," and "The Pill," but White couldn't leave well enough alone. And the results were typically Jack White—an iconoclastic synthesis of country and rock in the service of Lynn's legendary voice. As you may or may not have heard, the White Stripes carefully drew the boundaries of their own spot on the map of Detroit's storied musical history, and then—with the sympathetic sound of Detroit compilation—invited as many buddies as would fit into White's attic to lay down the definitive sound of garage rock in Detroit and enjoy the fruits of the land. But the White Stripes' importance, if indeed they go down in history as anything other than a curious footnote, may well be measured by their ability to return a sense of mystery to rock 'n' roll. Now this is no mean feat, especially in an era of instant information that's become terminally obsessed with knowing the eating, sleeping, and mating habits of its canon of temporary media saints. The White Stripes are, if nothing else, an exercise in control. Even if Jack and Meg were once husband and wife, the White Stripes will always be brother and sister.

It's too early to pass any kind of judgment on the White Stripes. They may or may not be the kind of band that kids refer to as "seminal" when they grow up to be smug music critics. And as we all know, each and every one has a wee bit of saint and a wee bit of devil within them, with the remainder fleshed out by conflict. The White Stripes—Jack and Meg, to be specific—are certainly no exception.

In fact, they are a case in point, and that's one of the things that makes them so interesting. They acknowledge the fact that they're in conflict, but also actively aspire to be saints while indulging their inner devils. They engage, to paraphrase their lyric, in every way and leave the ironic detachment to the less imaginative artist. In that sense, they're very much a product of the modernism that characterized the art world around the time of their hometown's heyday in the 1940s and '50s. Yes, as people they are aware that the world has moved on. They enjoy the *Onion* and, gasp, Meg even has a cellular telephone. But the art they create together is something, as Woody Allen said in introducing *What's Up Tiger Lily?*, "wholly other."

Fell in Love with a Band

One Sweaty Night in Hamtown

Jack White took a step away from the microphone and a slight smile crept across his face, eventually giving way to a Cheshire grin. Both he and his red guitar had stopped singing—his amp simply hummed. Just behind him, Meg White sat idle at her borrowed drum kit, her right elbow crooked on her right knee as she flashed her own take on the Mona Lisa smile, visibly bemused.

They weren't done playing by a long shot, but for a moment, they didn't have to utter a word or strike a single note. On that Saturday night, March 13, 1999—the second night of a local rock music festival called the Hamtramck Blowout—it was enough for Jack and Meg to watch and listen. They listened to the two-hundred and fifty sweaty, drunken souls who packed into Paycheck's Lounge—a grotty dive in the middle of Hamtramck—sing every word (loudly) of the tender, cryptic song "Sugar Never Tasted So Good," a track from the B-side of their sophomore single, produced by the tiny local imprint, Italy Records. They looked out onto the faces of the local musicians and pals who comprised the core of Detroit's vibrant rock scene, grinning as the suddenly plentiful hipsters from the suburbs serenaded the band that had, until that point, been accurately described as Detroit's best-kept secret.

The pool table in the back by the video games and the jukebox had been covered with a plank of plywood and a few people had found their perch there. Even the grizzled regulars, who usually took up residence at the bar Monday afternoon through Sunday night, were forced to either stand by the door and watch in glassy-eyed bemusement, or go home for the evening.

It was half past midnight and the bar had run out of local brauswill, Stroh's. But for a fleeting moment, proprietor Johnny Paycheck—who for the past fifteen years had seen bands shitty, adventurous, and run-of-the-mill grace his rickety stage four nights a week—didn't seem to care. Sure, it was his name above the door, but the White Stripes owned the joint. And they hadn't even put out a record yet.

It was enough to make you forget that in just two hours, after the Hentchmen had to follow the White Stripes onto the stage, Paycheck's would once again be just another shitty local rock haunt. The White Stripes record label head, Dave Buick, was standing up front yelling "White Lines!!!"—a nod to the frequency with which the band's name was misprinted in bar ads. It is not hyperbole to say that the Stripes had the whole room in thrall, and that a majority of people in attendance— some of the forty or so local rockers included—would never get this close to the Stripes again.

Thing is, it almost didn't happen. Indeed, up until a couple days before the show, Meg White hadn't decided whether or not she wanted to continue in the White Stripes with her newly estranged husband. At the last minute, she had informed Jack that the White Stripes would take the stage. As Detroit radio jock Willy Wilson announced just prior to the Stripes taking the stage, "I've just been informed that this is not actually the White Stripes' last show." To which the crowd roared its approval. So one ending was narrowly avoided. It would have been, officially, the second band involving Jack White to have ended that weekend.

The previous evening, on the same stage, White had played the last show with country-punk outfit 2-Star Tabernacle. Later that night, at a techno club down the street that had been temporarily converted into a den of Detroit street rock iniquity, White would shed the red 'n' white duds of the Stripes for the more, er, rock, white 'n' black garb befitting the lead guitarist in Detroit street rock revivalists the Go— unfortunately he wouldn't last long in this band either.

In 2-Star, White shared singing, songwriting, and guitar duties with Dan Miller (a.k.a. D. Buell Miller, a.k.a. Old Man Miller, a.k.a. Goober), Miller's wife, Tracee, on bass, and drummer Damian Lange (who himself was doing double duty in scrappy R&B cover band the Detroit Cobras). Miller introduced the set, saying simply, "We're going to begin with a gospel number and end with a gospel number."

White was a wild-haired youngster, letting loose with his Robert

Plant meets Ethel Merman yelp—an unholy union of Johnny Rotten and that one guy in every half-baked band that thinks "this can totally work if we just practice four times a week!" Miller countered as the stern preacher in a three-piece suit, a full three inches taller than White (seven if you count the electric socket hair), and every bit a head-on crash between A. P. Carter and Lee Hazelwood. The band played to a three-quarter-filled but fully appreciative room, running its way through rejiggered Appalachian murder ballads by way of the Gun Club's sinister darkness like "Red Headed Girl," as well as edgy and darkly romantic country rock paens to the pitfalls of relationships, like Miller's "Who's to Say?" and White's "Hotel Yorba" and "The Union Forever"—all of which would appear later in these two fellas' careers.

Both Miller and White had grand ideas about what they wanted to do with the country music that so inspired them. Thing was, 2-Star Tabernacle was not the place for that to happen. 2-Star was what happens when you give guitars, amps, and microphones to two bright songwriters with strong personalities—the kind of eccentric dudes who could stop party conversation with an impression or a well-spun yarn whenever they so chose—and set them loose on the stage together.

The Go! was another story entirely. Put a mildly good-looking, charismatic frontman in front of a chugging rhythm section and punctuate it with seriously searing lead guitar. Add to the whole thing an absolutely bored populace of twentysomethings looking for a soundtrack to go with their kicks and a penchant for continuing the party until either the cops or the sun told them to stop and you've got the Go! The Go! weren't doing anything that Detroit street rock bands like Rocket 455 weren't doing half a dozen years earlier.

And Rocket wasn't doing anything the Stooges and the MC5 weren't doing twenty-five years prior. The difference was, most of the members of Rocket actually personally knew one of the members of the Stooges from doing time around the Detroit club circuit. Of course, with that basic formula for rock, you've also got—at its core—the Bob Seger System, Kid Rock, Poison, Aerosmith, and on and on.

Of course all of the aforementioned groups had someone burning with—for lack of a less-cliched term—the fire of rock 'n' roll. They were firing after something bigger than mere pop adulation.

The Go! of course, had Jack White. The buzz about the band had begun to build around Detroit's tiny rock scene long before White had signed on, but it reached epic proportions after he strapped on the six-string. Thing of it was, the band already had a frontman in the diminutive but strong-willed Bobby Harlow.

In March of 1999, the band had been successfully courted by Sub Pop Records and, in large part thanks to the early presence of Buick and White, it was the de rigueur show to catch if the offer was there on a Friday night.

But even when fans watched the Go! with their eyes clouded over by booze or made watery by cigarette smoke, they could see that White and Harlow were moving at two different speeds. And sometimes that tension works, but these two were on a collision course. When Friday night rolled around during the Blowout, the Go! were the midnight gig of choice for Detroit's hipster illuminati. You simply won't find an honest rock 'n' roll fan in the city who didn't think that was the band's peak line-up. There were maybe two hundred people squeezed into the joint and the band was playing a mere six inches above crowd level. They were careening off one another, both figuratively and literally. White—in his four-inch shoes—would lose himself in his riffery in front of the generally oblivious Buick only to get bounced into the diminutive and state-trooper-spec'd Harlow, who was nine times out of ten addressing his libidinous vocalisms to some lucky girl in the front row. Sure, he executed such classic rock star moves as the "langourous wrap your arms around the hunky guitar player" thing with White from time to time. But he was mostly keeping his eye on him, making sure the naturally charismatic White wasn't stealing too much of his spotlight. White seemed to sense this as he kept himself in his own world off to the side. And mostly Harlow would turn to Barre, the chord–blaring rhythm guitarist, and band cofounder John Krautner for onstage support. Meanwhile, drummer Mark Felis was the very portrait of Charlie Watts.

If 2-Star Tabernacle couldn't hold, the Go! was never meant to—at least not with Jack White as the lead guitarist. What the two groups had in common within the span of a year was the departure of one White who obviously had his eyes on bigger things—even if there was no way in hell anyone with an honest bone in their body would have predicted the extent to which the Stripes would succeed. If he wasn't willing to share the glory, he made it seem either (in the case of 2-Star) amicable or (in the case of the Go!) inevitable.

Either way, by the time the festival was over that Sunday morning, White would be playing solo at the Garden Bowl and thinking, if one should be allowed to offer conjecture on such things, the White Stripes were the only band that deserved his full attention.

Indeed, back to the White Stripes: If it weren't for the insistence of his estranged wife, Meg, Jack would have been standing on stage with Dave Buick (his bandmate in the Go! and the proprietor of Italy Records) on bass guitar and his seventeen-year-old nephew, Ben Blackwell, on drums. They would have been playing as Brown Cardboard (or some such name generated by the whim of what happened to cross into White's field of vision when the idea was hatched).

White, Buick, and Blackwell had rehearsed for the show. They were ready to, er, have a go of it.

"Well, Jack and Meg were having some 'sibling troubles,'" says Buick. "And they weren't going to play the show at all."

"For Blowout '99, the band that was gonna take the White Stripes' place was me, Jack, and Buick," says Jack White's nephew, Ben Blackwell. "It was called Brown Cardboard. Obviously we didn't play the Blowout. But we did play eventually."

"The one show that we did was July 4th weekend, 1999, a free show at the Stick, by the bar in the alleys area. We'd always talked about it after the Blowout. But surprisingly (for Detroit) we only played once," said the tow-headed, baby-faced scene fixture, prone to masking his fandom with a thin veil of cynicism.

Indeed, the Blowout evening's MC at Paycheck's, Willy Wilson, a longtime Detroit scene fixture and a jock from local public radio station WDET, introduced the Stripes with the thankful declaration that this evening's show was not, as had been previously reported, the duo's final performance.

So it was that at least three hundred people realized that they'd sooner or later have to share the Stripes with the outside world. Jack White was onto something and there was really no turning back afterward.

"I really don't think there was ever any doubt in Jack's mind that the White Stripes were his first priority," says Blackwell now with the benefit of retrospect.

The next day, Jack would play a show at the Garden Bowl with acclaimed pop songwriter and Royal Oak, Michigan native, Brendan Benson, who had recently returned home from L.A. and San Francisco when his relationship with Virgin Records had soured. White Stripes shows that year would be few and far between—they played a total of twenty shows the entire year—until they hit the road with indie gods on the decline, Pavement. After that, of course, it was merely a series of one defied expectation after another. "Surely," you might have heard folks at Paycheck's say that night, "this duo can't get any bigger than this. Can it?"

It did.

And it happened just a couple miles from where the onetime John Anthony Gillis and Megan Martha White began their domestic life together, a domestic life that has seen them from married couple to big brother and little sister, to big sister and little brother, to two-headed rock 'n' roll wrecking ball, to the pop world's most unlikely marquee names, cover stars, and gossip fodder. Oh, and they made a handful of great rock 'n' roll records in there somewhere, too.

It may very well be that Jack White is your third man, girl. However, it's a fact that he's the seventh son. It's funny that the one fact in White's real-world CV that could most easily be leveraged for mythic effect is the one tidbit he didn't deign to reveal until he was an established rock star, and even then he let it slip via a cryptic lyric, Coy boy.

But there we have it—a twentysomething-year-old blues aficionado given to little, er, white lies finally letting down his guard to boast in the traditional, culturally accepted rock 'n' roll manner and guess what? The cheeky bugger is telling the truth.

And that may be one of those weird, atavistic, real-life links that Jack White has to old-time Delta blues players. After all, the odds of a seventh son being born to a modern, urban family in 1975 must surely have diminished significantly since the turn of the twentieth century. Son House, Muddy Waters, Robert Johnson, hell, even youngsters like R. L. Burnside must have all been privy to the superstitions that surrounded the charmed seventh male child of a family.

In the case of the Gillis family of Southwest Detroit, their mythical bundle of joy, John Anthony Gillis, was born on July 9, 1975.

On July 9, 1776, The Declaration of Independence was read aloud to Gen. George Washington's troops in New York, and 196 years later to the day, David Bowie declared war on rock identity when he unveiled Ziggy Stardust in London.

A short three years further down the road, on July 9, 1975, Elvis Presley was working his jumpsuited mojo for the last time in Terre Haute, Indiana. Somewhere in Croatia, someone was certainly celebrating the 119th anniversary of the birth of inventor Nikola Tesla. Former Faces guitarist Ron Wood had recently replaced young gun Mick Taylor in the Rolling Stones and the greatest rock 'n' roll band in the world was taking a stand at the L.A. Forum when words like "greatest rock 'n' roll band in the world" and "taking a stand" still meant something in rock. The Detroit Tigers beat the Chicago White Sox 6–2 at Tiger Stadium at the corner of Michigan Ave. and Trumbull.

And not far away, Gorman and Teresa Gillis were welcoming the last of their ten children into the family home in Southwest Detroit, in the shadow of the Ambassador Bridge.

Jack was a pup born into a musical family—seven years younger than his next closest sibling. By the time he was out of short pants, three of his brothers (Stephen, Leo, and Eddie), plus a neighbor (Brian Muldoon) and a cousin (Paul Henry Ossy), as well as a cadre of itinerant interested parties, had formed a band called Catalyst. The band combined the elder Gillis boys' interest in Deep Purple riffs, a Jethro Tull approach to a quasi-druid vibe, the blues as channeled through the Stooges DIY sludge/street punk, and nonmusical prog-rock touchpoints like Aleister Crowley and the attendant literary nods that come with the study of Crowley, Buckminster Fuller, and numerology. They must have been a sight to behold as they commandeered the stages of such Cass Corridor shitholes as the Old Miami, a gang of serious-faced dudes conjuring the spirits to guide them to the place where the air met metal—or whatever. Leo, closest in age to Jack, and a vocal doppelganger for his little brother, especially in Jack's more theatrical moments, fronted the group. When you listen to Catalyst today, in fact, the vocal similarities are striking. The same nigh-on-falsetto tone, sense of drama, and inspired urgency are there. The only tell is that Leo sings of journeys to far away lands that might appeal best to an aficionado of magical arcana and little brother Jack lets loose on the arcane details of broken hearts and the interpersonal give-and-take that defines the modern life as seen by a hyper-observant mind that might connect to any teen with a pulse. When Catalyst weren't playing out, they were practicing in the attic of the Gillis household, a three-story house nearly identical to the other three-story houses that populate the Southwest Detroit neighborhood. The influence on young Jack was certainly significant.

The other sounds that could apparently be found circulating around the Gillis household were showtunes as sung by his folks Gorman and Teresa.

"I know his parents were really fans of Cole Porter and were always singing songs around the house," says one-time bandmate and frequent collaborator Dan Miller. "It was like any kid whose parents go around singing old songs. Except I think most other kids are like 'ah, my parents are being dorks or whatever' and I think Jack really appreciated that stuff and had respect and reverence for it. I think that's the great thing. He never shuts anything off."

Southwest Detroit is one neighborhood that thrives on the diversity and activity that comes with the infusion of an immigrant population. The Gillis family was as uniquely Detroit as it gets. The head of the working-class Catholic clan, Gorman, worked at Holy Redeemer Catholic Church, the spiritual beating heart of the Southwest Detroit community. Teresa Gillis raised their ten children in the same house in which they settled in the shadow of the auto industry and the prosperity it provided in the late 1950s. By all accounts, the Gillises were people who understood place, continuity, and perserverance. Hell, to stick it out in Detroit after the riots of 1967 shows that kind of backbone. But then again, Southwest Detroit had a sort of geographical immunity from some of the white flight that those riots induced. It was already working class. It was already Catholic. It already was populated with the kind of stubborn folks who weren't about to give up their home because the National Guard was called in when people decided to run riot over a city. It was off the beaten path in a way. The colossal Michigan Central Railroad station—once the hub of Detroit's tourist, business, and commerce travel—had officially closed in 1988. So, save for its position as the gateway to industrial Downriver, it was essentially a bedroom community for blue-collar industrial and auto workers, first-generation Puerto Ricans and Mexicans.

"Southwest is an old school city neighborhood," says Detroit Cobras guitarist Mary Restrepo. "But it's not that bad. He grew up in a Spanish neighborhood where it's not as much about guns. It's much more about knives, culturally. You don't hear about as many shootings in Southwest Detroit as you do in the rest of the city."

And if the neighbhorhood's blue-collar work ethic didn't rub off on Gillis, his family's work ethic surely did.

"I mean his brother built those two [geodesic] domes! They had a party and I had to go just to see the domes if nothing else and when I got to the end of the tour I got the idea that this was a very industrious, hardworking family," says Restrepo.

Jeff Meier—the guitarist for Detroit bands Rocket 455 and the Detroit Cobras—moved to the neighborhood around the time Jack graduated high school and describes it as "the only really thriving neighborhood in Detroit. But I don't know what it's thriving on. Maybe it's thriving on some not so good stuff. I don't know, but there's a lot of people living there and it's not all burned out. There's a lot of shit going on. It was like what the Lower East Side of New York was like the first few times I went there with Hispanic and black and white people all living together.

"You can go to neighborhood bars and hang out and there are party stores where you don't get mugged outside. I like it. I think the Hispanic community's really positive for the area. There's a lot of gang activity, which is the bad side of it, but it's also very tight knit."

It was also the kind of neighborhood in which urban artists could live on the cheap—the kind of neighborhood that would normally be ground zero for gentrification. But Southwest was in Detroit and modern urban-hipster gentrification wasn't really a worry in Detroit. Besides, the folks who moved to Southwest knew better than to mess with a tough neighborhood that actually works.

Gold Dollar proprietor Neil Yee also owned a house in Southwest Detroit.

It was in the family house in this neighborhood and whatever other practice spaces that were available to them—neighbor's basements, industrial buildings, and wherever else they could set up gear—that Catalyst set about crafting their sound. Appropriately enough, the Catalyst sound wasn't far in spirit or in execution from either the improv-drone-prone space-rock scene or the noise scene the city harbored since the non-Iggy members of the Stooges went underground and formed Dark Carnival.

And if the resulting compilation LP *Dogs in the Oven* (on the mercurially monikered Seven Ravens record label) is any indication, the bands—or at least Leo's lyrics—were as influenced by the architectural and numerological musings of Ian Anderson. In an odd way, the Catalyst recordings made from '83–'03 either prefigure or at least are of a piece with the sounds laid down by Detroit's so-called space-rock scene wherein bands like Fuxa, Windy & Carl, and a handful of others sprung from Detroit's west-side suburb of Dearborn (a mere stone's throw from Stripes and Catalyst's Southwest Detroit home).

If you head to Southwest Detroit today and drive down Vernor

Avenue toward the neighborhood police precinct—and past the fire station in front of which the White Stripes posed for the cover shots on their debut full-length—you may even notice two large geodesic domes. It is in these beautiful yet incongruous bubbles of urban pioneer spirit that the final sessions and mixing for the recently released Catalyst compilation were completed. Seems at least Leo shares his little brother's affinity for putting his money (not to mention time and discipline) where his mind is.

If the kids were musical, it wasn't at the direct urging of Gillis patriarch Gorman or matriarch Teresa. The Gillis boys' parents are remembered, by those who knew Jack, as the quirky near-retirees they were by the time the late '80s rolled around.

"His dad was just a quirky dude," recalls Jack's childhood friend Dominic Suchyta. "I remember his dad as retired almost all of our childhood. He had insane one-liners all the time. And it was a pretty Catholic neighborhood. So his dad was always preaching at me. Not in a bad way or anything, just preaching. There was a piano in the house, but it wasn't a musical house. It's not what you'd call your typical rock 'n' roll scene."

So it was that Catalyst and the music of his brothers were the first influences on a young John Gillis. When they weren't practicing in the attic, he'd wander up and beat on the drums just to hear himself make a racket. By the time he knew what he was doing he was hooked. And as soon as he was hooked, he set about finding coconspirators. And in a neighborhood like Southwest Detroit, where Catholic white kids eager to play rock 'n' roll were a distinct minority, that was no mean feat. But through the graces of his older brothers, young Jack would soon find a loyal foil for his active imagination.

Jack wasn't the kind of kid who had a lot of friends. He had a lot of brothers, instead. And by the time he was twelve years old, they were all but gone from the house. By all accounts, Jack understood that most adult notion of treasuring a few close friends rather than boasting a large circle of social peers.

That he grew up as a cultural and racial minority in the city of Detroit, actually in the city as opposed to the more lily-white suburbs, cannot be overstated as an indirect influence on the White Stripes: from their work ethic to their seeming creation in a vacuum to their reticence to trust outsiders, it alls springs from geography.

"There was just nothing to do in that neighborhood," remembers Suchyta. "You couldn't even shop there, really. The suburbs had everything. But we hated the suburbs. It was like the worst put-down to be called a suburbanite. We didn't understand the suburbanites . . . they had friends. We definitely identified with being Detroiters."

And to be blunt, if you were a white kid from an up-by-the-bootstraps Catholic family raised in Detroit—particularly Latino-dominated Southwest Detroit—during the 1970s and '80s, you wouldn't have a lot of pals. Particularly if you were the kid of a working-class clan that did its level best to keep your hyperactive ass out of trouble. Such was certainly the case with young John Gillis.

Thus was Gillis introduced to Dominic Suchyta, a kid from the neighborhood whose second-generation Italian-American parents shared the Catholic, blue-collar background with the Gillises. The two met in fifth grade at Holy Redeemer School, a parochial school attached to Holy Redeemer Cathedral—a massive Gothic church in the very heart of Southwest Detroit.

"Our school had two classes for every grade and he was in the other one," remembers Suchyta of his introduction to Gillis.

"I don't know why we hit it off. He's the youngest of ten, so he has a lot of ties in the community, so I think one of his older brothers knew one of my older brothers."

"When we first met he was listening to classical music. He had these record box sets of classical," recalls Suchyta.

The two guys did the normal kid stuff, of course, but they also found a common ground with their love of music.

"We were in the Boy Scouts together, played hockey together. We both played hockey together at Clark Park from a young age. I kinda envied his family because he had cool toys, because all of his older brothers had all their stuff still at his parents' house," says Suchyta.

Turns out Jack Gillis wasn't a bad hockey player, either. In one end of Clark Park every winter, the city set up an ice rink that offered community skating and open hockey. Gillis and Suchyta didn't turn down an opportunity to exercise the right of all kids born north of the Canadian border and lace 'em up at neighborhood pickup games.

"We were probably better than most of the kids out there, but that's probably only because you have a bunch of Mexican kids with rented skates skating for the first time," recalls Suchyta with a slight chuckle.

Regardless of why, the two did hit it off and became fast friends for the remainder of their time at Holy Redeemer. To hear Suchyta tell it, neither of them were exactly social animals. So by the time eighth grade rolled around when it came time to head to high school, the pair goaded one another into taking the test to get into Cass Tech High School—Detroit's renowned arts, music, and science magnet high school.

"I think we were each the reason the other one went to Cass Tech," says Suchyta. "We sort of made each other take the test—you had to take a test to get in and neither of us wanted to go to our neighborhood school."

Cass Tech is as close as Detroit Public Schools has to a trophy school. It sits, with its trademark "C" crossed with a "T" logo displayed prominently, looming over I-75 on the near northwest side of downtown Detroit. If you've not come to take for granted a set of wheels at your disposal, Cass Tech's not far from Downtown's sprawl of nothingness. And even now that his band has sold more than a million copies of its record, White's still not the school's most well-known alumnus. That'd probably be a toss-up between Motown legend Diana Ross and Lily Tomlin or John DeLorean who once graced the school's halls. Other Cass Tech grads include David Alan Grier, Ellen Burstyn, jazz musician Donald Byrd, Detroit mayor Kwame Kilpatrick, and a list of alumni that reads like a Detroit City Hall honor roll.

You get the picture that two kids like young Jack Gillis and Dominic Suchyta had a sense that if they wanted to get out of Detroit, this was the place where that ticket could get written.

Students at Cass Tech have to choose "majors"—courses of study that would be the students' focus for their four years at the school and a nod toward the intensity of college and life preparatory curriculum in which the school specializes. When Suchyta and Gillis enrolled, Suchyta elected the art curriculum. For his part, Gillis chose the school's business course. As Suchyta recalls, it was just as likely a decision made by necessity rather than long thought-out rationale. After all, you had to pick something, and Jack was a practical kid.

Still, music was the boys' first and shared passion. And both of them played in many of the school's musical ensembles.

"Jack played violin in the student class and trombone, too. He played trombone in a band when we were fifteen," recalls Suchyta of Jack's first musical ensemble endeavors.

But more importantly, outside of school they were playing, recording, and exploring their mutual love of music all the time. "That's all we did was play music," he says now, on the eve of his own band's—the jump-folk outfit, Steppin' in It—most recent trip to the West Coast to play a string of concerts and recording sessions. "There was nothing else. I look back and I honestly don't remember us doing anything else."

Family Values

Jack's brothers instilled in him a sense of defending yourself and your ideas, when they inevitably get called into question, by simply being older brothers. This fraternal trial by fire would serve Jack White well as he grew into an artist heralded by some as a paragon of independent spirit. This, of course, was not the intent. He was just Jackie Gillis, little brother and metaphorical punching bag.

"I remember him painting his porch at his parents' house. It was a chore that he had to do. And I remember all of his brothers coming by and telling him exactly how he was doing it wrong. And not just once, but one after the other, they'd come by, like six times! That's kinda what it was like, I guess, for him. He was the younger brother, so I think they were kinda assholes. I think that's where he got his stubbornness," recalls Suchyta.

But through his older brothers Suchyta and Gillis were on the receiving end of twenty years of accumulated musical wisdom and an apparent family heritage of going your own way. So even though by the time Gillis was old enough to make music of his own without being a nuisance to his older brothers they were out of the house, he had still been indoctrinated in their musical tastes by osmosis.

"Hanging out with them, they got us through a classic rock stage really early. By sixth grade we were listening to Led Zeppelin, Traffic, and the Who. So by the time we were in high school we were really searching for something else. We both got hooked on early blues really early," he recalls.

"His brothers were always pushing Deep Purple and the Who on him," recalls Jack's nephew Ben Blackwell.

Dedicated Followers of Passion

So it was that the two boys were simultaneously isolated from pop culture and wading deep into the river of American music while most kids were just content to act awkward and figure out how to slow-dance to "Take My Breath Away" or "Rub You the Right Way."

That doesn't mean they were unscathed by contemporary music. After all, they were going to a school in the middle of Detroit. They were two of only a handful of white kids in a school that was otherwise entirely African American. They merely took the smooth R&B sides they were forced to play as part of their curriculum in stride.

"Jack played drums and I played bass in some shows at Cass Tech that we put on," remembers Suchyta. "The school didn't have a lot of money and sometimes they'd do fashion shows to raise funds or whatever, and we'd be in the backing band for the fashion show. So we'd do 'Vision of Love' by Mariah Carey or some Anita Baker song—we didn't care for it, but we could play it," he laughs.

"At one of the Cass Tech shows, we were supposed to play 'Rub You the Right Way,' by Johnny Gill," remembers Suchyta. "I remember Jack getting booted off the drums. We had rehearsed the song over and over again, but somebody from our class came out and really wanted to play drums on that song and that guy was a little more proficient at R&B."

Just like Chuck Berry would have counseled 'em, they bided their time until the schoolbell rang to get their kicks. And while most kids were goofing around chasing after girls and spending their disposable income first on pop and chips, then on booze and smokes, Gillis and Suchyta were scraping their pennies together to pick up new sounds and the equipment to make their own music on the cheap. Occasionally the records were free.

"We were way into garbage picking. I remember him finding [the Stooges'] 'Funhouse' in the trash," remembers Suchyta. "But that wasn't so much good luck as it was because [neighbor and future collaborator] Brian Muldoon's brother was living next door and was cleaning out."

There wasn't a school bus that ran from Cass Tech to Southwest Detroit and waiting on the Detroit city bus was a full-day shot, so Jack and Dominic often found themselves hoofing to and from school. Thankfully, along the way was John King Books, a Detroit institution—three floors of used books, arcane maps, strange documents of historical significance, and, most importantly at the time, four records for a dollar—where Gillis and Suchyta would often score their fix; an armload of vinyl that would last them a week or two.

They'd occasionally—OK, relatively often—blow off school entirely to feed their love of music. They'd ride their bikes down Michigan Avenue, hitting the pawnshops that line the street connecting Detroit to Dearborn, Dearborn to Ypsilanti and Ann Arbor, Ann Arbor to Chicago. "We used to go to Vin's on Michigan at Fort Street or pawnshops looking for reel-to-reel recorders."

They made regular stops at Trapper's Alley—a sort of urban

mall–cum–tourist trap that's since been converted into a casino—in Greektown where there was a branch of the local Harmony House record store chain. Fortunately, right around the time Suchyta and Gillis were playing hooky, vinyl was choking out its last gasp and Harmony House was selling off its records at fire sale prices. Suchyta remembers one afternoon sojourn to the joint where Gillis scored the soundtrack to *Tommy*. They went home and devoured it over and over again that day, before retiring to the attic to make some noise.

Toys in the Attic

In The Gillis household the former Catalyst HQ had fallen into disuse right around the time that young Jack and Dominic's interest in making music was really taking off.

"We used to play in their rehearsal space, in Jack's attic at his parents' house," recalls Suchyta. "It had tons of equipment in it. It was funny: Since he's the youngest, only one or two of his brothers were still living there, so the attic was like an abandoned rehearsal space," he says with a laugh.

When Gillis and Suchyta got down to playing the music that they'd been ingesting nonstop, like it or not, it was in one of two places in the Gillis family abode—Jack's tiny bedroom or the fourth-floor attic. "His bedroom's tiny," recalls Suchyta. "Besides his bed and the drumkit, there's not a lot of room. But we recorded a lot of stuff in there. We did a rockin' version of Dylan's 'Masters of War' and 'Groom's Still Waiting at the Altar.' We recorded 'Song 1' by Fugazi. That was a bedroom recording."

If they really wanted to turn on the juice, they ascended the extra flight to the attic. Left up there was a ragtag collection of his older brothers' gear plus the odd record or book laying around like the flotsam of generations moved on.

After school, on weekends, during vacation—pretty much anytime they could squeeze in during their high school years—Jack and Dominic were playing along with, recording, and writing music.

"There was a light switch at the bottom of the stairs that controlled the lights up there [in the attic], so sometimes if we were too loud or too raunchy, Jack's dad would just flick the lights like 'that's it,'" says Suchyta with a chuckle.

Often, Jack would play drums and Suchyta would play bass with Gillis doubling back and putting down rudimentary guitar tracks. "When it was the two of us, we joked around that the 'band' was called the thirteenth floors," laughs Suchyta.

"We used to hang out in abandoned buildings like the recently closed hulking landmark Central Station and stuff and none of them ever had any thirteenth floor. And Jack was always into the number three and everything. So it kinda made sense.

"In the train station we'd throw toilets down the elevator shaft and stuff like that. It was on our way home from school, so we'd do that pretty frequently," says Suchyta, offering one of the rare glimpses of goofing.

"We'd take old stuff from those places, like, I still have a return address stamp from the Central Station. Cool old Detroit stuff like that."

Increasingly, though, they would play as a blues trio with Jack on drums, Suchyta on bass, and Jack's older brother Ed on guitar.

"Ed was the brother that was going to be cool with us," recalls Suchyta. "He was into the blues and he started the blues side project with us. Jack and Ed's singing voices are the earliest singing voices I remember." he says. And Jack's was nothing to write home about at the time.

"We called it the Fuck-ups," remembers Suchyta with a slight laugh. "But we didn't name it the Fuck-ups, other people named it that. He's the youngest of ten, so I think some of his older brothers called it that."

But if Jack's brothers gave them shit about their musical endeavors, they at least were kind enough to give them shows to play, too.

"The only times we performed together was at a party at his brother's house—like twice. Right in the shadow of Hotel Yorba," says Suchyta.

It was in this incarnation, that Jack Gillis took his first tentative steps toward songwriting. "He wrote a tune with lyrics," remembers Suchyta, "He wrote it on guitar. It was a lot like what they do now, a heavy rockin' blues tune, like 'Ball & Biscuit.'"

Jack's music always reflected his deep, deep love of Chicago's Southside houserockin' blues. Blues made by pickup bands of recently migrated Delta expatriates that are so loose that they can't help but ride the groove.

"There's one thing he'll have that the white-boy blues doesn't have and that's the Chicago blues sloppiness," says Suchyta today. "There are no changes, it's just a one-chord vamp. The white-boy blues were taking a Bo Diddley song and cleaning it up. That's the thing about Chicago blues—the drummer doesn't know where he is half the time."

That early love of the blues, which the two boys discovered together more than a decade earlier, hasn't changed one bit says Suchyta. "Last time I was at his place, we were watching blues videos, deep Delta blues."

In fact, White's habit of going downstream in the river of American music is exactly what sets him apart from contemporary rock-blues hybrid mongers. "Muddy Waters came from Mississippi to Chicago and he plugged in an electric guitar and it's raunchy and out of tune and I think that's where Jack gets his edge over folks that are listening to purist blues revivalists."

So it was that a short-lived trio called the Fuck-ups set the stage for the underlying passion of a band called the White Stripes, who would find a way to be the backdoor man and woman for revivifying Delta blues in the hearts and minds of discerning sixteen-year-olds in 2003. Of course, no one could have predicted it.

"After the Stripes hit it big," says Suchyta, "one of Jack's brothers called me telling me he had a royalty check for a band called the Fuck-ups."

This incarnation of their ongoing musical experiments also inspired Gillis to pick up the six-string and begin his transition from drummer to axeman.

"Looking back, it was shortly after that [his time with 13th Floor] that Jack started to play guitar in earnest," says Suchyta.

And so, the teenagers holed up in the Gillis household and set about finding their own musical path.

"We couldn't really do anything else. We didn't know *how* to do anything else! We didn't have a whole lotta friends—it's not like that was a problem—it was like let's jam," says Suchyta.

As for the neighbors, well, there wasn't much of a problem with the sound, and as the neighborhood was already a boisterous, largely Puerto Rican and Hispanic neighborhood anyway, there was a lot of stuff going on. Cars cruised the street with kicker boxes in the back, ice cream trucks trolled the streets, the highway roared not far away, kids played in their yards, yelling and running. Besides, the neighborhood was already likely accustomed to the sounds emanating from the Gillis attic—and they might as well get used to it, because once Jack really got his recording legs under him, the racket wasn't due to die down anytime soon.

"The attic really wasn't a sound problem except for the summer, when the windows had to be open," recalls Suchyta. "There was so much stuff going on there that I don't think they were gonna care if we made some noise. The neighborhood was definitely rough, but we didn't have any problems. We kind of didn't fit in, but it wasn't a big deal or anything."

Of course, it may be that the neighbors had a leg or two to stand on when it came to the volume of noise coming from the Gillis household circa 1992.

"One thing about Jack's guitar playing was that he was always loud. His amps are loud. We could never get him to be quiet. I remember blowing stuff up plugging amps into amps to get a louder sound."

But it wasn't just about playing louder according to Suchyta, the goal was make do with what you had and make great art from what was at hand. Chalk that up to their blue-collar background and the fact that both Jack and Dominic firmly believed you could get spoiled by nice gear if it got into unappreciative hands.

"We used to go to guitar shows all the time and I remember him getting a Mexican made red and white strat. I remember thinking how unfair it was that you could buy a new guitar and sound so much better instantly. That's where the pawnshop mentality came from—it not being fair to play new gear," recalls Suchyta. "We wanted to avoid the idea that you could get a guitar that's new and think automatically that you were good."

The two were a DIY dynamo before they were even out of high school. To make matters better, they didn't know any different.

"It's kind of funny because people ask whether it was extraordinary and I hadn't played with anyone else before! Now that you look back on it we were so young, doing so much, looking back, it's pretty extraordinary.

"I remember going back there when his parents still lived there and he'd be recording with a microphone covered with a Dixie cup, just to see what it sounded like."

"We had gotten a Teac four-track with an 8-channel mixer with a Simulsync at a pawnshop run. We were around sixteen. So I guess that's when we both started engineering," recalls Suchyta.

In Detroit, sixteen means a driver's license and a driver's license means freedom. Dominic and Jack used their newfound freedom to head to nearby Dearborn to expand their burgeoning record collections.

"I remember driving to Dearborn to buy tapes. We were playing 'I Shoulda Quit You, Babe' or some song that Zeppelin did and we didn't wanna play it like them. We just weren't really moved by the white-boy blues thing, the Brit rock—some of the things the Stones or the Yardbirds did were pretty great, but those were few and far between."

The tapes they ended up buying were those of Earl King, and Sonny Boy Williamson, and, of course, Robert Johnson. From there on it was a slippery slope down the mountain of American music from Son House and "Music Man" to Jimi Hendrix and the Stooges.

"We somehow got through our entire childhood unexposed to things that everyone else knew about," laughs Suchyta today.

"There was Metallica in there for sure, but . . . I remember hearing, for example, the Violent Femmes for the first time at my freshman orientation at Michigan State University. And everyone else seemed to know all about it and I was like 'What is this?!' "

The pair also used their newfound automotive freedom to start taking exploratory excursions into the suburbs.

"We'd go to this store on Nine Mile in Ferndale that had all this old weird stuff in it and we'd ask all these questions about all these reel-to-reels and no one would take us seriously," laughs Suchyta. But that wasn't new to the duo who at the time could have accurately been described as A/V nerds.

The automotive freedom also allowed the two guys to start checking out the coffeehouse scene that had sprung up largely in the suburbs by then at places like Gotham City in Ferndale, Planet Ant in Hamtramck, and other joints around town. There, Jack would occasionally read scribblings from his notebooks and journals at open mike nights. And it was also there that they would meet one Megan White, a Grosse Pointe native with a yen for quiet nonconformity.

Looking to the Future

By the time Jack was sixteen, his older brothers were looking out for him and had introduced him to Brian Muldoon, a neighbor a dozen-plus years Jack's senior, but who would be the first in a long line of masters to whom Jack would serve as apprentice as the young musician sought to find an outlet for the ideas running around his head.

"Sometime around when we were sixteen, Jack wanted to get into the reupholstery trade," remembers Suchyta. "He loved upholstery, and I think the Muldoons had lived next door to his parents. And so he started going over to Brian's shop and Brian would turn us on to a lot of great stuff."

"Brian's Shop" was his upholstery shop in Corktown. Muldoon, a master upholsterer and maker of high-grade suites would show Gillis not only the tricks of the upholstery trade that would later lead to Jack

White opening his own Third Man upholstery shop in the Russel Industrial Center outside of Hamtramck but he'd also introduce the young lad to the virtues of the garage and punk rock underground. The sound of bands like the MC5, the Stooges, the Flat Duo Jets, and especially Detroit's own garage blues primitives the Gories would catch Gillis totally off guard and would, even more than the learning associated with his ostensible career path, change his life forever.

"We'd play in the upholstery shop and Brian gave us MC5 records and Stooges records," says Suchyta. "We recorded [the MC5's] 'Looking at You' with just Jack. I distinctly remember taking the four-track over to the upholstery shop and recording that and getting a really good recording. And Jack was way into the Flat Duo Jets early on. That was one of the first bands that I remember that I hadn't heard of. And it was like wow, you didn't really need a bass player!" Suchyta ironically is now a bass player with Steppin' in It.

For Suchyta the next step was going off to college and continuing to explore his love of roots music at Michigan State University. Gillis for his part learned the trade that his older brothers had identified for him. And certainly not to the detriment of his upholstery apprenticeship, he also became more and more focused on playing music full-time. In fact, it was at this time that Gillis developed some of the signs of discipline and self-actualization that would come to his aid as he made the series of career-defining decisions that would eventually and surreally make him a Grammy winner. But that's down the line still. At the time, he was fleshing out some of the habits—never mind relying on god-given talent— that would come to define him as one of the more focused members of the Detroit music scene.

When it came to school, "He definitely put more effort into it than I was. I remember thinking 'why isn't this guy going to college?'" remembers Suchyta.

Gillis did take a few college courses in 1994 at Detroit's Wayne State University. But as he has stated in numerous interviews—and it seems totally consistent with his character—that he was dissatisfied with the level of commitment that other students showed in the classes he enrolled in.

He was already used to a near-monastic life of the pursuit of music. And he was developing the kind of habits that would carry him further than any of the instructors in WSU's College of Fine, Performing, and Communications Arts could.

"I remember Jack when he first started upholstering with Brian, he'd do something that I think was really strange, but then it made total sense like ten years later," recalls Suchyta.

"He used to time his rehearsals for drums. He'd play three hours every afternoon, for example. And there was a sign right above his bed that said 'learn to love upholstery,' and I was thinking 'this guy's a freak,' but it makes total sense now. And that blue-collar work ethic is definitely a part of the Detroit attitude. That and you don't really care about making money."

The scene at Muldoon's upholstery studio must have been liberating for a couple of teenagers that had previously confined their musical explorations to the confines of one of their houses. In the heart of Detroit's industrial center, at night, amplifiers, the Stooges, loading out to your car with the danger of lurkers jumping out of the shadows, it was the penultimate Detroit rehearsal space scenario. And Jack and Dominic were living it.

"There were some people we knew from school in a band called the Vegetarian Cannibals and they had put a tape out—and we wanted to do that, too. But I moved to MSU and we never got around to doing it," laments Suchyta.

Introducing Sister Meg

Toward the end of high school, on one of their soujourns to the coffeehouse in Ferndale, Jack Gillis had met Grosse Pointe resident Megan White. Grosse Pointe was only ten miles upstream as the Detroit River flows past Belle Isle, but it was a world away from the Southwest Detroit that Jack and Dominic called home.

"I hung out with Jack and Meg maybe a couple dozen times," says Suchyta. "It was our senior year that they met and that Jack and Meg started hanging out."

So the threesome would kill time like any other group of high school kids with wheels. The coffeehouse scene was really starting to become the central focus of late high school life in the Detroit area—especially in Detroit where getting anywhere meant driving anyway and the binds of high school social structures chafed most on the kinds of kids who were apt to kill time in the quasi-boho caffeinated world of coffeehouse poetry and the smell of freshly ground Arabica. Dominic, Jack, and Meg would often find themselves hanging out at Gotham City in Ferndale or Planet Ant in the Polish-American enclave of Hamtramck. "Meg was so quiet," recalls Suchyta. "I couldn't get anything out of her. She definitely didn't play anything musical."

When Suchyta moved away to attend university, only Jack and Meg were left. In retrospect, Suchyta can see how they could easily have adopted an us-against-the-world bond.

"Back then, there was only a couple other kids we'd ever hang out with. It was always just us," he says. "I kinda feel bad now because they didn't know anybody. Detroit's not really set up for folks who are underage. And they only had each other."

If Jack White's birthday is filled with the kind of auspicious historical coincidence that makes the cut as "compelling" in a bandography, Megan Martha White's bow into the world on December 10, 1974, shares precious little with history. It's almost as though she didn't want to make a big deal about it (if that's not a totally ridiculous statement, I don't know what is).

Grosse Pointe Woods, the specific enclave of Grosse Pointe in which Meg grew up, is closer to middle class than upper middle class. The stereotype is that all of the Grosse Pointes are incredibly well off, but that's not entirely true. Sure, members of the Ford family and a couple NFL team owners live in Grosse Pointe Shores, and Grosse Pointe Park is embarrassingly affluent. But the Woods is decidedly middle class, sharing a border with less well-heeled 'burbs as Harper Woods and the East

Side of Detroit (where Jack's sister's family, including Ben Blackwell, settled). The Whites lived on a street of well-kept little bungalow houses. A neighborhood that is best described as "nice"—obviously a great place to grow up. Right down the street was the Grosse Pointe Woods park where the neighborhood kids and parents would congregate for city league baseball games and general outdoor, family-friendly frolicking.

In other words, Jack and Meg couldn't have had more different upbringings. His was a large lower-middle-class Catholic family from Detroit's blue-collar underbelly. Hers was a small (one older sister) WASP family from the solidly middle-to-upper-middle-class side of the tracks. He was a demonstrative kid, she demure.

But what they had in common is striking. Both of their childhoods would have a lot to do with the musicians they'd become, Jack's bombastic and confident as though already tried by fire (even though he hides a deeply nervous and insecure side), Meg's deceptively quiet, the secret center of a world of her own creation (yet she exudes undeniable confidence).

"She was my cousin, Diane's, best friend growing up and they were inseparable," recalls Meg's neighbor Matthew Peabody. "She lived across the street from Meg and it's almost like every time I thought of my cousin, I immediately thought of Meg, too. They were always together. And she was always the quiet girl at Diane's side in junior high. My mom saw her on the cover of a magazine the other week and she was like 'I can't believe that's the little girl that used to do Diane's hair and makeup,'" muses Peabody. "They were these tight friends that did all the littlest friends things together."

Peabody, like Meg, also attended Grosse Pointe North High School. He remembers her as the artistic type. It wouldn't be unfair to think of her embodying a cleaner-cut version of Ally Sheedy's character in *The Breakfast Club*. If you had a nickel for every time someone used the word "quiet" when describing Meg, you'd have more money than she and Jack reportedly made when they signed to V2 records. And it seems that that's not a recent character development (and it also seems that she uses her quiet reputation to mask a wicked sense of humor and a keen observational eye that she shares only with a trusted few).

"She was in a lot of the art classes in my high school. My friends were in classes with her and she was always the quiet, obviously artistic type. Kind of like in the background. You didn't really notice, because she didn't really do anything to make you notice her. She just kept very much to herself. I know we used to have art shows at North and I'd see some of her stuff up in those, and she kind of had that vibe to her, like not tortured, but the quiet artist," summarizes Peabody.

"She seemed to have this schoolgirl innocence to her. You look back in retrospect and its something you appreciate now. It seems like in high school everybody tries their best to have this standout personality, which is kind of pretentious, but that's high school. And she was cool because she wasn't like that."

If you talk to anyone in her class, they're likely to say the same thing: she was just kind of there. She had a small group of friends and didn't go in for sports or music or anything else for that matter. At a relatively well-heeled school like Grosse Pointe North, where social status was based largely upon your extracurricular activities, that was a rarity. So much so that in high school, "no one knew her," says Peabody.

"She was just Megan White. I always knew her as Megan. And then I started reading that she was now called Meg and I thought, 'wow, a rock star name.'" He laughs. "Now she's this rock sex symbol, this quiet kid from the neighborhood."

When Peabody found out about the Stripes' success, he says it "blew me out of the water. Of all people. "Most of the kids from Grosse Pointe migrate back to the area after college," says Peabody.

"When they started blowing up, that became a topic of conversation all the time. If anything the big topic of conversation is how funny it is that people are coming around and trying to figure out their backgrounds. People are speculating about how Meg went to school in Detroit because she lived in Hamtramck, but she went to school in Grosse Pointe of all places. And the whole brother-sister thing was funny. I was like she never had a *brother*, not that I saw at least!" he laughs.

Future Gold Dollar proprietor Neil Yee was pals with Meg's older sister Heather and met the future Stripes drummer when she was a high schooler knocking around with her big sis on the Hamtramck open mike scene.

"I had actually met Heather at the Hamtramck pub open mike night in 1991, so I always knew Meg as the little sister and Jack as the boyfriend."

Apparently, the socially awkward, quiet Gillis didn't make a huge impression on Yee. "I always remember him being around and at the time I didn't realize that that he even played music."

Meg stood out in another atypical-for-Grosse-Pointe way, too. She didn't go away to college. Ninety percent of all kids who graduate from high school in Grosse Pointe go away to college—the city's like one big prep school—and those that don't generally go right into the family business. The most famous North student in the music industry up until Meg White was Gregg Alexander (a 1986 North dropout) of late '90s one-hit wonders the New Radicals.

"Not many kids at that time went straight to work out of high school and go to work at a coffeeshop or a bar," recalls Peabody. "The standard thing is you went to high school to prepare for college and then you went away to college."

It's safe to say that Megan White was not voted "Most Likely to Become a Rock 'n' Roll Sex Symbol" when the Grosse Pointe North class of 1993 accepted their diplomas.

Goober and the Peas

By the time Gillis graduated from high school, he had already set about making music a top priority in his life—moreover, he had already written and recorded at least one future White Stripes song, "The Union Forever," with his Two-Part Resin (né Upholsterers) bandmate Brian Muldoon.

But it wasn't until one of his coffeehouse jaunts that his course became clearer. It was there that he came upon a flyer left by Detroit cow-punk/proto alt.country outfit Goober & the Peas seeking a new drummer.

It was the summer of 1993 when Jack took the leap. Like Alice Cooper said, "school's out forever . . ." Except Gillis was really just entering another phase of his musical education.

Suchyta was a bit freaked out by his buddy's decision to try out for an established band: "I thought he was crazy," he recalls. "Here's this young kid and I was just like 'You're auditioning for a band?' They're gonna totally laugh at you. I mean, Goober & the Peas had just opened for Dylan at the Fox Theatre!"

Goober & the Peas had been a fixture on the Detroit scene since their start in the late '80s. Dan "Goober" Miller always described the band as a "freak show" and he was not far off. Known as much for their stage antics of chucking hay around at the audience and Miller's larger-than-life, high-wire, high-strung, high-energy urban cowboy persona as for the shit-kicking, hot-rocking reinvigorated cowpunk they practiced, the band was a live dynamo and a must-see, often packing 1,000-person venues across the Midwest.

Goober & the Peas had a serially monogamous relationship with their drummers, going from one to the next with alarming speed over their six-year existence.

"We had a real problem with drummers. Some people would play for just one show. So we went through fifteen official drummers and after each of those fifteen, we had auditions," recalls G&TPs frontman Dan Miller (then a.k.a. Goober).

"So I just put up flyers for [what would be] the last drummer—as it turned out, Jack was the last Goober & the Peas drummer. I think he said he saw it at Planet Ant because he used to hang out there. Then he called back while we were on tour and he left messages for us and he just sounded interesting," says Miller.

"There was something about his voice, even on the answering machine, I wondered 'where's this guy from?!' And then when I called him back I asked him about it. He said, 'Oh, I'd been watching *The Last Picture Show* and so I started talking like that for a while."

Jack swung by Dan's house for the audition—a ritual the other Peas were by now intimately accustomed to enacting. Drummer comes by, drummer sits behind kit, band strikes up a couple of songs. Drummer plays along, band makes a judgment. "We'd just say jump in and see what your instincts are and play whatever you feel like playing," says Miller.

In Gillis's case, he says, "There was no doubt about it, we all just agreed after we went through a couple songs."

"He just had his head down and he really played great. We'd had a lot of different kinds of drummers over the years—even some Neal Peart–ish professional-type drummers—and Jack wasn't that, but he wasn't horribly sloppy. I think he had taught himself how to play. More than anything, though, it was just his feeling for the music. The other guys just looked at one another and agreed. It wasn't 'we'll call you later' it was 'so, you wanna join?'"

Playing along in the basement is one thing. But at the time, Goober & the Peas were playing in front of good-size crowds, as large as 1,000 people at their shit-kicking hometown hootenannies at downtown music landmark St. Andrew's Hall. And they were touring—a lot.

"I don't think he had ever been to an audition before. He was eighteen years old, but it was so obvious that he was really good," says Miller. "But the other thing for as much touring as we did, we needed to make sure: Okay, he got the musical end of it, but is this a nice person? Is this a guy you wanna hang out with when you're on tour? And we just talked to him for a little bit and he seemed like a nice, good person."

"And we thought he would offset our evilness," he laughs.

The first show with Jack behind the kit was in St. Joseph, Michigan, a small town on the west side of the state, not known as a cultural mecca but a place where Goober & the Peas had booked a show anyway.

"We had such a great feeling [that night] that backstage before the encore, we were like 'so, what do you guys want to do?'" recalls Miller.

"Jack, do you want to play guitar and sing? And he was like 'Yeah!' I think we did 'Little Sister' or some Elvis song.

"The other thing I remember with Jack was that you've been playing with other people for a while, you get into a pattern of playing the same songs the same way," says Miller. "And he was inspired by Bob Dylan playing the same songs, but in different ways. And so Jack would change things up night to night and it did add something to the song and sometimes it would throw us off," recalls Miller of the bold gambit his young drummer had taken.

"But it challenged us, too. And playing the same songs the same way every night gets boring."

Unfortunately for Goober & the Peas (and fortunately for future White Stripes fans everywhere), the band's days were numbered. The well had begun to run dry, as so often happens with bands that plateau creatively as they begin to draw in larger and larger audiences.

They released one record in 1995 upon which Jack Gillis appeared, "The Jet Age Genius of Goober & the Peas."

"I think the thing that sucked about it was that it would have been a lot better if he had come along a couple years earlier, because by that time, we were losing our inspiration a little bit and my [older] brother [guitar player Mike] was out of the band at that point and it wasn't that much fun," says Miller.

"We had toured a little bit too much. It's always more fun when you're there at the beginning or when things are inspiring. It's that same thing that a lot of bands go through where you say to yourself: 'We could tour a lot and make a pretty good living doing this touring Europe, and we'll get good guarantees and all that, but man, I felt a lot more inspired playing in front of nine people in Wichita on a Tuesday night than I do playing on a Saturday in front of 1,000 people at St. Andrew's or in Chicago."

In 1996, Goober & the Peas decided to cut their creative losses and fold up the tent for good. But by no means had Miller stopped writing music and Gillis had only just begun. While Miller took some time to figure out his next musical identity, Gillis returned to his upholstery business, Third Man Upholstery (motto "Your Furniture is Not Dead") in earnest and redoubled his efforts to master songwriting and six-string playing daily after work with Brian Muldoon and their band Two-Part Resin, so named after one half of the formula for an upholstering compound.

That fall, he would also marry his first love and crosstown sweetheart, Megan, and subsequently take her surname. But even as he was playing stripped-down cover versions of his favorite songs (as well as a smattering of originals) with his mentor and friend Muldoon, Jack White had a concept cooking for a different kind of duo, grounded as much in his affinity for artful pretense and Tin Pan Alley pop perfection as in his abiding yen for down 'n' dirty blues and Detroit's gritty rock history.

For whatever it's worth, John Anthony Gillis and Megan Martha White got married at a small service in the tiny town of South Lyon—about forty-five minutes northwest of Detroit—on September 21, 1996, with only a few friends and family in attendance. What's more, and maybe all that matters in the big for-public-scrutiny picture, is that they were relatively young—both were twenty-one. They began their life together in a small apartment in Hamtramck where they lived for several months before finally settling into the same home in which Jack and his nine brothers and sisters grew up when Jack's parents moved out of the neighborhood.

By the time the young couple moved into the house, it had seen better days, but it was cozy and an odd combination of rustic and art-filled—particularly for a house plopped right in the middle of an urban block in the shadow of superhighways connecting Canada and the United States. The Whites would soon find their home the ad-hoc headquarters for not only their band, but for White and Miller's next venture, the short-lived country-rock quartet 2-Star Tabernacle.

2-Star Tabernacle

2-Star Tabernacle was from the get-go an object lesson in dynamic tension. Sometimes it soared incredibly, sometimes it never got off the ground. White and Miller dueled (from the audience's viewpoint at least) for center stage; drummer Damian Lange was behind the kit, a sort of rockabilly-looking Buddha with arms swinging and landing improbably on just-in-pocket rhythm; and Dan's better half, Tracee, statuesque and plunking notes on the bass like she had just learned the instrument. Their repertoire was coaxed from Hank Williams, Sr., by way of Jeffery Lee Pierce's smoking Gun Club.

Miller had been stewing over the concept for 2-Star for some time, knowing full well he'd have to do something so completely un-Goober to even begin to shake the self-described "freak show" carnival barker persona that he had taken such care to develop for the past seven years. It doesn't seem entirely unfair to think about 2-Star Tabernacle as Miller's rebound date—an outfit constructed as much for the purposes of cleansing the artistic palate as achieving anything lasting. 2-Star's live shows were often the scene of many a Goober fan yelling out requests for Goober & the Peas' college circuit cult hit "Hot Hot Women and Cold Cold Beer." These requests were usually quashed by Miller's withering gaze and a few words of unambiguous arch-Baptist preacher discouragement. In this context, White was the hot-shot rock 'n' roll kid, the wildcard in platform shoes seething at Miller's right hand. If his and Tracee's presence alone didn't make the break perfectly clear, then the unnerving menace of such White stompers as "The Union Forever" and the unsettling quietude-unto-bluster of Miller's stalker-with-a-heart-of-gold lovenote "Who's to Say?" should have been a clue.

It fell together as necessarily as it fell apart two years later. And by the time it was done, both White and Miller would have bands on their hands that meant as much to them—and more to some fans—as Goober & the Peas ever did, with White focused solely on the Stripes and Miller forming Gothic-country quintet Blanche.

"I think when Goober & the Peas ended, I wasn't really thinking about getting a band together," says Miller. "But I had it in my head a few months later that I wanted to get this noisy melodic band like Gallon Drunk together. And then I thought, well who would I do that with? Tom [a.k.a. Junior] Hendrickson who I had always written songs with in Goober was living in Nashville at the time. So I just started writing songs by myself. I didn't know who else I would get in the band, but I kept in touch with Jack and we started working on 2-Star stuff."

Miller was at that point in his music life where he had to figure out how to make ends meet and (hopefully) avoid a standard-issue day job. In Detroit this typically means avoiding a gig, working in some capacity under the patronage of the Big Three (Ford, General Motors, and Chrysler). But Miller side-stepped that.

"I had been talking about it, but I had never really made the time to do it. So I started substitute teaching and it would be so boring because when you sub, for the most part you're just babysitting, you're not actively teaching anything—especially high school kids. So I would just sit there and have songs go through my head and try to write songs. Then I started doing some four-track stuff and I saw Jack and we were hanging out and we just decided to start working on stuff then," says Miller.

Their first show was at the Peas' old stomping grounds, St. Andrew's Hall, in December of 1997 at a legal defense fundraiser show for local pop culture and humor weekly *Orbit* magazine (for which Miller wrote occasionally). 2-Star only did a couple songs, but they immediately started to draw attention that was equally gawker delay and admiration.

Jack, of course, had also been writing songs. Besides "The Union

Forever," future White Stripes singles "Hotel Yorba" and "Dead Leaves and the Dirty Ground" were also 2-Star-era songs. And the band covered the traditional spiritual "Wayfaring Stranger"—which Miller would later make a live staple in his subsequent band Blanche and which White would record for the soundtrack to the film *Cold Mountain*.

"We started 2-Star without a clear focus, but he had written some songs and I had written some songs. Mine were slower, traditional country at that point along with some Gallon Drunk–ish songs. And I think those were too country for what he was feeling because a lot of his songs were these faster things, so we'd rehearse them together, and they all kinda sounded good together," says Dan of the pairing. If 2-Star started without a clear focus, it's not inaccurate to say that they never really found that focus, with Miller finding his songwriting voice again and White coming into his own as a writer.

"2-Star was always going in a million different directions and we were never able to pick just one," recalls White.

Tracee was just learning to play the bass and, with three experienced musicians, including her husband, in the band, she was, perhaps rightfully, a wee bit intimidated. ("Her only experience was knowing what music she liked listening to," explains Miller.) But one day, at practice, White put her fears at ease with a simple compliment of her bass-playing simplicity: "I always remember Jack saying to her when she had this real basic bassline, he's like 'God, that's great! I don't think I would be able to play as consistently as you play because I would just get bored and try to change it and that's not good for a bass player to have, that attention deficit disorder.'"

After a handful of shows, it was clear that White was starting to gain the kind of confidence that allows a creative, hyperactive mind to become exceedingly prolific. He started bringing songs to the 2-Star table more and more frequently. Indeed, it was during this period that he also took his first tentative steps to penning songs for other bands around town such as the Hentchmen and Rocket 455, trying to mimic their songwriting style and use that mimicry as a reflective lens for his own work in the nascent White Stripes body of work.

"I just remember when we'd practice in our basement and we'd work on one of my songs until it came together and sounded really good," says Miller of what became clear to him was the beginning of the end of the band. "And Jack, especially toward the end kept bringing in these new songs. And a lot of them were similar, especially in the beginning, but they were always so lyrically perplexing. Like I never really understood exactly what they were about and I loved that. The imagery was really great, and they had this abstract quality to the lyrics. It reminded me of the Gun Club in the feeling and darkness."

2-Star Tabernacle only made one officially released recording. And that was with Detroit-via-Chicago R&B wildcard Andre Williams, who had had a hit in 1967 with the novelty dance number "Bacon Fat" and had enjoyed regional success on the R&B circuit recording for such Detroit-based labels as Fortune and Northern during the '60s.

The unlikely pairing happened by coincidence. 2-Star Tabernacle was playing a show with the Demolition Dollrods at the Magic Stick. Andre had been making a record called "Silky" with Mick Collins and Dan "Dollrod" Kroha. And he turned up during 2-Star's soundcheck that night.

"He came up to us and he said, 'You know, I like country music, too. We should do a record together,'" remembers Miller.

The A-side of the single for Chicago-based alt.country label Bloodshot Records was called "Jet Black Daddy, Lilly White Mama." The B-side was a cover of the Hank Williams, Sr., song "Ramblin' Man." The session took place in Jack and Meg's living room with the band, Williams, and Rocket 455/Detroit Cobras guitarist and Southwest Detroit neighbor Jeff Meier manning the boards.

"The idea was to keep it really soulful," says Miller. "Not intentionally lo-fi, but to have that edge to it. And Andre showed up for the session in a nice white hat and white suit, so he fit in well with the 2-Star look," chuckles Miller.

"They had the stuff in the can and the version of 'Ramblin' Man' that they did sounds to me like staring to the gates of hell—so amazingly apocalyptic," says Bloodshot Records co-owner (and Detroit native) Rob Miller.

"I'd known Goober . . . and didn't like them, to be blunt. He mentioned Jack and I knew him from other bands. You know, shitty little garage bands from around Detroit," he laughs.

The resulting songs are a rickety pair of numbers that found Jack providing a stark vocal harmony counterpart to Williams's husky, whiskey-soaked baritone growl on "Ramblin' Man," and a spare, rhythmic piano choogle to the Williams-penned "Jet Black Daddy . . ." But it's the song that didn't make the cut from that session that points toward White's growing confidence in his own material and the contemporaneous development of the White Stripes sound and vision. "The Big Three Killed My Baby" would become the White Stripes' first true signature song, in their hands an acid attack on planned obsolesence and the intellectual and cultural brain rot that Detroit's automotive industry had wrought over the years.

"Jack wrote 'The Big Three Killed My Baby' for Andre," remembers Dan Miller. "And I just remember him trying to describe it to Damian, he had the driving guitar part and I had a complementary part to that that sounded cool. And we'd play it and Jack was like 'it sounded great, but it's just not what I imagined it would sound like.'

"He was trying to get Damian to play something way simpler, but that wasn't Damian's instinct. But Jack just wanted everything stripped down with that Gories feeling."

Further complicating White's vision was Williams, who had his own ideas for the song. "When we recorded it with Andre it was so funny because he was just like [adopts Andre's trademark sleazy growl of a voice] 'Yeah, it sounds good, but let's get a little Spanish beginning to it!' he had this intro thing where he said 'They downsized the eeeassy way!' and then it would build up into the song," laughs Miller.

"And that was the first year where there was a big deal made of El Niño, so he threw that in there, too. He wanted to do something like 'stay in school' or something. Make it topical. You know 'this is for the kids!' So he sang the beginning and Jack sang the rest of it and Jack's voice was really hoarse that day, so it's just a really bizarre recording," marvels Miller.

"[Andre] was so funny," says Miller. "When we did that session, we were doing a cover of 'Ramblin' Man' and we wanted to give him some room to sing the way he wanted to sing, but stay within the constraints of the song, because he was always just drawing everything out, kind of out of time. So we were kind of like 'well, you gotta start singing the chorus at least before the chorus ends' and he'd be like 'Oh, so you're kinda saying like I'm in jail, but I can go wherever I want, huh? I see. All right, fuck it! Let's just do the song.'"

In the early days of the White Stripes, 2-Star and the Stripes would often play shows together.

One such show that ended up being a harbinger of things to come was an October 1998 show in nearby Toledo, Ohio, at which the White Stripes were billed first of three bands as the "White Lines."

The show in Toledo, opening for 2-Star, was the first White Stripes show I ever saw," says Ben Blackwell. "As I look back on it, it was a little rough, but at the time it was explosive for me.

"It's still probably one of the favorite shows of my life. There were probably twenty people there. I knew all the songs, it was just that I couldn't get into the clubs to see 'em! Somehow, I got to Jack's, and Jack drove to Toledo.

"2-Star played as well, and Dan and Tracee were always like, 'We could see the Stripes getting really really big,'" continues Blackwell.

"And Jack always thought they were crazy. He'd always say, '2-Star's the money band. 2-Star's gonna get really big.' But the White Stripes were definitely where his heart was. There's a tape of the show and you can hear people in the crowd talking and after the White Stripes played, a guy in the crowd says 'I don't know what that was, but I sure like it.'"

"When we went down there," recalls Miller, "people didn't know 2-Star either, so it was an introduction to both bands."

By the time 2-Star called it a day in March of '99; White was churning out songs at an alarming rate and the White Stripes were starting to get a little traction locally, beginning to draw people besides the same fifty folks who showed up for rock 'n' roll shows on the Midtown circuit regardless of who was playing.

"When he started writing White Stripes stuff it reminded me of the early Modern Lovers," remembers Miller. "Where there's something kind of dangerous about it, but there's also something really sincere and sweet and a little bit evil. So when he and Meg started the White Stripes I thought the songs were so great. And when we'd get together in 2-Star Tabernacle, it would push me to be a better musician and a songwriter," he recalls.

"And I think it's helped everyone in town take it to a different level. But being in a band with him at that point—and I'm sure anyone who has worked with him will tell you that—it's pretty intimidating to play with somebody that talented and that focused and that driven."

A Revisionist Stripes Mix Tape

The White Stripes, of course, didn't just spring from a vacuum. And you don't just jump out of the gate playing Son House covers and nothing else. We take for granted that the White Stripes are huge fans of Bob Dylan, Loretta Lynn, Blind Willie McTell, the MC5, and the Stooges. But there's music that falls between the cracks when thinking about the influences of the Stripes, a collision of cultures that all collude to make them as musically elusive as they are accessible. After all, they certainly weren't listening to strictly Detroit-made music as they laid out the blueprint for what would become their signature sound. They were plundering their pasts and filtering the sounds through their unique sensibility. In fact, a faction of the Stripes' naysayers are fond of mentioning that the band isn't doing anything that hasn't been done before. That's part of the point. Through homage, the Stripes find their unique synthesis.

"Jack is really great at articulating and justifying their shameless referencing of their heroes," says Steve McDonald, one half of the seminal L.A. power-pop group Redd Kross and creator of the White Stripes tribute project Redd Blood Cells. "Maybe in time he's got to think about it enough that he's really defined why it's relevant to him and why it should be to other people. I think there's a lot of relevance to looking to the past, especially things that have been discarded by the mainstream and paying homage and drawing inspiration from that."

So here's a warts 'n' all mix tape into which, ideally, any old Stripes song could be plopped and it wouldn't feel out of place.

"Outta Here"—The Gories

One of the seminal Detroit garage-blues band's most primal moments. Big, fat, dead-simple floor toms, sparse guitar strikes, Dan Kroha's desperate, high-pitched tale of being sick to death of the same people in the same places and longing for a place where he can really let down his hair. If that doesn't sound like a template for some of the Stripes' work, then you aren't listening hard enough.

"So Tired"—the Beatles (Lennon)

If you adhere to the theory that every songwriter is a John, Paul, George, or Ringo, then Jack White is a classic John. And this piece of seemingly tossed-off confessional speaks to the exposed emotional nerve that White also makes effortless. Slow, naked, confessional jams from a rock band? Yeah, that's the Stripes.

"Dignified and Old"—the Modern Lovers

The Modern Lovers were one of the bands identified by White early on as an inspiration. And it's easy to see why. JoJo's ever more sophisticated faux-naif persona became more and more infatuated with simplifying to its essence American music while still injecting a healthy dose of un-healthy strangeness to his lyrics. One has to wonder who would win an arm-wrestling match for Jack White's songwriting soul: Jonathan Rich-man, Bob Dylan, or Leadbelly. My money's on Leadbelly, but that's just because he's bigger and has done time.

"Vision of Love"—Mariah Carey

Hell, even the best rock 'n' roll drummers have to start somewhere. Miss Carey's polyoctave histrionics may not have found their way into the Stripes' sound, but as one of the artists whose music Jack had to re-create while at Cass Tech High School at least she was a benchmark against which Jack and Meg could measure their derision for modern recording technology's trappings.

"King of the Rambling Spires"/"20th Century Boy"—T. Rex

Both for Bolan's dandy persona as well as T. Rex's influence on White's glammy/arena guitar progression. Its medieval tale of a king's return touches on the Stripes' mythologizing, theatricality, and progressive rock underpinnings. The latter tune's multitracked vocals, gut-punch guitar attack, and loose groove anticipate a sound to which the Stripes would later aspire.

"Bohemian Rhapsody" & "Another One Bites the Dust"—Queen

They don't make rock bands any more theatrical than Queen, from Freddie Mercury's leonine strut to Brian May's outsize riffery. While at first people compared the Stripes to Led Zeppelin by saying White was like Plant and Page rolled into one, Queen's core duo are more and more the appropriate touchpoint as the Stripes grow more confident. And "Seven Nation Army" coexists nicely with "Another One Bites the Dust" as a jam readymade for sampling.

"Psycho"—the Sonics

Volume, intensity, and perversity in the face of normalcy. The Seattle protopunks made frat and garage rock obsolete by redlining it only to have it mainlined by every would-be Detroit rocker worth his or her salt. These guys let the Detroit garage scene know the real rock 'n' roll score.

"Jack on Fire/She's Like Heroin to Me"—Gun Club

Okay, so the name of the first one makes it an obvious choice, but this bleak tale of a man gone astray from his own soul is riveting. Its neighbor on the Gun Club's "Fire of Love" record was a cover that White busted out when he played solo back in the day giving the original's sinister malevolence a hiccupy urgency all his own. More importantly, the Gun Club's records point to a punk rock–informed path for Dylan-obsessed rockers. And obviously White studied it well.

"Fly Me to the Moon"—Peggy Lee

Why not the Peggy Lee version? You gotta figure that's the one that White would pick. Or maybe he would add his foppish theatricality to the Frank Sinatra template. Either way, the fantasist and the romanticist are both engaged by this infectious classic.

"Minnie the Moocher"—Cab Calloway

It was Cab Calloway that influenced the White Stripes' version of "St. James Infirmary Blues" and it was Calloway who could be seen grinning from the stage before the band took the stage at some of the more re-cent White Stripes shows (as well as the soundtrack to *The Music Man*). It was Calloway's old-school style, presentation, drama, and classy the-atricality that inspired the Stripes crew's zoot suit uniform, and it's his feline storytelling that inflects White's vocals. Plus, Cab's older sister was named Blanche. Go figure.

"Lazy"/"Space Truckin'"—Deep Purple

Machine Head cuts, the epic former track designed to blow your mind the latter to knock your block off. The majesty of rock in all its pomp and circumstance, Richie Blackmore's volume and Ian Gillan's flash seem to dovetail nicely into the latter day Stripes output.

"You're So Mystifyin'"—the Kinks

Perhaps the songwriter to which White tips his hat the least and tips his hand the most is Ray Davies. You could pick any of the master's songs, really, but this one's got good rhythm and is a smart attempt at speaking to a girl who confuses the song's protagonist, who won't admit that despite his confusion, he's trying to charm her.

"Song 1"—Fugazi

There's little doubt that a young White, exposed to Fugazi to the extent that he actually recorded "Song 1" in his bedroom, was inspired by Ian McKaye and company's DIY politics. And laying ears on the visceral stop/start dynamics of "Song 1," it's no wonder.

"It's Too Darned Hot"—Cole Porter (writer)

The singer would love to be with his baby tonite, but curse it all it's too darned hot. Talk about conjuring up an image with minimal words! Cole Porter was the master and White certainly absorbed a thing or two from the showtunes that his folks sung around the house throughout his childhood.

"Cross-Eyed Girl"—Brendan Benson

Released in 1996 before White really hunkered down on crafting his conflicted modernist neoromantic persona, Benson already had it mastered—and he had nailed the pop song craft with one hand tied behind his back, to boot.

"Mill Stream"—Flat Duo Jets

From their debut record, this proto-Stripe-ian North Carolina duo layered the raunch of rock 'n' blues on top of this Depression-era sunshine romance tale. The result was the kind of cognitive dissonance that would characterize the entire Stripes career. And the Hentchmen did a decent cover of it, too.

The Early Days of the White Stripes

It was Thomas Edison who said success is 99 percent perspiration and 1 percent inspiration. Sure, Jack White expressed more admiration for Nikola Tesla than the "Wizard of Menlo Park," but considering that the White Stripes dropped Edison's name in their early singsong romper-stomper "Astro," it's not a big stretch to figure that they picked up on that axiom and adhered to it like it was handed down on a stone tablet. In fact, that's one of the underlying dynamics that sets the White Stripes apart from many of their contemporaries. What they seem to know instinctively is the result of years of carefully observing the little victories and mistakes of others and taking copious mental notes. Their ability to be spontaneous is predicated on the idea that everything that can be accounted for has been.

The band started with an idea: A brother and sister discover instruments in their attic. They decide to play some songs together, but not before dressing themselves up, like kids picking their own clothes for church on Sunday—in an entirely red and white palate. Red for anger and passion. White for purity and innocence. And the number was three—one for Jack, one for Meg, and one for the White Stripes. The kids had been busy listening to Jonathan Richman, T. Rex, the Gories, Bob Dylan, AC/DC, and the Gun Club. The idea was fleshed out by a husband and wife couple with a penchant for theater and visual arts, respectively. The flesh was pressed into action. The action created opportunities.

Opportunities were seized. When you lay it out, it sounds simple. But anyone who's ever talked to either Jack or Meg knows that even though they're a couple of the most "present," engaged people you're likely to encounter, you always get the sense that there's ten other things going on behind the front. It was that way from the beginning, from the idea.

The quote attributed to George Washington on the inside sleeve of the Stripes' debut single "Let's Shake Hands" reads like a band mission statement: "We take the stars and blue union from heaven, the red from our mother country, separating it by white stripes, thus showing we have separated from her, and the white stripes shall go down to posterity representing liberty."

To say that they were just another garage rock band is to ignore entirely the White Stripes' pretension, and here the word *pretense* is used both in its classic sense, hinting at some deeper thought than three chords and a modified surf backbeat, as well as in the critical "damn, that's pretentious," sense. Let it never be said that Jack White had no ambition.

Even during his tenure in Goober & the Peas, Jack was still jamming as regularly as possible with Muldoon. But Jack was young, experiencing his first flush of rock 'n' roll life and getting his creative juices flowing at a breakneck pace. Muldoon was a family man, White's senior with his own well-established business. It's a story as old as rock 'n' roll itself: Friends make music together for different reasons and when it becomes apparent that choices need to be made, they get made. White chose to follow the siren's call and Muldoon's schedule didn't support his participation in playing out more often.

Suchyta sums it up nicely: "Jack wanted to play more than Brian could and that's when Meg came in."

The newlyweds were living together in the former Gillis household. It was only a matter of time, really, until they began playing together.

"The way I saw it was that she took Brian's place," says Suchyta. "And then it got creative because she's a creative person. She was just this really artsy girl. She also knew a bunch of artists, too. She introduced Jack to this artist that only drew Captain America. There was this circle of expressive people."

That circle of expressive people included the Millers (Dan worked

as an actor to pay the bills and Tracee was a respected painter in town);
musician and photographer Steve Shaw, who had recently cofounded
the Detroit Cobras; Neil Yee, who, besides owning and operating the
Gold Dollar, was involved with the city's theater and poetry scenes; as
well as a score of other folks on the downtown music scene that crossed
over heavily with the city's visual arts community. In fact, through
White's acquaintance with Shaw, Jack was informally tied to the Stooges
through the Asheton's post-Stooges punk multimedia-art projects. In
other words, chances are, if you met a musician in Detroit, they didn't
describe themselves as one. They were more likely a painter/musician,
writer/musician, web designer/musician in addition to the job you did to
keep a roof over your head (record or bookstore clerk, barista, bartender, art mover, temp worker). It was, of course, the same as any "bo-
hemian" community across the country, except in Detroit, the crushing
effect of inactivity, burnout, or apathy were ever present. After all, if
you wanted to stick around the scene, you had to keep pretty busy to
stay ahead of the boredom that led to the depression that led to the bottle that led to being just another anonymous face in the bar. And no one
that lived, worked, or played along the Cass Corridor and environs
seemed content to just punch the clock like the other schlubs in town.

The Whites were among the musicians that could be regularly found
at downtown art dives attending gallery openings and cross-pollinating
the ideas that were flying around their noggins.

Jack White busied himself during the day reupholstering furniture for
a small and spotty clientele, but he and Meg didn't exactly have a huge nut
to hit each month when the bills came due. They lived cheaply in a cheap
part of town in a house that Jack had purchased from his parents. Meg
bartended at a suburban House of Blues knockoff barbeque joint called
Memphis Smoke where the clientele enjoyed a handful of Heinekens or
Sierra Nevadas while indulging in Stevie Ray Vaughan–style electric blues
cover bands. She wasn't the only drummer behind the bar, either. Also
slinging premium ales was the diminutive-statured, big-hearted Wildbunch drummer Corey Martin (a.k.a. Martin M, a.k.a. M).

Jack also continued to dabble in his passion for sculpture. He created found artworks from objects he picked out of the garbage, forgotten or obsolete toys, trinkets, and treasures.

"I remember going back to his house during college after his folks had moved out and he had cleaned up his basement—which after years of having ten kids playing and living in the house was understandably trashed—and he's got Dr. Pepper cans cut into trucks and wagons and cupholders and all this stuff all over the place," remembers Suchyta of White's industrious approach to making art where you found it.

White showed off his disdain for the auto industry and interest in forensic science with a series of sculptures that were box-mounted cross-sections of children's cars—metal toy cars literally cut longways and displayed like so much industrial taxidermy. He did most of the work for his own edification, but he did participate in one show with Muldoon and a few others at the Russell Industrial Center in 1996.

Ben Blackwell kept a piece from that show: "Some people call this my retirement fund," he jokes, It's a four-by-four-inch piece of hardwood floor taken from the gym of White's old school—mounted with a thick, four-inch coil of auto spring—to another piece of wood. It's simple, like a makeshift toy made by a kid whose parents didn't give him any. It's the kind of urban reclamation art practiced by dozens of city bohos in Detroit to both more and less acclaim.

The most famous piece of White sculpture is, of course, the *Triple Tremolo*, featured in the CD art for the Stripes' sophomore record, *De Stijl*. The piece manages to combine Jack's idiosyncrasies and passions into one neat package. The three-by-three red-painted box contains a Leslie speaker (a speaker often used by organ players and is valued by musicians for the warm and eerie tones it generates by dint of its oscillation). The *Triple Tremelo* is hand-painted and contains strategically placed acoustic holes and baffles. On its front is a window with a peppermint circle that twirls hypnotically when the device is turned on. Between the peppermint twirl and the Leslie's comforting whirr and hum, it's a wonder White didn't sign on for the carnival sideshow as a traveling mesmerist. It's impressive in its detail, with its arrangement of holes, the brilliant red, and dapples of black in simple patterns. White designed and built it while his blues-slinging cohort, Johnny Walker of the Soledad Brothers, wired it up so that it actually worked.

Suchyta remembers that the *Triple Tremelo* had its origins in an insider tip on a would-be trash score.

"Jack reupholstered some stuff for Holy Redeemer and there was a Leslie speaker in the church and we knew the boiler room maintenance guy," recalls Suchyta.

So Jack took it and eventually transformed it into a piece of signature art. Typical.

Peppermints, red, white, black, obsolete technology repurposed, homemade art and technology, collaboration with kindred spirits—the *Triple Tremelo* is 100 percent pure metaphor for Jack White in the White Stripes.

The Whites also goofed around with their pals the Millers and others making music on the Millers' front porch on warm summer nights and creating home movies just to entertain themselves.

"He was inspiring to me," says Miller. "I remember he and I talking about liking super 8 movies. I was telling him about some idea that I had where I wanted to do this and that, but I didn't have a video camera, just a super-8 camera, and I was worrying about getting the sound right and blah, blah, blah and he was like 'Let's just do it! Even if it's horrible, let's do it!'

"He just works that way and it's his nature that he's just manically driven to get things done," says Miller. "It's such a great quality for a musician to have because it carries through to the way he records things and to writing."

Of course, the other thing the Whites were doing when Jack wasn't making outsider art for kicks was simple pickup jamming in their attic.

"Them jamming was just them jamming. They were just seeing what was going on," remembers Blackwell of Jack and Meg's exploratory efforts playing together. "He had his own upholstery shop and Meg was working and that's just how they spent extra time. They'd go see shows, they'd mess around upstairs. They never thought much of it."

"We were sitting around the attic and I'd be playing," recalled Jack in a 1999 interview during the recording session for their debut full-length. "Meg sat down behind the drums and was sort of watching. And like, for example, for [the song] 'Screwdriver,' she just pointed across the room at a screwdriver sitting on the floor and said, 'Write a song about that.'"

All the goofing around in the attic gave the Whites an idea. And Jack, being the vocal member of the group, was the band's first evangelizer.

"Before he started the White Stripes," recalls Miller, "he said, 'I have this idea for this band,' and he just spelled it out completely: Focusing on red, white, and black, having the peppermint thing and the stage aesthetic, how he wanted the band to be presented, the childlike quality, everything."

Blackwell remembers exactly the first time he heard about what would become the White Stripes: "It was at my uncle Al's wedding—which would have been summer of '96—Jack was just telling me that him and Meg had jammed and he seemed really excited about it," recalls Blackwell.

"And that it was primal—that it was basic. I was fourteen at the time, so that was a new aspect of music to me. He would of course later turn me on to the Gories and stuff like the Stooges, so I would understand better where he was coming from."

More specifically, recalls Blackwell, Jack was attempting a hybrid of a few of his favorite things.

"He said in a really early interview that if there was anywhere he was getting his inspiration, it was from the Gories and the Flat Duo Jets. And I think that was the idea to start upon. Both those bands, as great as they might be musically, are kind of lacking lyrically. And Jack really had an admiration for Dylan and poetic lyrics. And that's what he added to it."

While there are those that might find that a bit of a stretch, White did have a knack for the spare, telling lyric even from the get-go and even when he was blatantly aping his idols. The ambition to write literary lyrics was sorely lacking from garage rock at the time. So it's fair to say that one of the Stripes' initial intents was to "Trojan Horse" a bit of lyrical pretension into the world of chicks, cars, and Pabst Blue Ribbon. But first and foremost, it was two kids messing around.

Early on, Jack made perfectly clear that his main intent, no matter how obscured by feedback, volume, and attitude, was on crafting a great melody.

"I write a lot of the songs on acoustic guitar and I like to do a lot of open E blues tunings," he told WDET jock Willy Wilson in 1999. "And I write some on piano and then we transfer them over to guitar and drums. It's a totally different instrument. It's more reverbed out. As punk as it would be live, if the melody can come out on the piano then that's what I can transfer over. As long as there's a melody there."

And he wasn't shy about displaying his open-mike poetry-reading literary side, either. One example of White's literary aspirations—and a telling homage to his idol Dylan—was the early Stripes staple "Wasting My Time" in which White intoned that if he was wasting his time, then it couldn't be better spent than by "recalling every rhyme/from the book, the page, the line, the word, the letter," finishing with a dramatic vocal decrescendo. It was so textbook Dylan, that it's easy to confuse it with his reading of Dylan's own "One More Cup of Coffee," a cover the Stripes worked into their early sets and which would appear on their debut record in 1999.

The motivations were clear from the get-go even to outside observers like music journalist and Paybacks leader Wendy Case: "The fascinating thing about that whole trip is that clearly Jack's plan was already in place by the time the White Stripes played their first show," she says. "Right down to the peppermint thing."

But in typical White fashion, he deferred attention away from his own poetic aspirations and hung the White Stripes' raison d'être firmly on Meg's shoulders.

"When we started, our objective was to be as simple as possible," Jack told the *Metro Times* in 1999. "Meg's sound is like a little girl trying to play the drums and doing the best she can. Her playing on 'The Big Three Killed My Baby' is the epitome of what I like about her drumming. It's just hits over and over again. It's not even a drumbeat—it's just accents."

"They toyed around with different names, like when they were actually practicing and had the idea of being a band," says Blackwell. "I don't think they ever got to the point where they were calling themselves anything besides the White Stripes. But Bazooka or Soda Powder were names that they were toying with."

Thankfully, those names weren't chosen. Not that "the White Stripes" was a grabber from the get-go. "I remember the first time I saw the name and hadn't heard the band," remembers Detroit City Council, Dirtbombs, and Bantam Rooster member Tom Potter, "I thought they were some stupid hardcore band from the suburbs or something!" Devoid of its current attendant pop culture association, one could easily see the name connoting a hardcore band as easily as a cover band or anything else for that matter. Band names, like unusual children's names, are inherently stupid until the members and the music establish the band's personality. Exhibit A: Led Zeppelin.

But Jack always had an eye for the detail that hooks the casual observer. In both of the inserts to the first two singles are hand-typed quotes from George Washington and Marquis de Lafayette that imply some sort of greater cultural context to the band's seemingly blood-simple rock 'n' roll. And that kind of forethought was certainly aided by the duo's isolation.

"I think the fact that they were isolated and didn't know what was going on was ultimately to their benefit," reckons Blackwell.

"Because they were sitting there toiling away in their attic just practicing for like three months before they'd even played a show. So they come out and they're doing something totally different, totally well . . . despite what other people might say about whether they could play or not."

Blackwell was in on the White Stripes quite literally from the ground floor. Or, at least, that was his vantage point on a lot of the early White Stripes practices. "I was at fucking every early practice, man. But it's hard for me to say what they were like because I'd sleep through them. I'd come over after school and they'd be practicing up in the attic. And I'd have a pillow or something and I'd curl up under a table while they were practicing. They'd say 'Ben whaddya think of that one?' and I'd say (in sleepy voice) 'Oh, it was OK . . . I was sleeping.' And I think about it now and I'm like 'Wow, I slept through a good two dozen White Stripes practices' . . . in the room! Not like I was downstairs."

The Whites' domestic situation certainly influenced their anytime-the-urge-struck-'em practice "schedule." "They'd just go through a song till it was right," said Blackwell. "You know, a basic band practice. I think it would be spontaneous, too, you know, if they were just hanging out and Jack and Meg were both there, one of 'em would say, 'Hey maybe we should practice that new song. Let's go upstairs' and everything would be set up. You wouldn't have to schedule anything." It sounds downright idyllic, indeed, childlike.

Jack and Meg started hanging out at a new joint in a relatively dicey section of the Cass Corridor called the Gold Dollar. The Dollar was not the garage-rock haven that it has been made into by revisionist history. It was a dive, to be sure, a former drag and exotica "show bar." And it was about half a mile farther down the Cass Corridor than most rock tourists had ventured before. Its pale blue exterior with the Gold Dollar logo was the only thing distinguishing it from the half-abandoned buildings that surrounded it. The parking lot was a nightmare of potholes and tight squeezes on crowded nights. You'd take a left into the bar from the typically flyer-and-free-weekly–paper crowded, er, "foyer," open the door to the bar and be greeted by the doorperson—sometimes Tom Potter's better half, Katy, other times the ubiquitous Corey, and, later, Gravitar/Detroit City Council/Bogue guitarist Mike Walker. Behind them was Yee's "office," a recording setup/mixing board from which he ran sound and watched over the joint. If a band showed up too early for soundcheck, they might even catch him stealing a quick nap in the little cubby. The bar was to the right along the entire south wall, a massive Gold Dollar coin propped up on the mirror behind the liquor bottles, earplugs, and Off Woodward recordings. CDs were for sale by bands like Stun Gun, the Wildbunch, and Maschina. The two-tiered ceilings were low enough to trap the smoke and sound, and if the singer of the band was tall, like Dan Miller or Jack White, the view of them could very well be cut off. There were a couple rows of linoleum-covered tables and that's about it. But the place—per Yee's whim and whimsy—was wide-eyed in its programming. Poetry, short plays, oddball bands, and misfit sonic artists were just as likely to be onstage (especially in the early years) as any rote rawk acts. Every year, the downtown music scene admitted what it truly was—a surrogate high school for freaks and misfits—and threw itself a prom with themes like Purple Reign and "Night on Disco Mountain." It was the kind of place books get written about.

Bartenders like Amy Abbott held court behind the Dollar bar from 1997 till its closing in 2001. "How can one describe the Gold Dollar experience? It pretty much had everything you could want in a rock club—anywhere you sat or stood was a good angle, its setup was conducive to watching bands," she recalls.

"Neil had a good, pure idea when he started that we all sort of sullied along the way. There was definitely a sense of belonging and family, and I think a lot had to do with its location. In the early days its location kept the tourists at bay so you really just got the people that wanted to be there as opposed to the folks that thought it was the place to be. The ladies' room was pleasant, the men's like an oversize cat box," says Abbott "The building was decrepit, and I was always suspicious that the smoke eating machine was just a ruse. Mostly though, we worked really hard to make it far . . . everyone that worked there was asked to work there, we kind of singled people out that would make good employees. When you have the ability to choose who you surround yourself with it makes things more harmonious. No one really needed to be an asshole. I really tried to treat everyone with the same service and courtesy because to me there is nothing worse than going into a bar and being treated like shit by the staff just because you don't know them or hang out with them. Also for me I really liked dressing up in various disguises or looks as a way of keeping myself entertained. That is what was fun about the Wildbunch (a.k.a. Electric Six) in the early days, they would go along with out curious themes—like Thanksgiving Eve and Prom."

And, to make matters more mercurial, anyone could get booked at the Gold Dollar so long as they met one of Neil Yee's two criteria: "You had to be either good or a nice person," laughs Yee.

The White Stripes, being both, were among the early regulars. They hung out there because Yee had asked Meg's sister Heather to be the place's first bartender. But the fringe benefit was that in 1996, the bar's first year, Yee opened the stage up on Sunday nights—even going so far as to provide guitar, drums, bass, and amps—to aspiring musicians. White was one of them and he took the opportunity to get some stage experience in on those Sundays.

One of his first real conversations with Jack told a lot about the kid at the time.

"Jack offered to make some wooden sign or carve something for the bar," recalls Yee. "I was like 'carve a wood sign?' I didn't even know what to make of that. Then I figured everyone just liked the 'I just found this place, and I've discovered this dive' aspect of the bar. And it was authentically that. I was kind of impressed with carving wood, but I had no idea how that would fit in with what I was doing."

"He did a chair for me," Yee continues. "He did a great job, fantastic. He did more than I expected. I think that's how he paid for the first few White Stripes recordings.

"After I'd seen him with other bands, I remember them coming in to the bar. I know Meg has always been reserved. Jack, I didn't really know as well, but he seemed like he was really, really quiet," says Yee of the young couple. "They seemed like little kids, which I guess they were at the time."

Of course, Yee had known Meg for a while through her sister Heather.

"In the early days, they just started showing up and I know that Meg, like Heather, had no goals or aspirations of being in a band. And things just kinda happened," says Yee.

"I think that things happen to Meg for the most part rather than Meg making things happen. I remember when Heather called me and said Meg quit her job because they were touring too much and I remember thinking that that was the last person I'd think would quit their day job!"

Yee recalls one afternoon on the shores of Lake St. Clair (the near–Great Lake out of which the Detroit River flows) that sticks out in his head as typically Meg-esque.

"After the White Stripes had started, Heather and Meg were taking their mom out on my sailboat," he says. "It was really windy and my sailboat had a really unreliable motor. So we just went and picked up rocks and stones and shiny things. And that's sort of typical of them—looking at little things that no one else might notice and collecting them. Heather lived in my house and she had the weirdest collection of trash-picked items, large pieces of metal, all sorts of stuff."

The White Stripes' first "real" show was an afterthought. First of all, they had already played at least once at the Gold Dollar (and perhaps another time at a Hamtramck coffeehouse called Planet Ant, also on open mike night). They had apparently struck such a chord with the assembled drink and java sippers that barely anyone can remember whether or not it actually happened. Even Jeff Meier, who was friends with Jack and Meg, is vague at best with his recollection. "I think I saw them. Maybe it was just Jack. But I'm pretty sure Meg was playing, too."

"We like to say we formed on Bastille Day, 1997," said Jack White.

There are very few soundbytes that have been uttered by the imminently quotable Mr. White that more closely encapsulate his puckish attitude toward his and the band's history. He's simply a man constantly aware of the myth he's spinning about his band. "We like to say . . ." Instant disclaimer. Caveat Emptor. He knows that fans want a sexy story, not the reality of the mundane. After all, rock and roll, as rote as it has become, still breathes the air of escapism. Jack and Meg White realize this. But in the interest of those calendar-obsessed fans, contrary to—or in perfect keeping with—the White Stripes myth, their first show wasn't actually on Bastille Day (the French Independence day celebrated July 14) in 1997. They did play an open mike night at the Gold Dollar that week, but the 14th was a Monday that year and open mike nights at the Gold Dollar were always on Sundays.

Thankfully, Gold Dollar proprietor Neil Yee also had an actual live website at the time that can be referenced and so what is sure is that the first *documented* appearance of the White Stripes live is at the Gold Dollar on August 14, 1997, opening for Meier's band, Rocket 455, and then again the next night, for the Hentchmen (which, for the record, was supposed to be their first gig).

"I had met Jack outside the Magic Bag," recalls the Hentchmen's John Szymanski. "He and Meg were coming out of a show and so were Tim (Purrier, Hentchmen guitarist) and I, and he just said, 'Hey, you're the Hentchmen!' And he gave me his business card, and it was for Third Man Upholstery. So I filed it away. A few months later, we had a gig booked at the Gold Dollar and I was talking to Jeff Meier and he said, 'Well, you oughta have my friend Jack's band open.' And I put two and two together and found the card and called him and he said 'yeah.' So it was that simple."

That same weekend, Rocket 455 was scheduled to play, so Meier tapped the Stripes to kick off the show for them, too. At the time, the people who were going to see garage rock shows in Detroit were a group composed largely of other musicians and sundry scenesters in a nonexistent "scene."

"When they first started playing, there are so many people that said they were at the first show that weren't," says Yee. "I'm like, 'you weren't there, either.' Even their first shows after the one or two open mike nights, there weren't that many people there."

Typically, opening bands at the Gold Dollar would only hold the casual interest of friends and family, and even then people rotated in and out of the building, alternating between watching the band and standing around outside enjoying the sights and smells of the Cass Corridor in the summertime. Many of the people that came out to see Rocket also came out the next night to see the Hentchmen. And the shows have grown legendary only in the hindsight of people who may or may not have even been there.

What is generally agreed upon by those who were there was that the White Stripes were an opening act and as such had to suffer the indignity of being on the receiving end of the Detroit hipster mafia's often too-cool-for-school attitude. Which means that despite their best efforts at being outrageously different from the blue-collar rock that the Hentchmen and Rocket were plying, the main reaction to the band was "uh, yeah, they were pretty good I guess."

Meg rocked the white and red Coca-Cola Zubas as her stage attire and Jack was already making people talk about his hair, which at the time was the shaved-side "whitewall" with a mushroom of eye-length curls on top.

"I didn't really think anything," remembers Szymanski. "Because, at that point, it was like any new band is worth having play with you, you know? So we didn't hear them beforehand or anything. Maybe he mentioned the Flat Duo Jets or the Gories, so he was dropping the right names. I thought he was pleasant and everything.

"Of course, even then the vision was already there," he continues. "They already had the peppermint drumhead. He put his guitar amp on that riser thing. I remember the crowd being mixed. There was maybe like twelve people there. Maybe there was more at the Rocket show."

The "riser thing" was a trademark of early White Stripes shows and a particular point of pride in Jack's presentation of the band. He would haul into the club an hourglass-shaped midcentury modern table, place his amp on top of it, and drape it in red fabric so, for all intents and purposes, there was no amplification to be seen on stage, merely an enigmatic red lump on a funky table from which throbbed the most urgent, forceful guitar tones and some of the most graceful, understated sounds to be heard on the balls-to-the-wall garage rock scene.

"I remember carting that around thinking *Why do I have to do this?!*" recalls the Stripes earliest roadie, Blackwell. "Now I understand that he wanted to make it more than going to see someone down at the bar. He wanted to make it more of an event—short of pyro and smoke machines. He made it an event in his own way."

Suffice it to say that there were those that saw something different right off the bat, and for whom that difference was intriguing enough. The shows were rough, but the idea was there. The concept—such as it was—was a sturdy construction. The songs were slower, clunkier, and more raw on the edges and in the middle. Early tunes like "Astro" and "Canon" were delivered with White's firebrand vocals dominant; his guitar riffs were more chunky than articulate.

"The first time I remember encountering Jack, Steve Shaw and I were just hanging out drinking one night and we went upstairs at the Garden Bowl and either the Soledad Brothers or Johnny Walker solo was playing in the corner by the bar and I remember noticing Jack with his New Wave haircut sitting there," says Dave Buick. "He was dressed all proper. I'm not even positive if it happened, but I'm pretty sure at the end of the show he did a couple songs with Johnny. And I remember Steve and I thought that both of those guys were really good. That was in the springtime of '97. And then I remember three or four months after that going to see Rocket and Jeff's buddy was opening up—and that was the White Stripes.

"He had talked up Jack—and I don't want to get Jeff in trouble—but he seemed like he was kind of making an excuse like they might be kind of hard to take or something. I remember him kind of saying 'my friend's band is opening up' as a kind of disclaimer. I listened to most of it from outside. And then the next night, I liked it even better and then three or four shows in, I already knew all the songs. I got hooked pretty early."

What grabbed Buick and so many others right away was the passion and raw soul the White Stripes displayed. To him and others, it was the same as the first time they saw the Gories or the Hentchmen. Not a lot backing it up, not a lot of polish, but a lot of raw energy.

"The Gories and the Stripes music wasn't the same," says Buick. "But it made me feel the same way. It made me feel like there was something new starting. It was right after I had put out my first records. It made me think 'Oh, cool, there's something else I can be excited about.'"

"The first time that I saw them perform it was really, really spine-chillingly great," enthuses Miller. "It's one of those things where if someone describes a film they really love or reading a book and seeing the movie, sometimes it's not the same thing at all and you have high expectations. The expectations were so high the first time I saw them after hearing him describe the White Stripes, but they nailed it."

Others weren't as initially impressed.

"This is where I get myself into trouble, but I thought the show lacked any real dynamics," says Detroit photographer and former Dirtbombs drummer EWolf. "Perhaps it was the mismatch of having Jack who is at least aspiring to be a virtuoso as opposed to Meg who was a student at that point. A lot of my favorite bands were bands that didn't have any mastery of their instruments, but they shared that lack of mastery. It wasn't negative, but it didn't win me over completely."

On the other hand, at least they were trying something with diverse roots. And it's important to remember that outside of the tight downtown scene, other people were making music that was as inspired and twisted as the Stripes if not more so. "A lot of the bands in town seemed to take a good idea and run it into the ground," says EWolf. "It's fine to draw your influences from a particular point in music history, but show that you have something else going on. I was a big fan of Mule at the time. Their sound was so bombastic and off-kilter country and was such a weird fusion of blues and country that people couldn't grasp what it was."

"They were doing it really well for a band that had never played a show before," says Blackwell, who wasn't old enough to get in to see the Gold Dollar shows, but vividly remembers uncle Jack's excitement at the result.

"It was ultimately accepted by the scene pretty immediately. I remember after a show or two Jack saying to me, 'The guys from the Hentchmen love us! They want to do a benefit so that we can record an album!'"

Around the same time that he had met the Hentchmen, White made the acquaintance of one Johnny Walker (né Wirick), of the Ohio blues duo the Soledad Brothers. The Soledads had grown out of the Toledo-area blues-rock trio Henry & June, which had released a 45 on Detroiter Marty Klotz's Human Fly label ("Lowdown Streamline" b/w/ "Going Back to Memphis") in 1995.

The Soledad Brothers were a distillation of the kind of blues that White attempted with the White Stripes, except without all the pesky baggage of '60s pop, folk, classic rock, and musical theater. They struck up a friendship immediately that would lead to one of the more productive ongoing collaborations of kindred spirits on the Detroit music scene with White producing a few of the Soledad's singles and their debut full-length at his home in Southwest Detroit. It was one more way the perennial outsider White was actively creating a community of likeminds around himself and further ingraining himself into the fabric of the Detroit music scene.

"I was playing at a lounge in Detroit when Jack struck up a conversation about slide guitar," Walker told Australian writer Shane Jesse Xmass in 2000. "He was really pumping me for information. I could see that he was really enthusiastic about playing blues, and he had good taste. For many years after we would talk smack and play guitar on his front porch. We recorded a lot of good stuff on his front porch. Jack White is worth his weight in brilliance. He played snow shovel on the Italy single. He had to stand twenty feet from the mike, on the sidewalk, because the shovel was so loud. You are still able to hear his hollerin' 'In My Time of Dying' on the record. We also recorded a version of 'Little Red Rooster' on his porch complete with distant Southwest Detroit gunfire. Very tasteful."

Indeed, this acceptance seemed to be very important to White for both pragmatic and personal reasons. Pragmatic because you need someone to open for and play with and personal because he wasn't sure there were other freaks out there like himself that found solace in the dusty grooves of deep cuts dug from the record bins. He was wrong, of course. Detroit is full of such people. And the White Stripes started to fit in right away.

"They weren't necessarily adopted, just accepted. Like wow. There's other people who like the same music as me. I'm willing to bet he'd never met anyone else who liked Love before. But now he could talk to somebody about Love and they'd say, 'Oh, have you heard Arthur Lee's solo record?' And Jack'd be like 'What? Solo record?' and that person would say 'Oh, yeah, *Vindicator* or whatever,'" says Blackwell. "So I think that was just opening a new door to a bunch of new opportunities."

Also in attendance at those first couple shows was Jim Diamond, who had just moved to Detroit from the Michigan state capital Lansing. Diamond wasn't easily impressed.

"I remember seeing the White Stripes at the Gold Dollar opening up and Jack had some kind of Split Enz hairdo. So I was like, Who's the Split Enz kid?" says the Ghetto Recorders owner with a chuckle.

"Anyway, I thought, 'The girl's kinda cute' and 'He can't really play very well, all right whatever. It's like Bantam Rooster with a girl.'"

It was during one of these early Detroit shows that Jack White made an important connection to his songwriting growth. Singer and songwriter Brendan Benson had recently returned from California to his native Detroit after extricating himself from a recording contract with major label Virgin Records. He had heard little about the Whites save for knowing that Jack was also in 2-Star Tabernacle with Miller, when he ambled into the Gold Dollar.

"I walked into the Gold Dollar and I remember hearing Jack singing and thinking *oh, it's some chick* or whatever, some girl singing because at the time his voice was just sooo affected," he recalls. "It became less affected as he perfected it, but I remember turning the corner and seeing this guy who I had seen around town, kinda, and I was surprised to see him on stage. And I was sort of dumbfounded. I don't normally like going to see bands, but I remember I just couldn't wait for the next song and hoping it would never end and, at the same time, wondering *What the fuck is going on?!*"

What Benson picked out right away was the naked honesty and raw emotion that White was already getting across in even the White Stripes' earliest shows.

"It was so strange that I barely noticed the red and white motif," laughs Benson.

"After that show, I made it a point to meet him. I said, I gotta become friends with this guy and I have to like pick his brain and I want what he's doing to rub off on me," says Benson. "It was totally premeditated. I wanted that. I wanted the Midas touch. Because I was struggling, I still am, I mean, fuck, I think about things so much. I beat myself up about how hard it is to write a song from the heart.

"Having worked with [songwriters] Jason Faulkner and Jon Brion—not to say anything negative about them—but it is kind of this school of music that is sort of cerebral. Jack was like the antithesis of that. He was just the raw emotion. In every way.

"I mean, I don't think he could really play that well at the time and that's what I love so much about him. I think that he's loud and when you're that loud and distorted, you can make all kinds of cool sounds. But he's got finesse, too. That's something a lot of people don't have. The guitar is just like another appendage. He's never uncomfortable, it never seems to get away from him, and if it does, he just reels it back in."

Soon he had Jack over to his house/recording studio on Detroit's East Side. "I remember the first time he came over, I was showing him around the house. I was showing him upstairs, showing him some guitars and he was smoking a cigarette and there was no ashtray around and so he was ashing on the table, just ashing on it. I was horrified. I thought you know, just fucking uncouth and crude. I didn't say anything. But in the end, when we went to leave the room, he was like [brushes imaginary ashes into hand] 'Oh, sorry.' He was just like oblivious. That's what I like about him. I like to think back on that. He's a strange guy and that's so cool. To know someone who's genuinely so strange."

White's ability to stay true to his inner weirdo shone through from the get-go when it came time to perform with Meg as the White Stripes.

"The other thing that struck me was their interaction on stage," Benson recalls.

"I knew they were married, and the way that he was referring to her as his sister was . . . I thought of this whole sexual thing at first. Like wow, kind of backwoods, kind of . . . I couldn't get my head around it. But I knew that it was cool."

"The other thing was that he would flash fingers at her. Maybe it was because she couldn't play and he was kind of cueing her on the sly. But

I'd like to think it was kind of a James Brown thing. Because other times it was like 'two times: bam . . . bam!' So I thought that was amazing."

Indeed, at their early shows, Jack played the necessary dual part of bandleader and frontman to its fullest, though, both surprising the gathered dozen or so people with his keening Tin Pan Alley–meets-glam-rock falsetto and his startlingly aggressive guitar attack while also counting off beats to Meg by waving his hands in the air, counting with his fingers, or shouting it out.

"Jack coaching Meg onstage, I think was part of the show," says Blackwell. "But I think it would fluctuate."

"Sometimes she really did need it," says Blackwell. "I knew what Meg knew on drums and what Meg would need help on and what she wouldn't. She was just learning the drums after all."

And other times, still, Jack would appear to get fed up and ignore her mistakes entirely and just carry on and hope she caught up.

"I don't know how deeply Jack thought about any of it," says Blackwell. "It's almost like too many bands practice too much. The Stooges, the Gories, the Ramones, they weren't bands sitting there being perfectionists. They were practicing onstage. I think Jack knew that from studying those bands. So I don't think it was him thinking they had to get to a certain point before they could play a show. It happened when it happened, like lightning in a bottle or some other Jim Croce shit."

Likely the real answer was somewhere in between showmanship and willful ineptitude. Either way, the mix of menace and entertainment created a dynamic stage tension that hasn't dissipated to this day. Audiences could sense that Jack was frustrated with Meg's imperfection and they could also sense that she had no intention of budging an inch from what she was doing. With her pigtails tilted slightly starboard, her brown eyes peering up with her stick rested on the tom, she seemed to say "screw you," "I love you," and "let's get this shit moving" in the same glance and each with equal intensity. Even though White had already written songs like "The Union Forever" years earlier, Meg simply wasn't able to work the traps consistently enough for them to add the song to their setlist. They wouldn't start playing the song as the White Stripes until late 1999 and it wouldn't turn up in recorded form until *White Blood Cells* in 2001. But they were growing and people could see the learning curve drawn in the air connecting Jack's growing ability as an interpreter of the blues and his first-thought-best-thought punk spirit with the duo's ability to stick together.

Still, they were first of three bands on both of those bills at the Gold Dollar and there is such a thing as Detroit Rock Standard Time, which dictates that all bands push the time they are to go onstage to the very last minute and the people that come to see the shows do likewise. The result is often that opening acts simply and regularly get missed.

"At the Gold Dollar shows, people would only really start to show up and it would only really get crowded at like a quarter to one in the morning or something," recalls Buick.

"So people definitely weren't there for the White Stripes shows. For the first year, at least, people weren't there," he continues. "The White Stripes were always first on the bill and slowly but surely more people would come for them and more people would pay attention and there were more people there early who didn't want to see the Subsonics or Rocket, but there'd be people showing up to see the White Stripes and singing along."

By the time the White Stripes were invited to play the 1998 Fourth Street Fair—an annual outdoor street gathering held every July that features many of the best and brightest rock acts slogging it out on the downtown club scene—they had begun to hit their stride. Local promoter and scene gadfly Greg Baise remembers this show as a touchstone of the early Stripes' progress.

"I remember they played on the Park Stage," recalls Baise. "And it was one of those shows by them that just sticks out. I'm not sure exactly why. Meg was drumming barefoot, and it was summer and Jack's in-between song banter had gotten more interesting."

And by that time, they had worked their signature tune "The Big Three Killed My Baby" into a real showstopper. It was a sweltering day and the normally nocturnal musicians were only blinking reluctantly into the light when the Stripes took the stage early in the afternoon.

But they were enough of a known commodity to draw a crowd of sixty or so curious souls and accomplished enough to keep 'em watching at rapt attention.

Pleased to Meet You

Wednesday nights at the Garden Bowl—the bar downstairs from the Magic Stick that doubled as the watering hole for bowlers rolling 'em on the oldest lanes in the United States—were reserved for the rock 'n' roll bowling league that hosted such weekly gladiatorial challenges as the Rolling Bitches (a.k.a. Dave Buick, Jack White, and Greg Siemasz) against Team GASH (a.k.a. John and Mike Hentch and Willy Wilson) as well as teams composed of members of the Waxwings, Rocket 455, the Sights, the Clone Defects, and other hometown heroes, various and sundry local promoters and itinerant drummers and bass players. The evenings would start civilly enough, to be sure, but it wasn't an uncommon sight by the end of the evening to have beeramids as tall as men and drunken declarations of love and war that would be forgotten once Thursday morning opened its sleep-encrusted eyes.

"There was a lot of the Italy Records contracts, or lack thereof, that happened at bowling league," remembers Buick.

"I have a vague memory of us talking about doing the second record and also about the Hentchforth idea—with Jack playing bass with them—there. At least I'm fairly certain. You don't remember a lot when you have a beeramid the size of you," he laughs.

And, while it may sound like 20/20 hindsight at the service of mere trivia, White was a damn good bowler. Seriously serious about it, too.

"Jack was a really good bowler, a fast bowler. There was a time when he actually shattered his ball on the pins," recalls Buick.

It's not surprising that the oft-bandied about (at least in the post-Stollsteimer dust-up press) encounter with Sights drummer Dave Shettler was supposedly over a bowling ball.

More often than disagreements, though, informal agreements were made. It was there the budding entrepreneur, Buick, would agree to release records by his band buddies on his nascent Italy Records label. It was just such an informal agreement that led to the White Stripes debut.

"I started Italy for two reasons," says Buick. "One was to have an excuse as to why I was quitting my full-time job. Not like I ever had spent more than an hour a week on Italy. But I needed an excuse to tell my boss and to tell my mom. The second reason was because I always wanted to be a part of a music scene and have something to do with records that were in kids' record collections, and I couldn't play music and I had some money, so I was like, I'll put out some records.

"The Dirtys were having a record come out on [German-via–New Jersey garage punk label] Crypt and I thought, well, you don't' have anything else out, so let's put a single out here so you can have a Detroit single out before that record is released. And they were really too slow and too drunk, so they ended up being the second release." Of course, the White Stripes ended up being the third release.

"I kinda liked the fact that a lot of people were very vocal about disliking the White Stripes. I don't know why that turned me on, but for some reason it did. All these people that were talking about how annoyed they were. And I just thought it would be cool to have a single out that would anger so many people. Even though the one song 'Let's Shake Hands' is such a nice song that it shouldn't anger anyone!" he laughs.

People, he says, didn't understand why Jack whined or why they didn't have a bass player or didn't understand why Meg wasn't a good drummer. And that appealed to his inner confrontational punk.

"The sentiment is so pure, but still the music pissed people off.

"I approached Jack at some holiday show. I remember I was there with Steve Shaw and Peggy from the Gories and some other people and Jack walked by and I asked him about it and he was really confused," muses Buick.

"He said he didn't have any money! That he didn't have the money to do it. I don't even know what he thought I was gonna do, he just said that he couldn't afford that. Which is kinda cool, cause it seemed like at that point, Jack had no intention or no knowledge of the music scene or the industry. It just seemed like he was doing it for the sake of doing it."

This stands as a stark contrast to the confident, assured White who studies his various moves and seems to pick just the right one every time. But it also points to another ongoing thread in the success of the White Stripes as they built from baby band to worldbeaters.

"He has always seemed like he knows what he wanted," says Buick. "But maybe he's just been learning how to get it along the way. Because he was kind of naïve about the whole situation at first. And I'm not saying it like I was anything more than a guy that had put out two local singles. But the next time I talked to him, I explained that I'd pay for it and I'd give him a certain amount of singles and he was like 'yeah, totally' and a month later he had the stuff all recorded and in my hands," says Buick.

"As soon as I told him that I'd pay for it, he didn't waste time with anything."

"They had a ton of great songs at the time," remembers Blackwell, "like 'Jimmy the Exploder' and 'Screwdriver.' I remember telling Jack that they should record some of those." Blackwell was the one person to sit in on the majority of Stripes rehearsals. "It just goes to show you why I'm not in the White Stripes, I guess."

The first White Stripes record just may have been their perfect recording. Had they pulled the plug after "Let's Shake Hands" (backed with the disturbingly sublime cover of the Terry Gilkyson-via-Marlene Dietrich tune, the nuptially ambivalent "Look Me Over Closely"), the Stripes would doubtless have gone down in record collector history as an outta-left-field oddball act that could have existed comfortably with a cult of thirty or forty fanatics. Of course, as long as we're laying down revisionist history, we should assume that at least Jack would have gone on to make a handful of singles on obscure-o indie labels. Hell, that's exactly what the White Stripes did until 2001. But we digress.

From the opening sludgy moments of "Let's Shake Hands," simple-as-rock bliss guitar attack and crest-and-crash-riding surf rhythm battery to Jack's hyperactive falsetto ringing true like a desperate, plaintive puppy dog in heat—"oh-wo-hooha-babae less be friendsss."

Lacking a better plan, White either settled for conventional greetings as practiced by the rest of society in which he saw no role for himself or opted for a socially acceptable form of romantic, idyllic handholding. Either way, his guitar pronouncements assured that he was finally vindicated in his desire to simply hold hands. "Can't come up with a better plan/put your little fingers in mine/baby/let's shake hands."

It is also an anthem of the strangest sort. A surf-rock with vocals that attempt to squeeze some sort of "can I get a witness" call and response into its terse two-minute runtime. "Well there's something there in the air/Jump up and let me know when you're there baby let's be friends!"

It would take fellow Michigander Andrew W.K. four years to top that kind of open-hearted, open-chorded absurd openmindedness.

The menacing stroll of "Look Me Over Closely"—sort of a cross between the Cramps and Kurt Weill—meanwhile was a strange choice of covers for a newlywed recently betrothed to his first true love.

Further, the Whites tapped their Southwest Detroit neighbor Meier to man the recordings. Since his early ill-fated attempts to record the Gories in a disused Cass Corridor apartment, Meier had established a little bit of a name for himself and had earned a reputation as a punk-friendly hit-it-and-quit-it recordist. He'd helmed forty-five sessions for not only his own bands Rocket 455 and the Detroit Cobras, but he'd also branched out to capture the sounds of the Hentchmen and the Dirtys—a self-destructing punk-rock quartet from Port Huron, about an hour away by I-94 as the eighteen-wheelers roll.

White had heard these recordings and—coupled with his knock-around friendship with Meier, and the duo's shared love of the home-made feel of old blues and R&B records—was suitably impressed enough to enlist him.

"We were hanging out all the time," recalls Meier, "and it just seemed like the logical thing to do. I think I recorded the Dirtys right around that same time. So he probably heard that, too."

So one day, as 1997 ticked over to 1998, in Jack and Meg's home, the White Stripes and Meier holed up in the parlor of the White house to record two simple songs. Meier recalls things going just as smoothly as any recording done by friends at home for a tiny locals-only DIY punk rock label.

"It was a sunny day. I don't think they played the song that many times. I think we only had a few takes to choose from and I think it was pretty obvious which one was gonna be the single," he says.

"He just let me do what I always do. He had a little bit of input," says Meier. "I did what I always do, bare minimum sound isolation with a lot of room sound. I'm not really concerned with isolating things, but just get enough to control the sound a little bit. It was pretty much a one-take. It was pretty quick and to the point. I don't remember spending a whole lot of time on it. It was all done in two to three hours.

"Then they did that 'Look Me Over Closely,'" he remembers with a slight widening of his already perpetually wide-eyed gaze.

"And I didn't know what to make of that. I appreciate Broadway, I guess," he laughs.

"I remember we did the music first. So he went and redid the vocals another day for 'Let's Shake Hands,'" says Meier.

"But he did the vocals for 'Look Me Over Closely' that day. And I remember him doing these little theatrical thespian moves," he recalls with a slight flourish of his arms indicating only a small percentage of the drama White injected into the effort.

"It was like he was doing Broadway. I don't know if he had been in plays as a child or whatever, but he was doing these big gestures like he was recording a song from an operetta. It was unexpected, but it wasn't the first time where I've recorded or seen something unexpected. I thought it was cool. I wish there was a DVD of him singing it. That would add to the whole feeling of the single," Meier concludes with a chuckle.

"Jack, I just think had a feeling, like a sentimental feeling," ventures Benson about the record's wide-eyed embrace of minimalist poetry.

"Like other garage bands might have been singing about some foxy chick or whatever, but he was singing about this thing which was real juvenile. Like being in love at the age of six or seven, like this real puppy love kind of thing. Like 'Let's Shake Hands' was like 'let's touch,' it's just brilliant. It's certainly more vulnerable than the rockers who were putting up a front.

"With the rockers it was all innuendo or cliché or cryptic, encoded. But his stuff was like, 'do you remember when you were on the playground and you wanted . . . ' when you try to describe it, that's what's horrible, because it's so hard to do, but a song like 'Let's Shake Hands,' was [that feeling] for me."

Meanwhile, following its March '98 release the world outside of Detroit paid essentially zero notice to the White Stripes. The single wasn't flying out of Buick's house/label headquarters.

White set himself apart from the other "local rock" rabble by paying attention to details like personally handing the band's singles to area writers and taking a minute to talk to them about the record, about upcoming shows, and generally walking the line between self-promotion and amiable chatting like an expert politician. This is diametrically opposed to the musicians who send their records in the mail, never follow up, and then send bitchy e-mails three months later when they weren't reviewed. After all, half of life is showing up and White showed up.

"We sent out a few promos to *MRR* and *Flipside* and some dumb garage magazines and stuff like that. That gets a couple nerds with beer bellies into it, you know?" laughs Buick.

"It didn't sell well right away. I pressed 1,000 and it took a pretty long time to sell 'em out. It took so long that for a couple years I was just giving those singles away," he says. "I got another going for multiple hundreds of dollars on eBay and I really wish I had a bunch of 'em now!" says Buick, who now runs downtown Detroit record-store–cum-label Young Soul Rebels.

Nine months and twice as many White Stripes shows later, Italy released the White Stripes' second single, "Lafayette Blues" b/w "Sugar Never Tasted So Good" and if ever there was a reason to pay attention to B-sides of singles, it was this record. The A-side was a jarring rockabillyhued stomp and rave-up litany of the myriad Detroit-area street names with French origin pronounced as the French might as opposed to how Detroiters had become accustomed. For example, Livernois Avenue, a main north-south artery leading out of the city is pronounced on local traffic reports as "liver-noy" instead of "leevernwah." It was a cute inside joke punctuated by a non sequitur rave-up preceded by the intonation that White was "ready, ready, ready to . . . rock 'n' roll!"

But the B-side was the chink in the armor that let a few observant local geeks in on the White Stripes' secret weapon: Jack was nurturing his inner poet and that poet was married to his growing ability to craft a stunning pop tune. "Sugar Never Tasted So Good" is a disarming exercise in minimalist storytelling. With just a few words, White suggests an entire landscape of regret, possibility, and youthful folly. "And her words like a daisy/until my mind gets lazy/I must have been crazy not to see. . . . yeah-ah." Looking back on a love lost, recalling it with the enigmatic title phrase "sugar never tasted so good," and ending with the very blues-like admission "what a fool this boy can be" over near-droning, chock-a-block acoustic guitar strums, White the mesmerist made his first appearance (he had come close with "Look Me Over Closely," but his inner showboat eventually won the day).

"Sugar Never Tasted So Good" was a watershed tune.

"I think the moment I realized there was a lot more going on than what I originally suspected," says the platinum-blond rock Amazon Wendy Case, "was when I bumped into Jack—and I was doing rock journalism at the time—and I was talking to him about his record and a few of us walked up the stairs together at the Stick and Brendan Benson was onstage. And we got to the top of the stairs and both of us stopped and realized he was doing 'Sugar Never Tasted So Good.'

"I already knew it was a really good song, but to hear it in a different context was really riveting. It was the first time I realized that there was something much heavier going on than just the simplicity of the band or of the idea. That there was really some great songwriting going on."

What took Case by surprise was the newly displayed evidence of the care that was going into crafting his songs.

"It was no longer just a tossed-off kitschy idea of 'Oh, I'm going to get my girlfriend or my wife to play drums and I'm just gonna bash out some chords and yelp over them.' Suddenly when you hear the song out of context, you really started understanding that there was something greater than the whole going on there."

The single was again recorded in the White's house and the B-side boasted the kind of dusky hand-holding intimacy that would later charm their budding legion of fans when they re-created it for the song "We Are Going to Be Friends."

Since the release of the first single, White had become the de facto in-house producer for Italy Records. Actually, the house in question was usually Jack's and the recordings typically went off in his living room. For a year and a half or so, White had a hand in nearly every Italy record (45s all) that hit store shelves. During this time, the old house on Ferdinand became ground zero for the downtown garage rock crowd. For his part, White seemed to use this period to boost his own confidence in getting the sounds in his head down on tape with local and imported yokels as his willing test subjects.

"He recorded all of them from number three to twelve or thirteen," says Buick of White's contribution to the labels catalog. "I was more like his right-hand man and Italy was just like what he was doing," he laughs.

"The front room was kind of always changing," remembers Blackwell. "I think Jack was interested in trying every different possibility. If you call that experimental or not. The drums would be in a different place every time you'd go over there. Same with the amps. There was good separation in the room so he was able to record the basic tracks live. I can remember that every different session he'd done for the Stripes or the Greenhornes or the Soledad Brothers the drums being in three to four different spots. He didn't have a set way of recording in that room.

"For most of the bands it wasn't really like he has a strong idea, he just hears it and knows what it should sound like," recalls Buick.

Buick remembers, in particular, one informal recording session for Cincinaiti R&B revivalists, the Greenhornes, single "Stayed Up All Night."

"The Greenhornes were walking around with whiskey and we were drinking whiskey and beer and we went up to the store to get an RC adapter for some piece of equipment. Me and Johnny Walker went up and get it. At the same time we bought a bunch of suction cup dart guns at this drug store in Southwest Detroit. The whole session was pretty much the Greenhornes and Me and Jack sitting around in his living room having a dart gun war and he just happened to be recording at the same time.

"He knew what they should sound like and he set up real quick and had some drinks and played darts. It wasn't like he was Phil Spector in the studio. And it's not like he was goofing around. I think that it's just early on he figured out what was going on."

"If you have a band like the Greenhornes, a five-piece recording live to four-track, you go where people fit," says Blackwell.

"Actually they were playing as a six-piece, Johnny Walker was playing harmonica for that. That was a big party, that session was. Like the recording was an afterthought to having a party. There was probably like twelve people there, me and Buick and Shelby [Murphy] and Ko [Shih]. It was like 'Hey what are you doing today. Let's record a single.'"

Besides singles by the Greenhornes, White also manned recordings for Arizona punks the Fells (who thought enough of White to travel to Detroit just to record and play a couple knock-around shows), his roommates and blues comrades the Soledad Brothers, and, later, visiting Grand Rapids synth spazz freaks Whirlwind Heat, who White stumbled upon at Buick's insistence and with whom he would also form a lasting bond.

They warmed up for They Come in Threes, Buick's roommate, Chris McInnis's band, and, recalled White, "I immediately ran up to them afterward and said would you please just come to my house and record—if you want a place to stay tonight you can.

"But they were driving back to Grand Rapids that night so it didn't work out. But I called 'em up again and convinced them to come down. They didn't think I was for real about it. But they came to my house and did like five songs," White told WDET's Willy Wilson. Thus began a working relationship that would later bear major label fruit in 2003 when White released the Heat's LP "Do Rabbits Wonder" on his V2-distributed imprint Third Man.

That White was busy might be an understatement.

"At the time, Jack was playing with everybody in town," remembers Szymanski. "I remember him doing demos with Danny Dollrod, and Jeff Meier was recording them and he did a song for [Rocket 455 singer] Mark Wahl's wedding—he did the Velvet Underground song 'I'll Be Your Mirror.' I think him and Jeff Meier." One of those bands he ended up playing with was the Hentchmen.

"I think it just came from hanging out, because he was hanging out with Johnny Walker and they'd be jamming together and I'd sit in with those guys here and there," says the Hentchmen's John Szymanski.

At the time, the Hentchmen were looking for a bass player to flesh out their sound. And for a brief period, White was the de facto fourth Hentchman, playing on a 45 featuring a cover of the Yardbirds' R&B psych number "Psycho Daisies" and Lennon/McCartney's infectious ode to jealousy, "Some Other Guy." Jeff Meier was called in to produce (or coproduce or engineer or whatever informal agreement was never made about credits at the time).

"Jack was so accessible at the time we just asked him to come over and do it," says Szymanski.

"And he was more than glad to do it. He came to all the practices. He was just really involved with whatever he could be. We just rehearsed for a few weeks and did the recording. When we did the single he sat in with us at that show. And they were still not very big at that point."

Live they performed the MC5 chestnut "Lookin' At You" (which the Stripes would whip out occasionally in their future live sets and which White had learned playing with Muldoon) and "Some Other Guy."

"We were bowling one night and we said to Dave 'let's do a single.' Actually, it was Jack's idea to do 'Some Other Guy' cause he was listening a lot to the Beatles BBC Sessions and I think he just said 'I want to do 'Some Other Guy' with the Hentchmen at your next show' or something like that. So we were bowling and I suggested we record it as a single for Italy. Because Italy wanted to do a Hentchmen single and at that time we wanted to do something a little different so we had no problem letting Jack guest on that. To his credit, Dave followed through with that drunk idea."

Jack's enthusiasm, drive, and omnivorous musical consumption was at this point, firmly rooted in rounding out the garage rock side of his CV and the Hentchmen singles helped immensely.

"The single we did at Jack's house, because he wanted to play piano on it and he had a piano at his house," remembers Meier. "They had good chemistry. The Hentchmen, they had their shit together, so it was just like it probably took longer to set stuff up than it took to record it.

"I think the Hentchmen brought out straightforward rock 'n' roll from him that the Stripes didn't."

In August, they hunkered down to record a six-song twelve-inch EP with White called "Hentchforth." Meier was called in again to produce.

"When we did 'Hentchforth,'" says Meier, "I was working at a place in Pontiac. It was an old auto factory that a guy bought and turned into suites, and I was working at this shop. I asked the guy who ran it if we could use it for the weekend. And it was a pretty big, nice-sized room with high ceilings and there was an office where I set up my stuff. So we spent the weekend doing that. And that's kind of where me and Jack had a falling out. That's kind of the end of the story for me and Jack. He was starting to get a rock star attitude and I kind of called him on it," says the soft-spoken scene vet Meier of his quickly dissolving friendship with the budding rocker.

The release of the "Hentchforth" EP, the "Lafayette Blues" single, and the "Psycho Daisies" 45 were all celebrated on the same night at the Gold Dollar on October 23, 1998. The show was a knockout with the White Stripes displaying a growing sense of confidence (and that's a relative term when it came to their early live shows) with Jack starting to fill the frontman shoes he'd laid out for himself and Meg showing hints of discovering her intuitive-if-rudimentary signature playing style. A reinvigorated Hentchmen joined by White headlined and Italy Records probably made a couple hundred bucks that night in record sales from the one hundred or so in attendance, which was probably spent providing libation at one of the traditional after-parties at Buick's place in Detroit's historic and funky Woodbridge district.

For the Stripes record, Buick and White hightailed it just to get a few copies in their hands in time for the show.

The manufacturer had some potentially bad news for Buick, who had requested that the records be printed on white vinyl.

"He said, 'Well, I can get 'em to you, but they're not going to be all white vinyl, they're going to have swirls of whatever color I have in the press, too.' And I was like, fine, just send 'em, I'll take one hundred. So he sent me one hundred and (of course) it just so happened that the color that was in there was red."

It was the White Stripes' brand of serendipity.

So Buick and White picked out the records with the most attractive red swirls and set about twenty records aside. He and White hand-painted the labels for these as a sort of special one-night-only faux collectible lark. There's nothing like record nerds being given the keys to the castle and the pair relished the irony of creating a collectible record that presumably no one would really ever want to collect. Maybe White knew better or maybe he was just putting his usual handmade stamp on his product. Reality is probably somewhere in-between. Either way, he took the remaining thirty or so and gave his own imprimatur to them as well. Into each of the records he placed hand-addressed franc notes (a nice little visual pun on the A-side's lyrics). For example, he gave Buick a fifty-franc note, his family twenty-franc notes and ten-franc notes to everyone thanked on the single. He popped five- and two-franc notes into the rest and gave them out to folks like Dan Kroha, the Hentchmen, Jeff Meier, and other scenesters who had given the band a leg up over the past year.

"That was all Jack's idea. He went to the trouble to do that and give them to people he assumed would never get rid of them—and still he went to the trouble to make them collectable!" says Buick.

"Someone just sold the hand-painted one that I did for $2,600. One that Jack painted sold for $2,075 just the other day," says Buick. "So mine sold for more than Jack's! And we thought we were ripping everyone off for charging $6 for 'em at the show! We thought, *Hell yeah! We can make some money!* We split it up and we each got like, thirty dollars," he laughs without a single hint of regret.

"There's that issue of *Record Collector* where the White Stripes are on the cover as 'the most collectable modern band' and it's true. And that's one of the reasons why."

Those personal touches are one reason people are still finding the White Stripes more engaging than other indie bands. It's one of the reasons people think Jack White is a control freak. His near-obsessive attention to detail hints that he might have had success imagined the whole time—or at least the kind of success he'd find on the indie circuit. Even the studious White likely had no idea of the mainstream pop culture impact he'd one day have. But for now, he could control the little things that made the band into more of a multimedia performance art project than a traditional rock act.

Living Room Sessions

In November of 1998, an informal, semiregular "unplugged" night at the Garden Bowl became a sort of songwriting watershed on the downtown Detroit music scene. It started like most things in Detroit—out of sheer boredom.

Ko Shih was bored out of her mind. She'd pulled Sunday shift at the Garden Bowl and the only folks who were coming in were a handful of half-hungover musician pals and, gasp, bowlers. It had the standard-issue bar tchotchkes all over the wall: Retro-Replica signs touting locally made Vernor's ginger ale and Stroh's beer, a few Budweiser-related ad banners, a charming hint of neon, a scattering of linoleum-topped tables, and a gaggle of fliers and other reminders of rock shows yet to be upstairs in the Magic Stick. The Garden Bowl bar that Shih presided over was more of a holding tank than a watering hole. The Majestic Theatre complex also houses the Majestic Theatre (duh!), the cavernous show palace in which Harry Houdini received his fatal blow while taking a punch from an audience volunteer. Also in the complex was the Majestic Café, a sorta-chic eatery where visiting bands would spend their meal comps and the Magic Stick, the 500-person club that was fast becoming a de rigueur stop along the touring circuit. And then there was the Garden Bowl, the oldest bowling alley in America—no, seriously—and the adjacent bar. The Garden Bowl was one of the few places in Detroit that seemed to be honestly desegregated. Adventurous white suburbanites shared the lanes with black Detroiters in a rare embrace of diversity occasioned by the common bond of rented shoes and knocking the shit out of ten wooden pins.

Folks ordering rounds for their bowling teammates and people either waiting for the doors to open for the show upstairs at the Magic Stick or seeking a shorter bar line away from the throngs of elbow tippers made up much of the crowd. But by the time Sunday night rolled around, the place was usually a ghost town where you'd often as not find Jack White nursing either a beer or a cheeseburger while shooting the shit with the gregarious Shih. If ever there were anyone more suited to presiding over a dead night at a downtown bar where hipsters felt at home and left alone, it was Shih. With her deadpan "what the fuck do you want?!" hostess attitude, a Camel Light–inflected tone that could cut through even the loudest bar chatter with the slightest of ease, and a diminutive stature coupled with a mod fashion sense and relentless energy, simply, she owned the joint.

And sometimes it seemed like the only distraction from boredom was the blackboard upon which Shih would often draw or scrawl cryptic messages to her buddies who'd gratefully accept the occasional comp'd beer.

"What happened was that I got put on Sunday nights to bartend and it sucked because no one came in and I just sat there for ten hours straight all by myself," Shih says.

"Sometimes Jack or Tom Potter came in. So I just asked Jack, 'Why not come in on Sunday, bring in an acoustic guitar, and do [Dylan's] "Nashville Skyline" all by yourself?'"

"And he said no, I don't want to do that, I wanna do something else," Shih recalls.

"So he ended up coming in and doing a set solo with electric guitar. And it was great. Mindblowing. After that, Tom Potter did one. Johnny Walker did one, and then it became a regular occurrence."

And so a tradition was established. Jack would curate one every two months or so, but in between, every Sunday night for about a year, various members of bands or new outfits testing their live sea legs would set up on the floor and work it out. Often, they'd take the slings and arrows of their peers, attempt ill-advised covers, and basically engage in the kind of shenanigans that people might usually reserve for fucking around in their basement. Except nobody in this little circle of friends had a basement to speak of. And besides, it was more fun doing it in public. And, to make matters more irresistable, Shih compensated performers with a bottle of Jack Daniels for their efforts. And she'd keep the crowd well lubricated with Stroh's, too.

"They called 'em Living Room sessions and for good reason," remembers Blackwell. "Because it was like playing in your living room. And that was the allure of it. It wasn't pretentious. I guess it was just lucky that there was just so many talented musicians that were a part of it. You know that if you took two steps you'd run into five people that knew all the songs you could play—even those songs were both just on an Italy 7-inch."

The momentum was flowing. White and Shih's little diversion soon became the place to be for the thirty- or forty-musician core of that scene. From Brendan Benson to imports like Cincinnati's Greenhornes to stalwarts like the Hentchmen and short-lived novelty acts like the Fighting Pinheads.

Jack used the Living Room sessions to workshop some of the songs that would turn up recorded as late in the White Stripes discography as 2003.

He turned in crowd-silencing, moving versions of "You've Got Her in Your Pocket" and "Same Boy You've Always Known" at the time. And he also established his grip on covers that would become later Stripes live staples.

"It was great hearing him do [Dylan's] 'Isis.' I was so fucking stoked to hear him do that because that's one of my favorite songs. And of course, that song has like 1,800 verses and I was like 'no way is he gonna remember it.' Sure enough, he fucking remembered them all," laughs Benson.

For Benson, the whole scene was a revelation after his stint on the cynical end of the music biz when he was living in California.

"Music started to mean something again to me," he recalls. "After living in California, I was getting way too caught up in business stuff. I had no friends and the friends I had were my manager and my A&R guy. So coming back where people were just putting on shows like that and somebody like Jack or the Greenhornes would play it. Or seeing [Clone Defects frontman] Punk Rock Tim [Lampinen] do an acoustic set. I was like 'fucking hell, man! Why did I leave?!'

"That made the shit legitimate. It was like our own little unplugged thing, and that sounds gay, but it seemed like a highbrow hoity-toity thing to do. But the irony was great. And I think it forced people to take things seriously. We have some good fucking songwriters here. Not that it mattered. Sunday nights at the Garden Bowl, you knew what you were in for, you were going to shut up and listen. Which is not always fun. I'm not a big 'shush' guy, but there's a time and place for it, and that was it. It wasn't totally quiet," raves Benson.

For some, like John Szymanski, this was the moment it became apparent that Jack was destined for bigger things:

"I remember going down there and Jack playing one of the songs we had just recorded that night," the Hentchmen organist and singer recalls. "I remember thinking 'If anybody deserves to be on MTV it's this guy.' And I looked over at [Dirtbombs drummer] Pat [Pantano] and I remember him saying 'It's good to be alive to be able to see this right now.'"

They might have been off the cuff affairs to some, but to White, each show was a special event.

The Sunday night after the '99 Hamtramck Blowout, White and Benson did a songwriters' swap with each of them performing the others' songs.

"It was his idea to do that. He was always thinking big," remembers Benson. "He'd always treat it as if we were two renowned old-timers. Even though most of the people had no idea what these songs were that we were doing. Or what the fuck was going on. But we knew and it was cool."

In fact, the White Stripes, by that time were already starting to cover Benson's "Good to Me" and Jack would return the favor to his pop collaborator/sounding board by releasing the song as the B-side of "Seven Nation Army" in the UK. But for now, it was just two guys working on songs.

"It wasn't anything thought out," claims Blackwell. "I guess a lot of what people outside of Detroit don't understand is with what ease you could get a show in town." And the Garden Bowl shows were no exception—for the select few bands that comprised the tight-knit downtown scene.

Nevertheless, the informality of the Garden Bowl shows that weren't curated directly by White also gave a shot in the arm to the activity of the little rock community. Shih would egg on the bands from behind the bar to play songs she wanted to hear—technically it was her night, so they rarely refused to at least try.

"The day before the Stripes played with the Hentchmen and [Florida-based honorary Detroit band] the Girl Bombs at the Magic Stick, the Girl Bombs and the Soledad Brothers did a set in the Garden Bowl and I remember that [2-Star Tabernacle and Detroit Cobras drummer] Damian Lange sat in and played with Johnny, and then Meg sat in on drums and Meg and Jack played with Johnny—it was just like 'hey who else wants to play?'" remembers Blackwell.

For the one-year anniversary of the "Living Room" shows at the Garden Bowl, in November of '99 White assembled a revue of sorts that included his father as a special guest. The already-claustrophobic place was packed. White had already achieved the kind of local celebrity that allowed the Stripes to have their debut record release party in the Magic Stick and come close to filling the 500-person venue. So the anniversary of this night that he had taken care to curate and nurture was particularly important to White.

"They did a song together," says Shih. Actually they did two: "Fly Me to the Moon" and a song from the *Music Man*.

"It was awesome to see Good Guy Gorman sitting there, singing," remembers Greg Siemasz. "He got up and did a little soft-shoe jig dance and he was wearing like a black batting glove, maybe for arthritis or something. But it was really cool."

Also playing that night were Johnny Walker, and the Waxwings' Dean Fertita and Kevin Peyok. The rotating pickup band did versions of Beck's "Cold Brains," and the Waxwings' song "Fragile Girl." The whole evening had a real sense of celebration to it.

"I think it was important for him to have his dad there," reckons Blackwell. "Jack has a great sense of history and that's really important to him. No matter if it was Carnegie Hall or the Garden Bowl to be able to do a show with his father was really a special occasion."

Benson concurs: "He was always even then thinking so huge. It kinda made you think it was bigger [than it was]. He was always thinking of something new, what else can I invent? And that was always great. He never did anything cheesy or desperate."

"Then he did one more after that—it was right toward the end of my stint at the Garden Bowl in 2000 and right when they started getting big," recalls Shih.

"That last one was booked under John Gillis and we didn't want it to be huge. We wanted it to be just like the first show, where all his pals and regulars showed up. Then the *Free Press* foiled the plan by saying it was Jack."

The Living Room sessions peak of activity also coincided roughly with the ongoing dissolution of Jack and Meg's marriage. Maybe White was keeping busy to distract himself. Talking to folks around town, it seems imminently likely that it was a form of self-therapy to play whenever, wherever.

Still, the event was the place to be, and Jack White was at the center of it. Even as he and Meg sorted out how to continue the White Stripes post-divorce, Jack was helping to create a fertile scene around himself and set about soaking in the influences of the songwriters and performers that shared the floorspace of the Garden Bowl with him.

Even though White might have seemed like he was the center of the scene, it always seemed like he maintained an observational distance.

"He was always kind of at odds with social environments," says Benson. "Like with 'the scene,' I think he was always struggling, because there wasn't much substance and importance in it.

"He was always talking about it and making observations about stuff that I just took for granted. I remember, him saying something one time, 'This person laughs at this other person when he says this, but if I say the same thing, he doesn't laugh.' And I'd wonder why he was even thinking about that."

Small talk was not featured prominently on Jack White's list of favorite things. He wasn't a crank or anything, he just didn't bother wasting time.

Broken Bricks

It was also at this time that White began workshopping songs he would use on later White Stripes albums with a group that would (erroneously) come to be called Jack White & the Bricks—it featured White and Benson on guitar, Waxwing Kevin Peyok on bass, and Blackwell on drums.

"It was called the Bricks?" asks Brendan Benson incredulously. "I guess I remember that, but we never called it the Bricks. It was always the Jack White Band if it was anything."

Ben Blackwell slapped the skins and remembers why it was called the Bricks: "Club Bart ran an ad that said 'Jack White and the Bricks' for a show that we never played." The band did later play Club Bart, but that's for the trivia files.

The genesis of the band was simple and pragmatic—especially in a music scene with musicians to spare. Jack and Meg were no longer a couple and the first album hadn't yet found its audience.

"After the first White Stripes album came out," remembers Blackwell, "they weren't really playing or didn't have much set up to play, so we were doing shows, too." The first "Bricks" show was on the Garden Bowl lanes on July 9, 1999, (White's twenty-fourth birthday) literally on the lanes themselves. The Majestic had purpose-built risers that could be placed over the lanes to form a makeshift stage.

"I don't think they had any other shows on the lanes," laughs Blackwell. "I know that after we played there's no way they had another show on the lanes. You're essentially by the ball return and people are putting smokes out on the walkup to the penalty lines and afterwards it was a mess. I was just trying not to get kicked out," says Blackwell. "At that time I thought 'wow this is pretty cool' and now I'm thinking 'wow that was *really* cool!'"

Most of the material that "the Bricks" rocked would end up on *White Blood Cells*. It's not that Blackwell necessarily had more innate swing than Meg, but he was a more conventional rock drummer and in that context, Jack could see what the songs would sound like with a full kit and varying rhythms.

"I never got the impression that he was hedging his bets on the White Stripes at all," says Benson. "I just thought he wanted to work on songs and see them in a different light."

"Jack kinda wanted to do his Dylan and the band thing," says Blackwell. "That's what I kinda got out of it.

"It was all Jack. Brendan had just moved back to Detroit, and set up his studio in his house, so we rehearsed once there. It worked. It was never billed as Jack White and the Bricks, though," says Blackwell for the record.

"After we played our last show, there was rumbling about playing another one. And maybe nothing worked well and that's why it didn't survive (laughs). It was basically songs that the White Stripes weren't doing. We never did any of Brendan's songs. A lot of 'em were 2-Star songs, too. We did "The Union Forever," "Now Mary," "You've Got Her in Your Pocket," "Offend in Every Way." And after the Stripes released it we did a version of "Candy Cane Children."

They also did knock-around covers of "The Seeker," the MC5's "Looking at You," and anything else that struck their collective fancy.

"The Bricks was kinda just fun. It never seemed too serious. I remember one time we were practicing. I was driving to Jack's house and I got into a huge car accident at I-75 and Clark," remembers the then seventeen-year-old Blackwell. "And I was two hours late for practice. I showed up and they were like 'what happened' and I said 'I got into an accident.' They were like 'yeah, right.' I asked them how old were you when you first got into a car accident? Jack and Kevin said they were sixteen and Brendan fifteen—so I made it longer than any of 'em! And then we looked at the car and then we practiced."

The Go! Sound

For a hot Detroit minute—actually a couple years from late 1998 to early 2000—the Go! were *the* Detroit rock 'n' roll band. Based around the founding core of prototypical singer Bobby Harlow (who cut himself from the same cloth as Iggy with a dose of Jagger thrown in for good measure), bedrock rhythm guitarist John Krautner (a.k.a. "the nicest guy in Detroit rock 'n' roll"), and the cool of drummer Mark Fellis, the Go! were a crew of outsiders that scrapped their way to the top of the Detroit rock pile. Their sound was a collision of glam rock strut, Stooges thuggery, and pub rock choogle. And in a way, they were a more chick-friendly version of their direct forebears on the scene, Rocket 455. Almost from the word go the band featured a revolving door of bassists and lead guitarists with many one-time members of Rocket 455—Marco Delicato, Kenny Tudrick, and Steve Nawara, namely—taking a turn playing with the band.

The period in which White was in the band—from mid-'98 through '99—was its most active and, arguably, its best.

At many of their early shows, Dave Buick could be found front and center, Stroh's in hand, delightedly bobbing his head. It wasn't long before the Go! had fired their most recent bass player Matt Hatch and found themselves looking for a bass player. Buick, who had never played an instrument in his life (this being the novice-friendly Detroit scene and all), volunteered his services. Eventually, Buick would find a way to wangle his pal Jack White into the band, too, thus cementing what many regard as the Go!'s classic lineup.

"When I was originally going to join the Go!, John and Bobby were going to teach me to play rhythm guitar so Johnny could play lead and then three days before a show that they had—that I was just going to be in attendance at—they called me up and said that they fired Matt Hatch and that I was the new bass player," recalls Buick.

"They kinda taught me the songs, so I had to play. And Jack and I were already buddies, so him and Meg were at the show. He was at all the shows, actually, and we were trying out different ways to have a fifth member in the Go!"

Future Go! producer and Outrageous Cherry mainman Matt Smith ended up being drafted to play a couple times, and Bobby picked up the guitar and sang. That didn't last very long at all.

"I said, well, why don't we have Jack play? and Jack wanted to be a guitar player in a band. So he guested on like four songs at the Gold Dollar one night and then he just ended up joining.

"Jack is a great guitar player and him being in a band, playing songs that were already written, let him just focus on being a sweet lead guitar player," says Buick. Of course, it helped get people into the Go!, too.

By the time Buick joined the Go! there was already a buzz on about the band.

"When I joined the Go! the buzz went down for a little bit," laughs Buick. "Then when Jack joined, at least for a while, we were one of the bigger bands in Detroit. People were always at the show. Shortly after he joined, we signed a deal with Sub Pop."

Former Detroiter and Sub Pop A&R rep Dan Traeger had been tipped off to the Go! by Andy Krieger of KISS cover band Ace's High.

So Krieger and Traeger were in attendance when the Go! played with the Demolition Dollrods one night at the Magic Stick (the White Stripes opened the show). Matt Smith was there with some demos that the band had been recording, slipped Traeger a copy of the tape, and it was as simple as that. Everyone at Sub Pop dug the Go! and the future of the band seemed to be a punched ticket to indie success.

Then they went into the recording studio. In 1999, the band checked into Jim Diamond's Ghetto Recorders with Smith on board as producer. The sessions started auspiciously enough.

"Right when we very first walked up there, Jack walked into the back room and ran and jumped onto the punching bag and bear hugged it," remembers Buick. "And the spring went down to the ground and stayed broken. So within the first five minutes something was already broken."

The recording of basic tracks—done in just two short days—went just fine, but soon after that, fissures started to show in the band's structure. Before the recordings were done, this lineup of the band was effectively finished.

"We played all the stuff live and we were just going to overdub stuff—and Jack did his solos live," remembers Diamond. "I think we were done tracking everything and I remember talking to Matt one day saying 'Yeah, Jack's ready to come over and do all his guitar solos again.'"

Apparently, Jack had thought his takes had a lot of flubbed notes.

"And Matt's like 'What!? No, this can't be! It's perfect, it's genius!,'" recalls Diamond.

"So that started a lot of tension. Bobby and Matt were in one camp and Jack was in another. Jack had very specific ideas about what to do and what to play. And then Matt had specific ideas about what to do and how it was going to be done.

"I remember one time that really kind of ticked Jack off was when Matt Smith made a comparison to one of our takes being like pearls before swine," recalls Buick. "And Jack always got mad about obscure references. He was anti–obscure reference."

Buick and White blew off steam while they were recording the vocals by dropping trou while gathered around the mike for the title song.

"Jack and I took our pants off," says Buick. "When people dig out the record, they might like to know that we were pantsless. We just wanted a real stripped down sound. There was something about the two of us being naked that seemed like a good idea at the time."

There's no doubt that both Jack and Bobby had very very strong feelings about the recordings. And so it was inevitable that they butted heads. It was a classic rock 'n' roll rivalry between the showy, electrifying guitar player and the flamboyant singer/bandleader. When the Go! played live, it was a two-headed rock beastie and nine times out of ten, onstage at least, the tension made for great rock 'n' roll. What made the band more exciting with White in the band than subsequent incarnations was the dynamic between the stage egos. Of course, White wasn't unique in this respect; Dion Fisher, who replaced White in the band, also had a very different, though no less galvanizing presence, kind of a robot shaking off a coating of rust and realizing he's on fire.

But in the studio, the tension just sat there and waited and stewed in its own juices.

"I think there's different versions of the recordings," says Diamond. "Some of the things on the record were rehearsals done at Jack's house and they ended up being the recording, because Matt had some theory about the feel or this and that and Jack said 'No, it sounds like shit.' "

"There's probably about twenty-five mixes of each song at Diamond's studio somewhere," reckons Buick.

The relationship between Harlow and White, by all accounts, went rapidly downhill. "I always thought Jack was easy to work with. He knew what he wanted to do, he knew how he wanted his band to sound."

Thing of it is, it wasn't really Jack's band.

"When we were recording the Go! record, I can understand why— not that Bobby would be an easy guy to work with—he would say that Jack was a hard guy to work with because they both had visions and when it came down to it, the band was Bobby's, so Jack had to go. Unfortunately for Bobby, and me and everyone in the Go!" says Buick.

"I don't know the whole story about Jack quitting or being asked to leave. I remember it as being pretty much mutual," says Diamond.

"I don't want to make anybody look like a jackass," ventures Buick, "but what happened was Bobby probably felt threatened and kicked Jack out. But it was understandable why Bobby wanted to kick Jack out and why he should feel threatened."

2-Star had broken up shortly before he left the Go! And both were for the same reasons: White was going to focus on the White Stripes.

Then the Go! signed the deal with Sub Pop and White wanted to stick it out with the Go! Harlow's response, according to Buick, was "Uh, Jack, I think you're going to focus on the White Stripes."

"He seemed to be like OK, fine, I've got this other band the White Stripes. We're working on our second record. It worked out for Jack obviously," chuckles Diamond.

The resulting record—*Whatcha Doin'*, released in early 2000—failed to find a core audience and the Go! soon became mired in recording and production snafu's with Sub Pop when they retired to the studio to cut their follow-up, *Free Electricity*. They were subsequently dropped from the label.

Apparently egos were soothed enough by the time the White Stripes released *Elephant* to allow the retooled Go! to open for the Stripes several times in 2003. It was a typically graceful way for White to say "No hard feelings after all."

Take a Bow

With all the action that was happening around the Garden Bowl, Jack White's involvement with 2-Star Tabernacle and his enlistment as the lead guitarist for locally popular street rockers the Go!, you could forgive Jack and Meg for resting on their laurels. But to their credit, they kept things moving in the White Stripes camp whenever they got a chance. Whether it was road trips opening for 2-Star Tabernacle in Toledo or one-hit weekenders to Pat's in the Flats in Cleveland or Club Shanghai in Toronto at the advice and on the glowing recommendation to club owners from their buddies the Hentchmen, the Wildbunch, and Rocket 455, the Stripes were an active—maybe a little more so, in fact—local band.

"Jeff Meier or John Hentch would hook them up," remembers Blackwell. "When they played Cleveland they played with the Girl Bombs. Or they'd hook up with the Greenhornes in Cincinnati. They met the Greenhornes the same way everyone met the Greenhornes—at the Fighting Pinheads show on August 28-ish of 1998," remembers Blackwell. "I had the first day of school. Once the Greenhornes played that show, they became quick friends 'cause they were playing here like once a week."

The first out-of-town show they did was in September of 1997. Somehow Detroiter Dan Burke was putting on shows in Toronto and the White Stripes got hooked up and played a gig at Club Shanghai—a neon-bedecked dance club in Toronto's Chinatown. "From Jack's description the show was horrible," says Blackwell.

"They'd hooked up with the Soledad Brothers and done two shows in Toledo. That's how things work. Just the simple thing of knowing someone in another town and reciprocating. It's never like questioned or overthought. Johnny Walker got ahold of them. He opened for a 2-star show in Toledo."

As the Stripes started to build their local following based on the strength of their two Italy 45s and catch their live groove by, "practicing onstage" as often as possible and making connections with local kindred spirit bands wherever they went, word started to spread and their confidence grew to the point where they were actively seeking a label to put out a full-length. The Detroit Cobras had recently released their debut record on L.A.-based Sympathy for the Record Industry, a label with the reputation for putting out some of the rawest sounds coming from the garage-punk underground. Memphis blues-punk killers, the Oblivians and '68 Comeback—bands that were much admired by the Detroit rock scene and were a sort of analogue to Motor City counterparts Rocket 455 and the Detroit Cobras—put out records for Sympathy at the request of enigmatic label head Long Gone John. Sympathy wasn't so much a label as it was one person operating out of his house in Southern California putting out whatever records he felt like when he wasn't busy collecting lowbrow art, punk rock memorabilia, and other kitsch apocrypha. The Memphis and Detroit branches of the Sympathy roster knew each other and exchanged shows in each others' towns. It was during one of these visits that the White Stripes' 45 began its trip to the ears of Long Gone John.

"I was the one that got Jack his recoding deal on Sympathy," says Jeff Meier matter-of-factly. "It was right around the time [the Detroit Cobras] record came out on Sympathy.

"['68 Comeback leader] Jeff Evans was in town a couple days after the [Stripes] record came out on Italy and I happened to have a copy from Dave. '68 Comeback played a show in town and I said 'Hey, I just recorded this, check it out.' And Jeff Evans flipped his lid and he sent a copy to Long Gone. And I think Jack was pretty well aware that I did that, but I don't know. I did call them and say, they're interested in doing a record with you, can I give 'em your phone number? I did get a thank you, so that's OK. I had no idea it would be as big as it was, I just thought I'd help the guy out.

"Jack and I had a little falling out after that," according to Meier, "He didn't really thank me. He thanked everybody else under the sun, but not me."

In an interview with Willy Wilson in March 1999, White seemed to disagree with Meier's recollection when asked how he hooked up with Long Gone John:

"Steve Shaw who's in the Detroit Cobras. He had sent them the two records on Italy and he liked them and I guess he was pretty busy because he waited a couple months before he called us and said he really liked them and he'd like to do a full album."

Even after Long Gone John expressed interest, and even in the face of no interest from the labels to which the White Stripes had submitted material, Jack thought through the decision to release a record on Sympathy with his usual hypercritical faculty. Tom Potter remembers the White Stripes frontman fretting over the decision one night when they were both at their usual spots at the Garden Bowl bar.

"I knew going into [making a Bantam Rooster record with Sympathy] that it wasn't a money deal. I knew the reputation," says Potter.

"I remember talking with Jack when they were thinking about doing something with Sympathy."

Potter gave White the sage counsel of hard-learned experience.

"The thing with indie labels is that they're kind of frustrating because they're run by people who love music. They love your music so much that they want to put out your record. That doesn't necessarily make them good business people. It doesn't necessarily make them bad ones, either. The White Stripes had sent stuff to Crypt and to In the Red and other labels and they weren't interested. Jack sounds too much like Robert Plant or this thing or that thing. They're indie labels, they're not in this to make money, so they're reaction is what it is. But John dug it. So he put it out and he was more willing to take a chance."

So it was that in the dead of a Michigan winter, on a side street around the corner from downtown Detroit's State Theater, the White Stripes hunkered down to record their debut, self-titled full-length at Jim Diamond's Ghetto Recorders. It was recorded over the course of four chill days in January of 1999. If the Stripes' first two singles showed very little hint of their growing obsession with country blues—with the onus of influence on those two records falling more on the Eddie Cochran, cabaret, and folk-pop spots on the spectrum—the debut slab was all about sludgy blues, mud-blasted with overdriven punk rock, and colored with Jack White's tentative steps toward a signature form of modern art–influenced romantic lyrics.

The sludgy, reverberated stumbling guitar notes of "Jimmy the Explorer" that kicked off the record seemed purpose-built to echo through the deserted concrete canyons that surrounded the studio, looking for a bored ear. By the time Meg kicked in with her off-kilter floor-tom-and-snare counterpoint, the White Stripes had perhaps accidentally achieved a sublime collision of ineptitude with meticulous minimalism. The song, of course, took flight, suggesting the striking haunted urban soundscape of the opening was no accident. "Now Jimmy/why do you wanna explode now?!" by the time the song was over, there were red monkeys jumping on the bed, green apples exploding, and Jack White loosing lupine hillbilly Robert Plant *whoops* before crashing to an abrupt halt. They followed it with a randy run at Robert Johnson's "Stop Breaking Down." By the time the Big Three killed Jack's baby the whole of the White Stripes' little world had busted, blown up, or died. So the song was a funeral dirge. Though bleak as all hell, the White Stripes seem so gleeful about it that even Jack's melodramatic howl when he finds out his baby's "DEAD!!!! Yeah yeah yeah!" in "The Big Three Killed My Baby," you're banging your head and smiling—and you're not sure whether the dead baby is literally his common sense, his woman, or his car, or all three. Besides Johnson's blues standard "Stop Breaking Down" and "St. James Infirmary Blues," as made famous by Leadbelly in the middle of the century, the Stripes chose to interpret Dylan's "One More Cup of Coffee" and follow Dylan's lyric and compositional lead with their original "Wasting My Time." But it's "The Big Three" that was the album's center- and "master"-piece. It begged the question of the Stripes' numerological obsession.

"That's a big thing for me," Jack told the *Metro Times*. "It came out the most on 'The Big Three Killed My Baby.' It's three chords and three verses, and we accent threes together all through that. It was a number I always thought of as perfect, or our attempt at being perfect. Like on a traffic light, you couldn't just have a red and a green. I work on sculptures, too, and I always use three colors."

It couldn't have happened anyplace besides Ghetto Recorders.

Ghetto Recorders started its life as a chicken processing facility in the mid-1900s. So it's only appropriate that Bantam Rooster was the first band to make a record there. When Jim Diamond moved from Lansing, in 1995, the anonymous gray door on W. Elizabeth Street led only to the home of Motor City Brewing Works owner John Linardos. Linardos had been using the space to birth his own home recordings, but once Diamond moved in, word began to spread.

Basically one big cement room, a disused freight elevator sits in the back and a well-worn red rug is set up on a cement floor opposite; this is where the bands actually record. Diamond's control room was behind a windowless door, behind a cinder block wall. He had no line of sight with the bands he recorded, so it was all down to ears and his efficient use of the talkback.

Diamond made his inroads into the scene starting in 1996 by throwing parties, with plenty of Motor City's Ghettoblaster beer on hand, and recording the bands as they played for the parties. These live sessions soon became the de rigueur place to be for folks on the Detroit garage rock scene that was just starting to really coalesce. The Detroit Cobras, the Dirtys, the Hentchmen, and the Dirtbombs all recorded raunchy, beer-soaked, and slapdash live sets that captured the fun, chaos, and raw energy of the time.

"When I moved in here, I saw the Hentchmen opening for Dick Dale and thinking oh, my god, here's this other band I like! I remember talking to John and Mike [LaTulippe, the Hentchmen drummer]—and I had just set up an 8-track and a little mixing board—and I was like 'you guys have to come over and record' and I just remember them looking at me like 'who are you?' Like some guy, some jerk wants us to come and record and I kept bugging the Hentchmen cause I liked them so much," remembers Diamond of his less-than-auspicious introduction to the scene.

The Hentchmen finally acquiesced and played a live recording party—replete with complimentary cases of Ghettoblaster beer and about thirty to forty friends packing the joint and creating a "live" vibe. It was a party to be sure, and its success spread word of Diamond's place throughout the city.

Diamond also did recorded parties with the Dirtys and the Dirtbombs—each of them cementing his reputation as man of taste and skill.

Bantam Rooster was also at the time in the midst of recording their debut record *Deal Me In*.

"That was the first record I ever did here," says Diamond. "Tom and Eric [Cook, Bantam Rooster drummer] were like 'man we gotta go to Easley in Memphis because Sonic Youth went there' or something and I was like, in a pleading voice, 'no, you guys, I won't even charge you anything! Just come down for a day, we can mess around, and I won't even charge you!'"

"So it just kind of went from there with bookings few and far between for a long time," chuckles Diamond.

"I think Jack probably had heard the Bantam Rooster record—I don't think he came up for the Hentchmen party. And the Dirtbombs were playing and recording 'Horndog Fest' then, too, so maybe he heard that."

Either way, says Diamond, "they must have come to me, because I just kind of dismissed them the first time I saw them."

Obviously they had gotten better since the first time he saw them. Long Gone John had given the Stripes $3,000 to make the record.

"That was a Long Gone budget," says Diamond. "Somewhere between three and four thousand dollars. For everything. So they came in here. I was probably charging thirty-five dollars an hour. I said 'I'll give you guys a deal if you book more than two days! You only gotta pay thirty dollars an hour!' So I think we booked off three or four days in a row," remembers Diamond.

"It took a while because Meg had never been in a studio and she had just started playing drums, so we did a lot of takes of things. I remember, I said 'why don't you do the second record here' and I remember [Jack] saying 'No I don't want to spend that much time just doing takes,'" Diamond laughs. "'It costs too much, so we'll do it at home and we can take as long as we want and then I'll mix it at your place.' Cause, you know, Meg's no Max Roach or whatever," says Diamond.

"I don't know if he was counting off to her because I don't have a window on the control room," says Diamond. "All I know is that all of a sudden I'd hear some sticks drop. So she got frustrated. We had to do take after take of things. So I'd talk through the talkback 'no, it'll be fine, just do it again. Just don't drop your sticks at that one point.'"

Even though the band was as well-rehearsed as could be, Blackwell remembers them writing at least one song in-studio.

"I remember right before they recorded the first record that they played 'Astro,' and it was just an instrumental at the time," he says. "And [Jack] just came up with the lyrics while they were in the studio."

The pair settled into the studio. They would take breaks and drink tea and smoke cigarettes. When visitors arrived to talk, Meg would sit on the thrift-store couches in the studio's main room, her legs tucked under her, quietly smoking and taking in the details of whatever conversation Jack was engaged in at the time.

"I think she was just observing the whole time," remembers Diamond. "I think she was thinking 'what are we doing here in the studio making a record. This is a dumb idea. I thought we just got married and you were going to be an upholsterer and I'm going to work at the Memphis Smoke!'"

"I don't know what her aspirations were because she didn't really talk about it. It was pretty much Jack's deal."

Meg was set up in the corner closest to the control room, closest to the couches. She needed to have a place to go quickly to warm her bare feet as she didn't wear shoes in the studio.

"It was cold and this is a cold cement floor and there was broken glass everywhere because we broke a bunch of bottles during some Dirtys song, so I told her, well, I wouldn't go barefoot," says Diamond. "She insisted. But she was cold the whole time. Of course you're cold, you don't have your shoes on!"

Mick Collins of the Dirtbombs had just bought a brand new Silvertone amp that Diamond and the White Stripes pressed into service. "Jack had a speaker cabinet, but we had to cut apart Mick's head so we could use it with Jack's speaker cabinet. Jack had one head that started smoking, like it burnt out, so we used Mick's head on Jack's cabinet."

They did everything live to tape with a scratch vocal and Diamond clearly remembers White having some very specific ideas about how he wanted the sound to come out.

"I remember I set him up with some mike, covered with a Crown Royal bag, and old RCA Mic from the '50s. I was like 'Here, use this, it'll sound older.' And he said 'no, it sounds too much like we're in a studio,'" recalls Diamond.

"And I said, 'well you *are* in a studio!'"

Jack didn't want the record to sound, as he described it, fake. He wanted to capture the live sound as much as possible. Diamond's response was, "If you want it to sound live, just go record it at the Gold Dollar!

"So we ended up putting all the vocals through a tape recorder from 1953. Like singing through the 1953 tape recorder and mike-ing it's little built-in speaker. So that's why everything sounds trashy. It was made to sound that way purposefully."

Adding to the live vibe, White decided to have Diamond fade the reverb down every time the music would stop so it didn't sound "phony," then he'd turn it up when the next song would start.

"Those wacky kids," he laughs.

"Jack always wanted it really loud when we were monitoring and mixing stuff and I'd say, 'God, you're gonna go deaf, son,'" laughs Diamond. "I had the amp in the corner kind of blocked off, but it was loud."

The record sounded extra big because they had Meg set up over by the control room and a mike up on the set of stairs that leads nowhere.

Asked whether recording the White Stripes' first record was more or less memorable than the dozens of other records he's produced since, Diamond notes matter-of-factly that the Stripes record was at the time merely another recording done at the behest of Long Gone John between 1997 and 2001 when the White Stripes left Sympathy and many Detroit bands who had recorded for the label followed suit.

"I don't know how many people have heard that record. I've heard people talk about the Stripes and say 'Oh, yeah, the White Stripes' three records are amazing!' Like the first one wasn't even heard," says Diamond.

Now, however, with the Stripes' exponentially increased exposure, he gets e-mails from time to time from people seeking tech advice on how he recorded one of their favorite records.

"I'll tell 'em he played the whole time through a crappy Japanese guitar and a DOD whammy pedal. I'm not going to explain what I do here in detail. Now you go off on your own."

Though the record only took a few days to record and mix, the cost of recording in a studio was new and none-too-pleasant for the young couple. "There's all this tension when boy and girl couples that are in the same band come in the studio together," says Diamond.

"Like Meg would fuck up and that would generate some tension because they had to do a lot of takes and they were like 'oh, god, this is costing us $30 an hour.' This record's going to cost upwards of $2,000!" he laughs.

With reels of tape, Diamond estimates the total bill for the record was a little over two grand.

Long Gone had given them around $3,000 to record. "They used the rest to get the dogs vaccinated or something," chuckles Diamond.

Picture Perfect

No matter how striking the music the Stripes made, part and parcel of the (now-relative) success of their debut record was the striking image of two red-and-white-clad innocents standing in front of a red-saturated garage door, staring out at unsuspecting record shoppers. Who the hell were these freaks? Garage bands weren't supposed to be so striking with their visuals. This one all but jumped into your hands.

Tom Potter sums up the reaction nicely: "I had heard the album because Diamond and Jack had both played it for me, but I hadn't seen anything like it with art and stuff. I walk into this record store and they had just put it on the wall, with the Ko pictures and Andy and Patti's layout and it just grabbed me. It just looked different. It looked like something you had to fuckin' own. If I walked into a record store, I'd just buy it without knowing anything about them. I thought, man, this is gonna go somewhere. That definition of somewhere was that maybe someday they could sell out the Gold Dollar, but whatever."

Call it curb appeal. The Stripes had it in spades and it would later land their record in the hands of the most influential deejay in Britain. But for now, they were trying to cobble together their first real record cover on a shoestring budget by recruiting friends and fellow DIY travelers.

Ko Shih (née Komelina Zydeco) recalls the photo shoot vividly: "Heather, Meg's sister, had done photos for them but she couldn't do it that day," says Shih. "So Jack asked me to take photos of them. He had everything planned out. I just came with film in a camera. I took pictures of them all day. The cover was in front of the fire station in Southwest Detroit. They had just painted it and so it was really red. Jack said 'we gotta get there before the paint gets dull.' I didn't think they were gonna use those pictures," recalls Ko, "'cause I didn't think they were that good.

"It was cold that day! It was horrible. In the middle of winter. They're wearing T-shirts and Meg's wearing a little dress. If you pull the whole shot out there's like snow everywhere.

"I remember in the sequence I shot them in Jack was doing something with his fingers, on the first one he had one finger on his leg, he did a 'one sign,' second 'two sign,' third a 'three sign.' He didn't say anything to me about it, but I figured it out. He's got to have done it on purpose.

"Mine was definitely different than [*De Stijl* photographer] EWolf or [*White Blood Cells* and *Elephant* shutterbug] Pat [Pantano]'s—mine was really like 'Hey you wanna come over here and take pictures. And afterward I went to the Rite Aid to get them printed.'"

Ballistic Design, the husband-and-wife team of Andy and Patti Claydon—who also ran the Flying Bomb record label on which the Stripes had originally released "Candy Cane Children"—were again tapped for design and layout.

"Patti did most of this one. Jack had photos and wanted to use three on the cover. I did a version that Jack didn't like, so Patti did the 'filmstrip' version, which Jack liked a lot," recalls Andy.

"He didn't like the typography, said he wanted something simpler, but Patti stuck up for the concept of a White Stripe outlining the text and adding motion to the filmstrip idea, and Jack said if she felt that strongly about it, go ahead with it. (Funny thing, that typography ended up on T-shirts they did later. . . .)

"I did the inside stuff and a lot of grunt work (scanning, color adjusting, photo editing)."

"Oh, and Patti had to digitally erase Jack's wedding ring from all photos at Jack's request [as] Meg had just left him," adds Claydon.

The Whites' marriage wouldn't be officially dissolved in the eyes of the state of Michigan until March 24, 2000, but even as they wrapped up production on their debut record, it was clear that the teenage sweethearts' relationship was in a rocky strait. Jack was couch surfing quite a bit out of respect for his bandmate during the period which Dave Buick respectfully refers to as the time of their "sibling rivalry."

"He spent a lot of time at my house. It was a bad fight. He was pretty bummed out for a while. Meg was Jack's first girlfriend."

But the White Stripes had consistently referred to themselves as brother and sister since day one. At this point, Meg was still "my little sister Meg" (she'd later age gracefully into "my big sister Meg") when the band walked to the front of the stage after every show holding hands to take a bow.

When he was interviewing Jack White for his film *Detroit Rock Movie,* filmmaker Ben Hernandez asked Jack why they had insisted on the "brother and sister gambit." Jack's response was simple: "He said there's a lot of married couples in rock music. Saying we're brother and sister is more interesting. More mysterious," recalls Hernandez. Sounds simple enough. It would take a year and a half of the myth being bought by no less a fact-checking authority than the *New Yorker* to spur a reporter from *Time* magazine to uncover "the truth" about the White Stripes.

In a hushed voice and a rush of words that sounded near-embarrassed to hear itself, Jack White answered WDET host Willy Wilson's inquiry: "Are you a husband-and-wife duo or a brother-sister duo?"

"It's a brother-sister duo. It's just something that kinda came together, a little bit on accident. We were just goofing around a little bit and it seemed to work out because it's kind of simplistic. It's something that wasn't too complicated. We've been together about a year and a half. Bastille Day was the first day we jammed."

And so the myth was propagated giddily by Wilson, who knew better, but chose to stay kosher on the front. For local music writers, that was one of those secrets kept because it gave them a way to wink to each other and the readers who were wise enough to just let the mystery be. It was fun pretending that you didn't know that they were exs or soon to be exs.

"I was always very supportive of what I called the White Stripes Mystery Machine," recalls Case. "I love that kind of stuff and it's so absent from rock anymore and it used to be that everyone was a great mystery. Were the Rolling Stones really practicing black magic? Did Jimmy Page really have a suitcase full of whips that he beat teenage girls with? I don't know if that's true or not, but I want to believe that it is. I don't need to know the finer details, as long as I know that it's a possibility—that's good enough for me.

"The first time that I wrote about them I told everyone they were husband and wife," explains Case. "Because at the time they were still married. And that was 1998. And the reason I remember that was because when Brian McCollum told the world that the *Free Press* had 'discovered' that they were married (in 2000) I wrote something to the effect that 'it's common knowledge that Jack and Meg were married blah blah blah.' And Brian wrote this thing back to me like 'if it's such common knowledge then why didn't you guys break the story?' and I just copied the column from like two years earlier," laughs Case. "Anyway, they certainly look the part of brother and sister."

So why did they carry on? Simple. They both knew they were on to a good thing. And Jack probably sensed that it would be damn-near-impossible to re-create Meg's vaunted "childlike" drumming. Without Meg, the White Stripes wouldn't be the White Stripes. It'd be Jack White playing with a drummer.

Whatever the dynamic between them and no matter how it changed, they carried on. And White Stripes fans have Meg to thank for it. For it was she that lit the fire under Jack's ass when he had the backup plan—with Buick and Blackwell—in place for the band's appearance at the Blowout in 1999. Even then, nothing was sure. The duo quietly an-

nounced that the Blowout show was to be their last. Maybe the an-
nouncement brought out the throngs to the show that Saturday in
March. Or maybe it was just that the band's abilities and the public's acceptance of their artful conceits had finally intersected.

"We were just going to do covers and a few of Jack's songs," recalls
Buick.

"And I was excited about that. And then, as we were practicing, the
day of the Blowout at Jack's house, Meg said, 'C'mon, we're blood, we're
family, let's get together and play,'" recalls Buick.

"And that show was actually the first time that I knew that the White
Stripes were gonna be a huge thing.

"I think at that time the first singles had just come out. But people
were singing along to all of their songs. And not even to songs that were
on the single. I think that that's when everyone knew that these guys
were gonna be fuckin' huge."

By the time the record came out in June of '99, the White Stripes
had played several other gigs in and out of town, touring in true DIY
makeshift style.

"A bunch of the touring around the first album, we toured in my '95
Ford Taurus," remembers Blackwell.

"Jack and Meg in the front seat, me in the back with the bass drum,
and everything else fit in the trunk. The first time they played Milwau-
kee we took my car. The Taurus is in the backyard. My mom wants to
sell it on eBay as 'the car the White Stripes toured in,'" laughs Blackwell. "She's like 'Jack said we could do it!' I don't know, it's like my first
car, and there's a weird sentimental attachment."

After honing their set on the road, the Stripes were confident
enough in their ability to draw a crowd to hold their record release at
the Magic Stick. Even if the place was only two-thirds full, the crowd
was starting to come around more regularly to the desperate strangeness the White Stripes presented in the guise of childlike innocence.

Memphis musician Greg Cartwright remembers the supreme confidence that Jack displayed even this early with no shortage of admiration.

"Taking on a Terry Gilkyson song was particularly cool I thought. You don't see that much outside of folk singers," he says.

"We asked them to open for us and they said yes. They were great and delivered the songs with bravado like they were already playing to huge audiences. Strangely enough, while talking to Jack afterward he informed me that they were no longer performing opening slots and that this was a special consideration he was giving us. Now, at this point all they had were a couple singles, maybe the Hentchmen 10" as well, but no real following. They hadn't done any real touring and had no reason to believe they would be well received. And I thought 'Huh, this guy's really visualizing his desires.' I felt a little extra respect for him right then and there. Self-fulfilling prophecy. Above all else that's what it takes to make it. Total belief in yourself and your talents. Even if you're a cocky son of a bitch like P-Diddy with absolutely no talent to speak of you can make it if you convince yourself you're already on top waiting for everyone else to wake up and smell the coffee."

Dan Miller: "When the first album came out, one thing I was so happy about, was that I remember hearing people talk about the Birthday Party or the Gun Club or the Beatles getting to a certain point wanting to experiment with LSD or smoking weed or heroin or whatever, and having people say 'to get lyrics that are this perplexing comes as a result of some mind-altering substance.' I just remember thinking when I listened to the first record how great it was that someone was just doing that naturally.

"That their mind is that fucked up that they're coming to this point without having to resort to that stuff. I just remember having that discussion with musician friends over the years, like, 'I really like that song.' And they'd be like 'Well, you know how they came up with that, they did this.' It's so great that these White Stripes songs, what was he on when he came up with these? Nothing."

Well, maybe the clock. White puts an enormous amount of pressure on himself to deliver, to create within a certain time period. It's first thought, best thought put into action at the service of tapping once again into rock's inherent but long dormant chaos, mystery, and power to unnerve.

"I think that's great, because in a way it strips rock 'n' roll of that romantic notion that what you do in a recording session is have all these distractions, video games, hangers-on, people always dropping by. It's great to just clear all that out and focus on the music. And I think that's the thing that if you are paying for it, you're gonna be more driven. It's just another deadline," says Miller

This attitude would set the precedent for every subsequent White Stripes recording—hole-up, hunker down, and get the job done as quickly as the material deserves. Then get out there and tour your ass off. The White Stripes knew from the get-go that records were documents and that, after a certain point of musical fluency, they were a knockout live act and that that's where they were gonna get their bread buttered.

The White Stripes caught a huge break when Philadelphia R&B revisionists the Delta 72, for whom the Stripes had opened, passed a copy of the debut album on to Pavement's road manager, Debbie Pastor, who in turn recommended it to Pavement co-mainman Steven Malkmus.

The Stripes were asked to open for Pavement—who were touring for their final album *Terror Twilight*—at three shows in the Southeast. It was the kind of totally unexpected happenstance that the White Stripes needed to galvanize their commitment.

Pavement were selling out 400- to 500-person venues across the country, and now the strange little duo from Detroit were front and center in front of the chin-scratchingest audience in indie rock.

When the White Stripes got asked, every chin waggler in town's jaw dropped. "It was like 'No way! You are opening up for Pavement?!' says Stripes' pal Greg Siemasz, who went on that tour with them. "Of course now that's laughable, but at the time there was only maybe a couple of bands that had done anything on that scale, like opening up for a big indie rock band."

And Pavement was now asking this childish duo to open up for them. "That was a really fun time because it was really innocent," remembers Siemasz, who helped lug gear on the tour ("roadie" would be too formal a term).

The White Stripes were suddenly bumped up from playing the Gold Dollar or a half-filled Magic Stick to playing capacity joints where a sea of faces was waiting not on their every move, but rather anticipating another hour they'd have to kill before the band they paid to see hit the stage.

"I remember having that feeling backstage, I looked out and I was like 'Oh, my god! you're just gonna walk out in front of that and play?!' And of course, Jack claims that he never gets nervous. But anybody that steps in front of eight hundred people and has to play their songs has to have nerves, at least until you're in showmanship mode. He was never scared. There was never a time when he said he couldn't do it."

The audience was a wee bit underwhelmed for the most part. Garage rock, such as it was subsequently labeled in the wake of the Stripes and the Strokes' 2002 breakthrough success, didn't matter to the indie world. The too-cool-for-school indie nerds of '99 didn't wanna rock. But it didn't stop the Stripes from stepping up to the challenge. And they made some converts by the sheer emotional force of their performance alone. After all, says Siemasz, "I don't think anybody that ever listened to Pavement would admit to liking garage rock. At the time it was like 'I listen to Sebadoh. Did you check out the new Tsunami record? It's great! Matador is the best record label ever!'

"As it was, there were a couple people that would see it and be into it," says Siemasz. "The audience would stand there and do their job and clap, or whatever, but if you watch a White Stripes show even today, there is always that point where they could be a disaster or they could pull it off. You even feel that today. Because there's only two of them."

At the same time, the fact that there were only two of them onstage added at least a spark of intensity and dynamics that was undeniable, even if they were just the opening act. White Stripes shows could still go off the rails at any given moment. Pulling off a full set was a tightwire act between two people who piled their interpersonal tension into their live performances.

"It was very dramatic at the time," remembers Siemasz. "All this stuff was going on with Meg and Jack, and Jack would get mad at Meg onstage. I mean, it wasn't like he was hiding it. There was no place for them to hide! You were watching the drama unfold onstage. At the end of the show, they were friends and family, but that was probably the most trying time for them. A lot of that excitement was like watching a play—you can't deny that there was some sort of weirdness going on between these two dark-headed weirdos onstage."

Jack's stage direction of Meg was even more pronounced and intense. They hadn't gotten yet to the point where it was all for play. So it was that Pavement audiences were treated to the high-pressure cooker of Jack and Meg, with Jack yelling in Meg's face not a staged affectation, but an urgent entreaty to stop playing that beat right fucking now!

"As far as being an audience member, it was obvious that there was more to it than just two people being onstage. Two people playing onstage can be boring, and it's the same thing that still intrigues people about them now and that's their dynamic onstage."

The White Stripes and crew wrapped up their four-day run on the Pavement tour at Athens, Georgia's, fabled 40 Watt Club and piled into the rented minivan and headed back to Detroit. It had been an outing that would leave the Stripes pumped about their prospects and encouraged enough to at least record their second record, *De Stijl*, at home in Jack's house in Southwest Detroit among the comfort of the wall-mounted taxidermy, the piles of videocassettes of classic films, and the comfort that's described in sports as the home court advantage. Of course, with a band like the Stripes that thrives on limitations and deadlines both fiscal and creative, that can be a blessing and a curse.

Jack as Yenta

In the wake of the release of their debut record, the White Stripes were asked to record a 45 for underground music zine *Multiball*. In the process, Jack would play yenta for his nephew Blackwell and one of White's childhood idols, Gories coleader Mick Collins, whose current band, the Dirtbombs, was struggling through a series of itinerant drummers and lineups.

"The White Stripes recorded their song around August of 1999," says Blackwell. "*Multiball* approached the White Stripes to record a split single with the Dirtbombs. So the Dirtbombs recorded their song 'Cedar Point '76' and the Stripes did 'Hand Springs.' I wasn't on the Dirtbombs recording, but I ended up on the picture sleeve. That's kind of how I joined the Dirtbombs. I was at Jack's house one day and Mick had called him, to talk about sending out tapes together for the single or whatever, and Mick just happened to say in passing, 'Oh, by the way, do you know any drummers?' and Jack said 'Oh, yeah, one second.' And handed me the phone and I hear, [in Mick's telltale husky baritone] 'Uh, hey, Ben? This is Mick Collins' and I'm like 'hey, what's goin' on?' 'You play drums?' and I was like 'Uh, yeah.' And I totally sweet-talked my way into the band. I think I impressed him that I knew that a part from the 'Theme from the Dirtbombs' was ripped off from the Jackson 5."

Jack White's Other Day Job

Of course, Jack White worked as an upholsterer, but it was a career that didn't exactly fit with the traveling lifestyle of a rock 'n' roller. Brian Muldoon and White's Two-Part Resin (who would later release a 45 as the Upholsterers) parted company amicably when Jack made the choice to focus more of his energy on rock 'n' roll than Muldoon could afford and still maintain his own upholstery business clientele. The mighty long road of rock 'n' roll is littered with the also-rans of day-jobbers who gave up the dream of the footlights and groupies (or whatever floated their boat about rock 'n' roll as teenagers) for the more domesticated life. For the ones that made the commitment, the rock 'n' roll lifestyle's early days are often comprised of temp jobs, shit jobs, and under-the-table jobs like landscaping, office labor, and, particularly it seems, record store clerk.

During the White Stripes' salad days, Jack worked as a production assistant on commercial photo shoots, lugging gear, hanging lights, and generally running errands. A good day job for a musician sticking it out, feeling like the big break is right around the corner. In Jack's case in 1999 it was both. His friend Dan Miller had been making a living for a while as an actor, model, and voice talent in commercials and industrial films for the auto industry (you can't escape it in Detroit no matter how hard you try).

So Jack was no different from hundreds of other workers and a good number of gigging musicians in that respect. The shoots were long and the downtime is a fact of life. So he packed up his ideas in his head and stood around the set, waiting to get called to monkey around with some equipment or get behind the wheel and drive from an industrial park in a northern suburb of Detroit across town to some storage facility to pick up a lighting rig, only to head to some office complex in bucolic Mc-Mansion clusters with names like Farmington Hills. It was a day job that surely allowed for maximum daydreaming when the options were braying talk radio or planning rock 'n' roll takeover maneuvers. But it wasn't all grunt work.

"Some of our stuff was music oriented," says commercial director Kevin Carrico. "And Dan would say, 'I know a guitar player,' and so he would bring Jack to the shoot." One of the first cracks Jack had at rock 'n' roll "stardom" was as the preening and posing lead guitar player jamming out the hit "Closer to the Edge."

"It was actually as an industrial film for Chrysler. We faked a rock band and Jack got to fake being a guitar player. He did a great job. I remember Dave Buick was there, too." Joining White onstage for the epic jam was also Kevin Peyok on faux bass and the Go!'s Mark Fellis on faux drums. They were all tailor-made for the part, of course.

But it was money, and the result was a kick-ass MTV-worthy bit of rock cliché. The "Closer to the Edge" video was a perfect example of the other side of the Stripes—or at least Jack's sense of humor. He really got into it, and it was hilarious.

"I got the tape of it and we watched it, he liked it. Some people in his position might have said, 'Oh, let's only have a few people see this,' it's embarrassing or whatever," remembers Miller. "But not Jack. He took it up to the Magic Stick and they showed it over and over again on the VCR that night. He really wanted to share it with people!"

"Looking back at the old photos," recalls Carrico, "from when he PA'd for us, there's this photo of him carrying this piece of equipment and it's just so weird to think that he was a rock star.

"It just goes to show you, always be nice to the PA because you never know what they're going be tomorrow. No one ever thought our PA would become a rock star," he chuckles.

The Year 2000

Before the buzz had worn off from the Pavement tour, Jack and Meg holed up in the house they used to share to record their sophomore LP, *De Stijl*. Freed from the time constraints imposed by hiring a studio, they were able to create a loose record that is probably their most relaxed to date. The record was a vexing mix of overt exercises in form. Cuts like "Apple Blossom," "Truth Doesn't Make a Noise," and "You're Pretty Good Lookin' (for a girl)" are some of the most straightforward pop confections White has ever concocted (of course, tinted with trademark White characterizations of emotional and physical damage and heartbreak). As if to balance the hooks, White also chose to record some of the more intense slide blues ever rendered to tape by a rocker. Raw, powerful covers like White idol Son House's "Death Letter" are given a gut-bucket emotionality by Johnny Walker's slide guitar. The echoes of the Cole Porter and the showtunes his folks spun in this house while he was growing up haunt the proceedings and the ghosts end up getting channeled through White's sweet, tortured croon.

On the White original "Hello Operator" he invokes playground pattycake rhymes to dig into his longing. As a whole, the record plays like a fertile mind trying its level best to digest all the sounds that are flying at him a mile a minute and mostly succeeding. If the White Stripes first record was a full-on primal blast, a stake in the ground from which the nascent band was meant to explore, then *De Stijl*, with its patchwork formalism, is the first tentative step toward a signature sound that would be honed on subsequent records. A stepping stone to be sure, but one that was alarming at the time to fans who had come to take for granted the primal fury of the Stripes' live shows. Typically, White threw everyone off the scent of what were his most baroque compositions to date by aligning the album with a 1930s Dutch minimalist art movement that broke their visual expression down to its bare elements to find the heart of expression. There's no doubt White meant what he said in the rambling liner notes about stripping away artifice, decoration, and unnecessary distractions, but the relatively large number of guest artists on this record as well as the by-White Stripes-standards-anyway busy-ness of the execution tell a different story. If White had it mapped out in his head, the first record was the thesis. *De Stijl* was the antithesis. It would take them until *White Blood Cells* to find their true synthesis. Furthermore, White had hinted in interviews that recording the record at home allowed for too many distractions, taking away from the intended focus. Still, it's a truly lovely record that caught a fair number of listeners by surprise with its earthy tones, piano-favoring compositions, and expanded palette. Surely no one could take the Whites' aesthetic ambitions for granted now.

At the record release show, in fact, on June 3, 2000, at the Magic Bag in Ferndale, Jack spent a good chunk of the night behind the piano. It was strange to see someone who was usually so kinetic and edgy onstage seated at the piano bench. But it also lent an intimacy to the songs that added a sneaky charm once you realized that some of the tales were really, really dark.

One might be tempted to read into the near-misanthropic lyrics sung to nigh-on-perfect pop tunes a distinct influence from his songwriting relationship with Brendan Benson. Benson's not so sure: "People say that, and I guess I can see why people say that. But I think the songs that I think maybe might sound like me are his weaker songs," says the songwriter. "So I feel like if that's true, if that's me rubbing off on him, that's not a good thing."

Benson has a simpler answer than the ones posited by rock critics tempted to read too much into *De Stijl*. "I think that just like anybody else, he's fascinated with music. He was just hungry, hungry to learn new chords, new stuff.

"Just like I wanted to get more down to the bare essentials of a song, the basic heart of the song. Maybe he wanted to experiment more with the theory of the song or the chord changes," reckons Benson.

"I remember when he wrote one song, he got all excited about this chord change and I thought, 'that's funny, he's so excited about a chord change.'"

If the White Stripes were experimenting with new sounds, their self-confidence with their visual presentation was greater than ever. It should be said that the White Stripes weren't doing anything new by positioning themselves as aesthetes. Rock 'n' roll is chock-full of musicians that fancy themselves visually savvy enough to integrate their art with their sound. But the White Stripes' genius was two-fold in this arena. Firstly, they've kept their goals as simple as their ability to execute them. They realized that they were not the hyper Surrealists in the vein of multimedia pranksters like the Residents and their skill wasn't such that they could toy with form in such a thorough way as one of their obvious idols like Captain Beefheart. But with the tools they had at hand, they were as integrated a multimedia experience as any of their contemporaries. The other point that should be stressed was that they were, from a marketing standpoint, operating in the rock 'n' roll arena at the turn of the millennium. As such, they stood out from the pack by making simple assertions and choices. In a drab arena colored by gray ambivalence and nu-metal arena rock mopery, their red and white garb, their little white lies, and their subtle theatrical conceits were magnified. But they were still simple enough for anyone to grasp and, like the hick at the modern art exhibit, lots of folks looked at the Stripes and thought, "Hell, I could do that!" All of this was really called into sharp focus with *De Stijl*, the product, and the growing critical appreciation for the band's efforts that eventually followed quickly in its wake. After all, even though the critical response to *De Stijl* eventually reached mainstream mags like *Rolling Stone*, upon the album's release, a good number of copies of the record languished on record store shelves. The overt, some might say pretentious, invocation of *De Stijl* at first turned off their previous, though small, core audience of garage rock heads. But it would soon provide fodder for the Stripes to reach out to curious minds and ears. The White Stripes, at the time of *De Stijl*'s release, were just as likely to be the cute little garage band as they were anything that lasted beyond the year.

The growing confidence in their visual expression was obvious to Detroit photographer and drummer EWolf, who took the photos for the record.

"I did work with the Go! so that was when Jack first became aware of my services as a photographer," says the former Dirtbombs drummer.

EWolf photographed the Go! on Sub Pop's dime two or three times. And he remembers that at that point in his fashion career, Jack looked "like he was cast out of the Cure. He had wild flyaway hair and was look-ing very pale."

EWolf must have done something right, as it was proposed that he shoot photos for the next White Stripes record. Though his photo-graphic CV includes work with major label acts like the Detroiters, the Atomic Fireballs, and many bands on Chicago uber-indie Touch & Go and other indie-world high-profile stints, he was relatively cheap. It helped that he had a reputation for being resourceful and creative in a pinch.

So Jack and Meg arrived at EWolf's storefront studio in suburban Oak Park ready for their first professional shoot.

"What was really cool about it was that he came in prepared," enthuses EWolf. "He had his design worked out. He had all of his ideas as to what the album cover was to look like. He described it to me. He said 'I want to do this thing, that related to this design school from the '30s'—so from the way he was describing it it sounded like an old, modern art movement.

"But at the same time it was almost going to look like a Kraftwerk album. How he proposed he and Meg were going to look it was reminiscent of that German school of design. He said that they were just going to be standing there in the midst of these shapes that he had already cut out and painted and conceived as being the cover design.

"No other band that I had worked with had done that," says the photographer. "I was usually responsible for coming up with the concept and the props and everything. So in that way it was reassuring that things were going to go smoothly.

"The rest we kind of did by the seat of our pants," laughs the easygoing EWolf. "He wanted some more shots of them individually and as a duo. So we made other sets to shoot them with. But he brought in the props—the peppermint-striped bass, the Leslie cabinet, and the guitar.

"It was a combination of Jack's instruction that he wanted to be photographed with those things and my direction once we had those things in place. Meg was really good at following direction.

"One of them was funny because it was a shot of Jack and Meg together and it was in a very small room in my studio and Jack is close to the camera and Meg is back in the corner and we shot it with a wide-angle lens so Jack looks like he's six feet tall and Meg looks like she's three feet tall. That one became one of their promo photos I think."

EWolf says Jack had "a directedness that's kind of uncommon. At that point, where a band scarcely exists, you don't find very many people that are so concerned and so in control of their image."

Happy Booker Goes to Detroit

Another piece of the White Stripes puzzle fell into place in 2000. In early 2000, not long after *De Stijl* was recorded, the White Stripes were introduced to and signed with their booking agent Dave Kaplan.

At the time, Kaplan was just starting his own booking agency and Detroit duo Bantam Rooster was among his very first clients after Kaplan had parted ways with his previous gig booking the Kilowatt Club in San Francisco.

"With the White Stripes, it was a deal where the album had come out and it was doing all right and they had another dude who was booking them, but Jack was unhappy with him," recalls Potter. "He had booked a couple of crappy shows on the East Coast and Jack was like 'Fuck this guy. We just did a couple shows where I know we're doing well enough, we should be getting more money or headlining!'

"I was like 'Jack, you're still just getting going. But if you're looking, I know this guy Dave Kaplan. Here's his number, I'll call him tomorrow to look out for your call.' And they were starting to pick up momentum and Dave knew about 'em a little already."

The Stripes and Kaplan clicked and soon Kaplan and his roster grew till it read like a Detroit rock who's who—Bantam Rooster and the Stripes, the Sights, the Electric Six, the Dirtbombs, the Detroit Cobras, and a host of other area bands joined the flock. When Kaplan and his roster got picked up by the international Agency Group, the city's collective clout got a huge shot in the arm.

The White Stripes had to start to contend with their current lot in life as a band on the road, playing close to one hundred shows that year—an exponential leap that signaled a redoubled commitment to making a dent in the public conscience. The record was barely registering with fans who hadn't witnessed the Stripes live and lived to tell about it, so Jack and Meg knew that they had to take the gospel to the people.

Partway through their summer tour that year, they stumbled upon a bit of free publicity in Los Angeles when they pulled up for what they thought was a headlining gig at the tiny club Spaceland.

Turns out Weezer was making an unannounced comeback show after a two-year hiatus in which they recovered from two-hit-wonder burnout.

Weezer wanted to play a show at Spaceland and the White Stripes had already booked it. The White Stripes were not budging.

"Essentially they just got offered the same amount that they would have made playing by themselves to open for Weezer," said Blackwell.

The Stripes reluctantly played before a rabid Weezer crowd. They may have made a convert or two, but more importantly, they were there, in stark red and white, in front of an overstuffed house full of kids, not crusty garage rockers or record collector nerds, actual record-buying kids. And they couldn't move because it was so crowded. No one officially counted the number of times Jack uttered the words "we're the White Stripes" that night, but with such prime ad space at his disposal, presume it was a lot.

"You kinda got a sense of what was going on, that there was this whole underground Weezer community. That was really, really weird," recalls Blackwell.

"It seemed to be like kind of a typical White Stripes set, but I don't think most people picked up on it. In my mind at least it seems like it was a pretty forgettable White Stripes set. There were probably one or two converts." By the way, according to Blackwell, Weezer played under the name Goat Punishment that night.

As the White Stripes touring machine rolled on, they picked up momentum. "The general feeling seemed to be that they were having fun," recalls Blackwell. "I mean like invariably every tour had some kind of car problem, and that was a bummer, but they never really had like a bad tour where they lost money or whatever. It's like that still, things just kept getting better and better. They've yet to take a step back. It was always like 'the show's sold out, we need to play bigger places.'

"It was only really through interviewing Jack that I began to realize his ambitions were much greater than anybody had supposed," reckons Wendy Case. "I just thought they were the cute little rock duo that showed up when no one else would play for fifty dollars.

"I don't think Jack charted his course according to what everybody else was doing," says Case. "Everybody else was content to stay home and be a hometown hero. Like Rocket 455 and folks like that who everybody really admired here in town, they didn't have any ambitions to be anything more than a regional phenomenon. It seems clear to me that at some point Jack was looking beyond that."

"It used to be in Detroit, we'd get the same fifty people, the garage rock crowd or the obscure music fans or whatever," said Jack in an early 2001 interview for *Hour Detroit* magazine, "but last time we played Detroit it's like we were on the road in that there were young people, old people, couples, kids, people holding hands. And that's what it's like in other towns. We didn't want to play in front of the same fifty people cause it's hard to break out of that mold. It's hard to break out and still have these people like you."

One of the first places that picked up on the Stripes was San Francisco. For whatever the reason, the city that birthed both Journey and the Residents (oh, and the Mummies and Supercharger, too) latched on to the Stripes early and hard.

"It was impressive to see that he was genuinely excited when he knew there was an audience growing in San Francisco. He said I know there's an audience there, I don't understand it, but I'm really into it. He was very demonstrative that he could tell that the tide was rising, that he was excited. But he expressed it in a really gentlemanly way, not like 'we're gonna get to San Francisco and kick ass!' or anything like that.

"I remember the first time they played San Francisco it was a Tuesday night in 2000. And the [rock club] Bottom of the Hill was sold out—on Tuesday night!" says Blackwell.

Electric Six frontman Tyler Spencer was living in California at the time and he remembers ambling through the line he saw wrapped around the club. "People were talking about how the White Stripes were from Detroit and how cool Detroit must be and how the Stripes had a song that consisted entirely of street names. It was crazy and it was really inspiring, too."

"I remember at the time, the White Stripes' Italy records and Sympathy records were distributed by Mordam and Revolver, and they both have offices in San Francisco," says Blackwell. "And I remember going into the offices and it was weird because people working there were like looking down the aisle, like 'the White Stripes are here!' they had all like really really adored this band. And I thought 'oh, well, they must always act like that.'"

Then he went back with the Dirtbombs a couple years later and was asked by the receptionist in a polite tone, "Um, can I help you?"

All of that action was just preamble to the big breakthrough tour that the White Stripes were looking for. If there's a single period in which the White Stripes' underground success was raised to the proverbial next level, it was during their August 2000 tour with the buzz- and crush-worthy grrl band Sleater-Kinney who were touring in support of their new album *All Hands on the Bad One.*

Sleater-Kinney hand-picked the White Stripes to open for them on fourteen dates in the Midwest and on the East Coast, putting the Stripes front and center before eight hundred of the most band loyal, open-minded indie rock fans on the planet in cities like Washington, D.C., Boston, and New York where the East Coast music press takes its tea.

Sleater-Kinney fans are "more than fans," according to Jimmy Draper, a San Francisco music writer and former webmaster for the Sleater-Kinney website. They take the endorsement of S-K very seriously.

"People still keep Sleater-Kinney like their secret," says Draper. "So they're more likely to give the benefit of the doubt to an opening act.

"More than the fans," figures Draper, "and even though Sleater have huge audiences, they [also] get so much critical press. I always assumed there were a ton of critics at these shows. I don't remember a lot of press stuff happening independently for the Stripes, so the Sleater tour meant a lot of critical exposure."

Jack White would seem to agree with Draper's assessment.

"I was talking to Meg about it the other day," remembered White in early 2001, "and I said 'the Pavement crowd really didn't get us or get into us,' but a year later, the Sleater-Kinney crowd really took to us. Maybe the timing was right. It seems to be really, really odd to end up in *Rolling Stone.* We don't have anyone managing us, no one's sending our records out to press or pushing us with radio or anything. Maybe the songs are just good. Maybe we're lucky."

"I think it was the fact that they were playing in front of crowds that they knew weren't necessarily their crowds, but they were really really receptive. The crowds knew good music, so it was a combination that just kinda of built up Jack's confidence." In particular Blackwell remembers a show at Oberlin University as being "just insane because the White Stripes were just so on that night, and Sleater-Kinney kind of got it, like they definitely saw the Stripes play an amazing show and they recognized that the bar had been upped. And they knew to up their performance."

It's odd and yet characteristic of the Stripes' sometimes polarizing effect that Draper recalls the same show as a relatively sedate Sleater-Kinney show (he'd seen upward of two dozen S-K shows by that point).

"It was like in a big cafeteria on the campus and it was surprisingly small. Maybe three hundred people. Alcohol wasn't served and you had to be a student to get in. I remember that the backstage area was a classroom."

Sounds pretty damn rock 'n' roll!

Whatever the subjective reaction of individuals in attendance, the White Stripes seemed to sense the crowd responding and seized the moment to up their game.

"That tour helped the White Stripes a lot spreading the word of mouth," says Blackwell.

"The Stripes were really breaking out a shell where Jack would play entirely different songs, different sets. It's when he first seemed to start playing songs that they'd never played before, like 'I'm just going to go into this and Meg can figure it out or I'll lead her on.' And it was just really amazing when they'd do that."

"Right before that tour was around the time they stopped using set lists, and it was kinda like Jack just pulling out covers that they'd never done before and they were doing a lot of stuff just impromptu. That's kind of when the White Stripes that most people know developed.

"It was surreal to hang out with a band you really admired every night," remembers Blackwell, who was on the road with the Stripes for a few dates that tour. "That was how it was with Sleater-Kinney. One night Janet let us stay in her hotel room, so it was like me and Jack sharing a bed and her and Meg sharing a bed. It was just like 'what just happened? I'm a stupid freshman in college and I get to do all this?'"

When summer camp ended for the Stripes and Sleater-Kinney, Jack and Meg got right back on the road. The results of their opening jaunt were immediate.

The Stripes road show rolled into Asheville, North Carolina, at the end of September 2000. A cursory stroll around the town scouting for thrift and record stores quickly let the Stripes know just how far they had come.

"We were walking down the street and people were passing and saying 'hi' to us and we thought they were just friendly," recalled Jack in the *Hour Detroit* interview. "But we kept walking and a block later, the whole front display of this vintage clothing store was decorated in peppermint red and white and the window mannequins were dressed up like Meg and I. The show that night was just packed and the people went crazy and it was a great show."

The White Stripes were pretty confident that *De Stijl* was picking up steam. The other measure of its success and the buzz building around the band was that other indie labels were sniffing around the band.

And by all accounts, once he started sensing the band's growing momentum, Jack became more curious about getting the band into a better label situation, one in which adequate reporting of record sales and tour support existed. Detroit Cobras guitarist Mary Restrepo is blunt: "Fuck accounting and reporting, it was littler shit than that. Jack was one of the first guys that made it over there [to L.A. and Sympathy HQ]. And he was like, 'I went to the garage and there was all of our tour posters.'

He said he was doing tour support and he wasn't doing anything! The guy did nothing."

As Restrepo notes, White was looking for the kind of label where you weren't constantly wondering where your songs would turn up next. "We went to L.A. and he'd hand you a CD compilation that you're on and you didn't even know about it. And you're like 'do you realize that I didn't even know this existed!?'"

Among the first labels that showed interest in the White Stripes was Sub Pop records, who already counted among their roster Jack's former bandmates in the Go! Except at this point, the Go! weren't exactly a high priority for Sub Pop as their record was kinda stiffing and the band was heading back into the studio to reinvent themselves and engage in an extended period of recording studio navel gazing.

Sub Pop A&R guy Andy Kotowicz and label owner Jonathan Poneman went to see the Stripes at the Sit 'n' Spin in Seattle and were promptly blown away. "We were pretty taken from them in a way that I didn't expect to be from the record," says Kotowicz. "The guy has some kind of star magnetism and he was an amazing guitar player.

"The other thing that was striking was their sheer ability to sell records—the amount of people that lined up asking for one of everything was just astounding. They were selling the 'Hello Operator/Jolene' picture disc among their stuff and people were just lined up for it.

I know that he and Jonathan and he had met before. Because the first time I met Jonathan was at a Go! show in Detroit," say Kotowicz.

"The first time I called him about the *Singles Club* record I told him that the record is exclusive and Sub Pop owns the tracks and he seemed a little sketched about that." So the White Stripes submitted covers of Captain Beefheart songs "Party of Special Things To Do" and "China Pig/Ashtray Heart" for a limited edition *Sub Pop Singles Club* 45. "I think that the fact that he did those covers was pretty savvy on his part rather than turning over his own tracks—not that I'm second-guessing his appreciation of the good Captain!"

"He had mentioned that there was a label in Chicago called Bobsled that was interested in putting out a record," remembers Kotowicz. "After conferring with Jonathan I called Jack and told him we'd love to throw our hat in the ring—this was summer of 2000. He was real flattered and he said he'd talk to Meg and get back to us. And the next time we talked he was like 'yeah, I appreciate it, but probably not.'

"It seemed like his attitude at the time was like if I'm not going to be on a major label, I might as well stay with Sympathy. They're like family at this point, so I don't want to upset the relationship.

"I drove up to his place to pick up the [Singles Club] tracks. And I talked to him again about it and he was pretty emphatic," says Kotowicz. "He was really polite about it and we had a pretty good chat."

White even showed him the "Closer to the Edge" video.

Kotowicz says Sub Pop was disappointed and, on a personal level, he was disappointed, too, because the White Stripes tapped a particularly deep vein of music that spoke to him. "Jack brings in that blues and Tin Pan Alley influence, and he had roots that a lot of indie bands just don't have, so they spoke to the historian in me and I connected with that a whole lot.

"At the time, it was like 'who would have fuckin' thought it?' One of the reasons we didn't go crazy and go after 'em from the get-go was because we thought, 'who's gonna wanta sign this two-piece garage band from Detroit,'" laughs Kotowicz.

"If anyone brings up the White Stripes," to this day, Jonathan always say the same thing: "Tell 'em we'll give 'em ten grand. I'll up the budget to ten grand."

Also in the running for the White Stripes' services at the time were the Beastie Boys' Grand Royal label and Mississippi-based blues specialty imprint Fat Possum, both of which had major label backing, but not the clout to spend the necessary dough on radio or MTV.

But the label that came closest to winning the place perceived-if-not-actual mini-lottery that surrounded the White Stripes was tiny Chicago indie Bobsled Records, who had put out *Low to the Ground*, the debut record by White Stripe pals, the Waxwings.

The White Stripes had engaged in real live talks with Salerno to put out a record, but the talks hit a really silly loggerhead.

"Jack didn't have anything cooking with record labels," recalls Siemasz. "And Bobsled offered them more money than Sympathy ever gave them and tour support and all that stuff. It came down to the spine of the record, the little chartreuse green Bobsled logo that was supposed to be the label identity or whatever."

But Jack wouldn't budge and wouldn't have it on there as it was. And that was that, deal ended over a ¾-inch band of green.

"Their career would have been nothing if they would have said, 'you know what, the green thing, keep it,' reckons Siemasz.

"Jack wanted it to be black, white, or red. And Bob didn't want that and he's probably kicked himself in the ass every day for it. But at the same time, if that would have happened, the White Stripes wouldn't have had the same opportunities. But that's the thing. God is in the details."

Indeed, when you get money flashed in front of you, it's tempting to cut and run. But the White Stripes had the foresight to say no.

"Jack thought about it," remembers Siemasz. "He said, 'If it's going to come down to him not doing that, what else is he not going to do that's not supportive."

All of this was only preamble to the real label lottery that the White Stripes would enter in only a few months after *White Blood Cells* hit the streets to nearly universal acclaim. The White Stripes, for now, had the leverage of having said no and stood their ground on artistic control. They made it clear that they were in this on their own terms, even going so far as to maintain the front that Sympathy was family and that they'd suck it up and stick with the label that they'd had occasion more than once to complain about. Buick is less cynical: "Jack decided to go with Long Gone John and Sympathy for the same reason he takes local bands on tour, because he's loyal to them."

The upshot was that they remained independent, and that was the more important thing.

"John Waters said something like 'success is doing what you want to do, how you want to do it," said Jack early 2001. "That's pretty much where we are and it's a pretty good place to be. The dream of MTV and playing huge places seems to be like death. If we had a hit with a video that wouldn't last. It would have to be a one-hit-wonder kind of thing and it wouldn't be sustainable."

He took the next few months to bone up on the machinations of the music industry, trying to find the extent of his limitations as a negotiator and figure out how the band could move ahead without a lawyer or manager in their camp and hopefully without compromising their treasured freedom.

Another piece of the White Stripes administrative puzzle fell into place in the autumn of 2000 when a superfan from New Zealand named John Baker contacted the band through Long Gone John with an offer too good to refuse—a tour of Australia. Detroit bands with whom the White Stripes were pals—the Dirtbombs, the Hentchmen, Bantam Rooster—had made a few trips to Europe over the preceding couple years to mixed success, but none of them had crossed the Pacific. This was uncharted territory. The White Stripes made the leap based on the enthusiasm of Baker.

World Wide Whites

The White Stripes launched their Web site www.whitestripes.com in October of 2000. Now this is normally nothing to get all excited about, but for a band that had taken such a decidedly lo-fi, anti-technology stance that they launched it at all meant that they were serious about getting the word out to people outside their small circle of underground influence.

It was also not long after they launched the site that the Stripes turned down their very first overture from corporate America. In late 2000, Johnson & Johnson & Co. had just launched their teeth-whitening product White Strips. When companies launch products, they put up Web sites. And when they put up Web sites, they do their level-best to buy up all the potentially confusing domain names. Some cyber squatters make a perfectly good living simply buying domain names likely to be purchased by large companies with deep pockets and cashing in. But when the White Stripes were approached, according to Ben Blackwell, with an offer to have whitestripes.com purchased for $4,000 to $5,000, Jack and Meg flatly refused them. At the time, Blackwell was the de facto webmaster for the Stripes. Also at the time, Blackwell who seems to share his uncle's penchant for occasionally telling stories that make for good quotes even if they deviate from hard reality, hinted that the amount might have been as high as $75,000. Certainly more dramatic than four grand, but for a band that was struggling to pay their bills and keep their van on the road safely, the offer should have been tempting, but it wasn't.

Blackwell was known and loved then (and still is) by White Stripes faithful as Stripeybeast, the nom du web he used when he sent out e-mail updates of Jack and Meg's adventures.

"When it first started I was doing it through my personal AOL account and it was maybe a thousand people at that point. But it ended up the first e-mail I sent they took me off AOL because they thought I was sending spam. Man! The things I do for this band," he says, mock-sobbing.

The tone of Blackwell's e-mails had a lot to do with the way fans talk about the White Stripes.

When Blackwell sent out an e-mail announcing the release of *Elephant,* he flippantly mentioned that if you put the six available album covers together correctly, they would tell you where to find the Third Sword in Zelda.

"Like obviously the most outlandish thing you could ever imagine," laughs Blackwell. "And people are online talking after it came out saying stuff like 'So where do you get the third sword?' and it's like totally over their heads. It got to the point where I was making the most absurd claims just to see how seriously people would take it. So I was saying like they were going to be posing for wax figures at Madame Tussaud's and that one got way blown out of proportion with John Peel asking them about it and them having to explain, 'no, it was kind of just like a joke'" laughs Blackwell of his work as a cog in the mythmaking machine.

"Who knows, by now they probably have posed for wax figures, so I'm more of a foreseer, a soothsayer."

Go to a Land Down Under

In November 2000, the White Stripes—at the behest of uberfan and soon-to-be Stripes' road manager "Jumping" John Baker—landed in Australia not just as the first garage punk band of their generation to see the continent, but also as a sort of surrogate representative for that whole scene. Bands that recorded for Sympathy for the Record Industry and Crypt Records and In the Red, bands that owed a debt to the Gories and shit-hot bands like the Oblivians. The White Stripes took the flight knowing that they'd have eight shows on the continent in a week's time. But the trip would change their perspective entirely.

When the White Stripes returned from this trip, they'd settle back at home for a couple months before heading down to Memphis to record *White Blood Cells*. And they'd return with de facto road manager John Baker in their stable, too.

But at the time, they were an unknown quantity that had taken the leap of faith and traveled across the Pacific to play a few shows for people who were observant enough to latch onto the band.

I walked into this record store here in Melbourne called Au Go Go," remembers Aussie rock writer Shane Jesse Xmass, "I just started flicking through the shelves. I was, and still am, a huge Oblivians fan. I was aware that it would be ideal to perhaps pay attention to things that were linked via that particular band, or thru the Sympathy for the Record Industry label."

So he made his way to the "W" section and found two pasty-faced Detroiters staring out at him.

"I wasn't sure about the qualifications being made in regards to the matching red and white uniforms. Without listening to the music it seemed like a cheap gimmick, but it needs to be stressed that this was before I listened to the tunes, and now it's more like an annoyance. I'm perplexed as to why they thought the uniforms would be a great idea to begin with."

Xmass had previously discovered the Go! in much the same way, but he didn't realize that the guitar player on *Whatcha Doin'* was the same Jack White from the White Stripes. Nevertheless, the record grew on him and when the Stripes landed in November 2000, he toodled over to Melbourne to catch the shows.

"The first time I met Jack and Meg was at their in store signing. For me there was a hurry to get down there. John Baker rung me up about twenty minutes before saying 'They'll be at Au Go Go in twenty, come down to do your interview,'" recalls Xmass.

"I was shit scared as I think this was my first in-person interview, I didn't even own a Dictaphone, and I certainly wasn't living or eating very well."

He could have left the intimidation at home, for despite the enthusiastic support of Baker and Long Gone John, who had also made the trip to Australia, he didn't have to elbow for attention.

"What struck me as an absolute hilarity, and a further example of how fucked up this world is, is that at the store there was less than ten people. Included in those ten people were people to do with the tour. I'd say entourage, but at the time the White Stripes didn't seem to have any baggage, not that I have any idea if they do these days.

"What I was aware of was that there were no fans," recalls Xmass.

"It amazed me to think that no one was listening to great rock and roll. I don't know if I felt disgusted or ashamed, but I was certainly worried that no one would be coming to the shows, as the White Stripes were playing a gig a night, from Monday to Sunday, plus in stores, and other shit."

Jack and Meg had been in Australia for three days and they were already recruiting would-be journalists as their ad hoc road crew.

"On the Sunday," Xmass recalls, "Jumping John had told me to meet him at the venue. When I got there he asked if I could help lug in Meg's drum kit."

The venue was called the Tote, and says Xmass, "It's a famous bar, but it's a bit hard for me to describe it, or bands that have played there, as I haven't grown up in this bar, or Melbourne to be even more precise. But I can imagine it to be like any other small, clammy bar or pub that has shitty rock and roll bands playing every night. It's definitely not a 'cool' place. It resides in a regimented and traditional working-class part of Melbourne, and the bands that play there and its clientele and the jukebox reflect this."

The White Stripes played with locals the Onyas and, says Xmass, there was a tight crowd, pushed into the joint, enough of a crowd where he remembers "Jack White telling some muckheaps to go outside. It was a relaxing show, but very on edge."

So from the seeds of those first few shows and the subsequent word of mouth, a cult of Stripes devotion sprung up far, far from Detroit. But the Stripes were also, remember, the ambassadors of the real live, pulsing, breathing American underground rock 'n' roll. They were the first band of that sort to make it Down Under. And as such, they got a lot of borrowed interest from fans of other Sympathy bands. And they didn't waste the moment to make converts. And, says Xmass, the White Stripes appealed to what he perceives as Aussies' keen bullshit detector, too.

"Melbournians tend to be able to smell a turd a mile off, they subject things to a 'realness' test, y'know pomposity and show-ponies don't wash big down here, so in that aspect the White Stripes were deemed to be solid, but they did that through their music, and after these shows the word got around. Australians run a mile from hype, and the White Stripes got big here based on musicianship and a groundswell that evolved from that musicianship."

Word spread amongst the Australian rock underground and the White Stripes had a minor hit with *De Stijl*. Indeed, when they returned touring for *White Blood Cells* more than a year later, the word had spread—both between fans and via an ever-more-adoring Aussie music press— and the Stripes would make enough of an impact to earn their first certifiable Gold record in Australia with WBC. Not unimportantly, it was before one of the shows on the *White Blood Cells* tour that Jack started toying around with a bass-like riff that would become the foundation of "Seven Nation Army."

But at the end of their week's invasion of Australia, the White Stripes were just glad to have made a couple hundred fervent fans halfway around the world before returning to Detroit and further adventures.

Family Feud

One could forgive the White Stripes for taking a breather after the hectic year they had had. But Jack was already moving on to the next thing. Over the past year, he had been nurturing a young band from the western suburb of Ypsilanti called the Von Bondies.

The Von Bondies had started their band-life as the Baby Killers, a sort of pastiche of instrumental Cramps-y numbers and straight-up garage rock in the Nuggets tradition. They were nothing to write home about, but once they changed their name and tweaked their lineup to become the Von Bondies, they started to connect with audiences. Primary among the reasons was the fact that in frontman Jason Stollsteimer the Bondies had a charismatic howler who wasn't afraid to learn as he went and who had been weaned on Screamin' Jay Hawkins and alt-rock agitators Nation of Ulysses in equal measure. They also had one of the city's most bombastic and swinging skin slappers on drums in Don Blum. It certainly didn't hurt that Jack White was dating the band's guitarist Marcie Bolen, either. The Von Bondies ended up on some plum gigs thanks to the association and White took the band under his wing as his next pet project, working with Stollsteimer on his guitar chops.

"We played at the Gold Dollar with the Detroit Cobras and the White Stripes and for them there was only thirty people," remembered Stollsteimer. "We only knew four songs and no one was there, so we'd just play 'em again. Playing a live show's like having three practices."

As 2000 wound to a close, Long Gone John had agreed to put out a Von Bondies full-length. Jack White would be the producer.

They had just recruited a new bass player, Carrie Smith, who had previously been a member of Ypsilanti hardcore teen band the Fags.

So the tweaked lineup began woodshedding material at the White house in preparation for their impending check-in to Jim Diamond's studio for a quickie two-day recording session.

Diamond recalls the *Lack of Communication* recording going as smoothly as could be for a band trying to get a full-length record out of two days' worth of recording. Of course, there was some interpersonal tension already brewing.

"Jack was dating Marcie at the time, so I think there was some tension starting between a camp of Jack and Marcie in one and then Jason. So there was a little bit of tension there. And I remember Jason being unhappy because when we mixed it, Jack would want Marcie's guitar up really loud and Jason would be like 'Hey, I can't even hear my guitar,'" remembers Diamond.

"The first record would have sounded like the music in our head, but we had no time and no money. But in our heart we know it could have been better if we had more time," said Stollsteimer in retrospect. "It does sound like a garage record cuz it was done in a day. At that time we were just excited to be recording a record."

"I was only in the band for two months when I joined, so there was no creative input. The first record was a Jack White and the Von Bondies record," said Smith.

It seems that the seeds of disagreement were planted here that would later come to bear violent fruit on December 13, 2003, when Jack pummeled Stollsteimer and was subsequently charged with aggravated assault. Stollsteimer allegedly figured Diamond should get coproduction credits for the record and White wanted sole credit—or something silly to that effect.

"I don't know what's going on with all that production stuff. I was never consulted about any of that.

"When everyone was here, everyone had ideas. Jack would be like 'try that,' and Jason would, too. Or I would. So everyone had ideas. There wasn't like demarcation of 'OK, I will twiddle the knobs. Jack, please tell me what to do. Jason, go play the guitar.' It wasn't like that. It was pretty average in terms of its collaborative nature. Everyone always works together. It's just varying degrees of who's in charge. It wasn't even a week. It was like four days and then I mastered it. Total bill was like $1,600 out the door," says Diamond for his part.

Commenting on the spirit of the recording sessions as they were taking place, Diamond notes, "It was fun. But they're all fun. There probably ended up being a little tension, but it wasn't serious at all. Everyone was getting along and having fun. There wasn't any ill feelings."

The ill feelings were abated so long, it seems, as White was dating Bolen and as long as Stollsteimer refrained from needling White in the press that resulted with the Von Bondies' growing success.

The Von Bondies participated in the Sympathetic Sounds of Detroit compilation, and when their record was about to be released in spring 2001, White was championing them whenever he got the chance.

"I just got done producing the first Von Bondies record at Jim Diamond's Ghetto Recorders studio," raved White in early 2001 to Wilson. "And wait till you hear this record, man, it's unbelievable. You just haven't heard rock 'n' roll out of Detroit like this in a while. It's heavy duty. It's just very along the lines of the Gun Club, I think, the songs that are on this record. They're just amazingly talented people."

The camaraderie lasted through a summer tour through the States. "At the time, Jack was saying we were the better band that night," says Stollsteimer of the summer tour. "At some shows they did, they were still trying to make a two-piece sound full. Now they have it down pat, but at that time they were just using the house guy and there's no way a two-piece is ever gonna get any credit from the house sound man. He's gonna be like 'two-piece, this is bullshit.'"

The Stripes also took the Von Bondies over to Europe that fall.

"They were incredibly important," says Smith of the UK and European shows. "The first tour in November of 2001, ten dates in the UK and as many in Europe, was so important. We got so much exposure and we had never gotten press like that before. At that point in our career we wouldn't have gotten that without the help of the White Stripes. It really let us put our foot in the door and get us in front of audiences that were there to listen. I will never try to take that away from them for doing that, it was incredibly nice.

"They let us share their tour bus and now, being more savvy, I realize just how expensive tour buses are and they let us stay on their bus for free."

But the good feelings didn't last. As the Von Bondies started to get more successful and get their own buzz, Stollsteimer's confidence grew and so did his on-the-record complaints about the sound of their debut record. He spouted off more than once to European journalists (since, at the time, American journalists were hardly aware of the Bondies' existence). By the time the White Stripes, the Von Bondies, and the Dirtbombs were billed together at Dublin Castle in April of 2002, the tensions in the dressing room were such that the Stripes weren't on speaking terms with the Von Bondies. For his part, White was reportedly calling out the Von Bondies as the rotten fruit in the otherwise shiny red basket of apples that was the Detroit scene.

When in 2002 the Von Bondies made the leap to major-label status and opted not to join White on V2 Records, but rather sign with the recently resurrected Sire imprint helmed by the legendary Seymour Stein, any formal ties between the bands were broken. White was no longer dating Bolen, Stollsteimer no longer sought White's counsel on matters, and the Von Bondies' stock was on the rise. The Von Bondies went into the studio with former Modern Lover Jerry Harrison to record their Sire debut at the Record Plant in Sausalito. Stollsteimer immediately started distancing himself in the press from the production work on the first record.

By the night of December 13, 2003, the mud had been flung and both bands had been on tour for so long, they truly at this point had a complete lack of communication. When White approached Stollsteimer at the front of the stage at the Magic Stick—while Brendan Benson was onstage—the Von Bondies frontman refused to acknowledge him, it was apparently the last straw for White, who according to the Stoll-steimer's police report punched him approximately seven times in the face. It was the eve of a full weekend worth of promotional press for the Von Bondies in anticipation of their debut record *Pawn Shoppe Heart,* so to cynics and conspiracy theorists, the beatdown smelled like a pub-licity stunt. But it wasn't. However, the journos and photogs that had to be sent back to New York and L.A. all left with a story to whisper to their gossip editors.

Both parties had lawyered up by daybreak, but if you asked around Detroit, there, oddly, wasn't a lot of sympathy for Stollsteimer. When asked to comment about the Von Bondies, one local promoter simply said, "My mother said that if I didn't have anything nice to say about someone, don't say anything at all."

In the ensuing publicity hubbub, Stollsteimer was made the butt of jokes and White was dubbed "battling Jack" and other such inanities. What's lost here is that two former friends ended their relationship in a brutally public way.

On March 9, 2004, Jack White pled guilty to misdemeanor assault in Detroit's thirty-sixth District Court. Outside the court, White pulled a note out of his red fedora and read to reporters: "This was a personal matter and not a press promotion. I regret allowing myself to be pro-voked to the point of getting into a fistfight but I was raised to believe that honor and integrity mean something and that those principles are worth defending."

In turn, the Von Bondies issued a statement of their own: "Unlike Mr. White, we have been consistent and unwavering in our statement of December 15, 2003. Jason Stollsteimer was violently attacked by Jack White in an unprovoked incident . . . as one of his penalties, Mr. White has been ordered to attend anger management classes. We are relieved that this chapter has finally come to a close; Mr. White will address his anger issues and both the Von Bondies and Mr. White can get back to doing what they do best: make music."

That same Tuesday night, at the Magic Stick, the Von Bondies cele-brated the release of their major label debut *Pawn Shoppe Heart* to a sold-out crowd breathing in the air of tension and drinking from plastic beer bottles among the seemingly beefed-up security presence. The White Stripes and their friends, family, and lawyers settled into the darkened corners of the Bronx Bar, a neighborhood joint in the Cass Corridor a few blocks away from the Stick.

"Jack lost his temper. He should go to anger management classes," says British music writer Everett True matter-of-factly. True was visiting Detroit shortly after the dust-up to document the "scene" and staying with Ben Blackwell.

"Jason wound him up and Jack punched him. I'm sure Jack had quite a bit of provocation and I think that's Jason seeing a good marketing opportunity."

When a scene splinters, it happens slowly. But when a couple of the most famous members of the scene get into a bar fight after engaging in a period of enmity that was never well hidden from the locals, it happens a little faster.

"Things have definitely changed over the last few years," reckons Potter. "but there's still a core of camaraderie. There's still that core of family where it's like you can fight with your family and talk shit all you want, but if somebody outside the family wants to talk shit, well, we'll fuck with them. And even that's got a little looser these days. Any of us that were around six or seven years ago still pretty much kind of adhere to that. The kinship still exists. It's gotten a bit more fragmented. It's gotten a bit weird around here, but it still exists."

And maybe the Stripes have simply upped the stakes, keeping everyone more motivated and honest. But, as Potter points out, it's pretty damn hard to up the stakes from the MC5, the Stooges, and Parliament Funkadelic.

"But they've upped the stakes for people who don't know," says Potter. "There are still lot of bands that are like 'well, we're gonna do what we're gonna do. It's nice that the White Stripes opened some doors for us.'"

The media seized on it as some sort of "death of the Detroit scene" metaphor, but to be honest, the scene was already, save for a handful of bands, evolving. The ones that were most closely associated with the White Stripes like the Dirtbombs, Blanche, and Whirlwind Heat publicly barely batted an eyelash at the media coverage and bands that were on the scene like the Hentchmen, the Paybacks, Saturday Looks Good to Me, and others simply went about their business. The rest of the kids that were rapidly replacing the largely mid-thirtysomething rockers that had been thrust into the spotlight in the Stripes' wake really didn't care one way or the other. They had their own new bands to worry about, their own DIY fantasies to fulfill. The Von Bondies, for their part, went out on the road in Europe, Australia, and the United States, touring as much as they could to support their new major label record, and no doubt hoping all the while that they could gain some momentum away from the gossip pages.

"I think it's unfortunate that people's feelings had to be hurt in that process. No band wants to be in that position," said Smith.

Sympathetic Sounds of Detroit

The Stripes always maintained their participation in Detroit's generally humble rock scene. The Stripes' patronage of kindred spirits as well as their ability to put themselves at the center of the action even while deflecting some of the attention is nowhere better evidenced than by Jack's inaugural curatorial effort, the 2001 compilation *Sympathetic Sounds of Detroit,* recorded over the course of a couple weeks in the autumn of 2000 in his attic.

"Long Gone John called up and said that he was going to be putting together a series of records from a bunch of different cities around the country and he definitely wanted one for Detroit because there's such a good music scene going on," Jack told WDET's Willy Wilson in spring 2001. "So he asked me if I wanted to take on the project. I'm not a big fan of compilations—maybe if it's a box set of someone from the '60s I like that—but this one was a different idea. We did the whole thing in my attic, all the same microphones, all the same amplifiers, the same drumset, and everyone recorded their song on the same equipment. So it ended up being more of a project than a collection of songs from everyone's albums from across lots of different time periods. It was all recorded around the same time period on the same instruments. So there's more consistency to it."

The same attic in which White and Suchyta practiced all those many years ago and in which the other Gillis boys honed their particular take on the collision of alternative and classic rock was the scene of the recording of the *Sympathetic Sounds of Detroit* compilation. So while that compilation has become a combination of Rosetta Stone and Cliff's Notes to real and virtual Detroit Rock City tourists since the Stripes took off, the original intention was both much more DIY and conceptual than the resulting compilation would suggest. It did all take place in a tiny, dusty attic in Southwest Detroit in the house in which John Gillis grew up and in which he once again lived as Jack White. The deal was simple: Jack had set up an 8-track recorder and tape machine, a couple mikes, a drum set (Meg's), and several amps. Bands would show up with their instrument and/or drum sticks (though Jack had some extras of those, too, in case a band forgot as some surely did). The light load-in turned out to be a godsend since the casa de White had three floors and the attic was on the fourth, up a steep staircase through a narrow door and into a room with the sort of ceilings that slope with the roof of the house. There was a wee window on the south side, the same side of the room in which Jack had placed the makeshift studio. In the opposite corner of the room sat the five-piece drum set. This was where the White Stripes practiced, of course, so the place was set up to easily accommodate a two-piece, but once five or six people in the room started packing in, things got a little tight. And there was White was perched over the recording desk, milking his Teac for all it was worth in an effort to create a sort of postindustrial, DIY-punk version of the Hitsville studios.

So there he was, perched over the desk, directing traffic, creating a part-studio, part-home environment in which his friends would record their tunes for posterity. It was, after all, his idea to do the compilation for Sympathy for the Record Industry, and while it was neither rocket science nor the first time a "Detroit" compilation had come about, it was certainly the most ardently structured environment most folks had worked in. This was a very real art experiment. Besides, then you wouldn't have had the opportunity to cram bands like the Cobras or the Dirtbombs into a cramped space, having written a tune on totally short notice, give them unfamiliar equipment, and record live. It's classic Jack White to want to sit back and watch what happens. Naturally the results were mixed. He was working on something that he didn't know whether or not it would be good.

Though White was beginning to rail against the oversimplistic "garage rock" tag, for the compilation, he indulged his inner Barry Gordy and his inner bluesman by putting bands in a demanding recording situation while asking them to interpret "the blues." "When we were recording, I had asked a few of the bands to play blues off the top of their heads immediately just to see what we got just to see what's inside them that they could immediately come up with that related to the roots of rock 'n' roll instead of something considered garage rock or rehashing what would be called garage rock."

Often, the bands' initial reaction was to look at each other in wonder, but White got some surprising results from Whirlwind Heat and some powerful performances from Bantam Rooster.

Jack, naturally, picked the bands via a lottery.

"I set up about twelve chihuahas and put numbers on them in a rolling ball," he deadpanned to Willy Wilson in March 2001.

"I just had a few ideas of who should be well represented on the record, bands that have been around for a while like the Hentchmen and the Dirtbombs. Those bands need to be on something like that. But I also thought it would be great to have some bands who were just coming out, who were just starting to play shows like Ko and the Knockouts and Whirlwind Heat. So we could have an idea of what's gonna be happening next year, what's gonna be coming out so we have some attention on those bands and lay the groundwork [for them]."

The compilation was one of those affairs that tend to be referred to as "seminal." It crystallized the "Detroit" sound that rode the second wave of attention once the Stripes broke—with bands like the Dirt-bombs, Bantam Rooster, the Hentchmen, the Paybacks, Whirlwind Heat, the Soledad Brothers, Ko and the Knockouts, and the Detroit Co-bras among the bands laying down tracks. It was a super-exciting time in Detroit. Some hometown kids were getting out and they weren't con-tent to have the outside world tell 'em that they were great. Nope. The Stripes did what they would become famous for doing—turning the spot-light back on the scene from which they had sprung. The White Stripes, for their part, had already recorded *White Blood Cells* for Sympathy for the Record Industry and were beginning to receive the critical glory that followed their recent tour opening for Sleater-Kinney.

But in the spring of 2001, when the *Sympathetic Sounds* compila-tion was released, the White Stripes were little more than an under-ground phenomenon that had popped up a few times in the mainstream press. Jack White was a local celebrity who had seen a bit of the outside world and was bringing back news of the world to his hometown. With the *Sympathetic Sounds . . .* compilation, he would have the chance to share his enthusiasm for his hometown with the folks he'd made friends with along the way.

"When some of these things came out and when they came out I was on the floor. I just couldn't believe it. So much good stuff is going on and this is kind of like a family project where everyone got together to make it a good album. I kept saying 'oh, the next band that comes over to record, what's gonna happen?' but every time it was another great song, another great recording," he said.

"I wrote liner notes for this record and I mentioned that bands in other cities, bands in L.A., they have a different focus, they already have a connection to making it big," remembers White. "They already have a friend of a friend who works at such and such record label or they have a Web site or they print up T-shirts before they even play their first show. I guess in Detroit you don't even have that vibe. No one has this notion that when you're first starting a band that this is gonna get big very quickly and we're gonna get an album out on such and such a label and I know a guy at that label. No one thinks about that here in Detroit. The first and the foremost is the music."

Indeed, in the liner notes to his *Sympathetic Sounds of Detroit* compilation, Jack White writes that no industry rep would be caught dead in Detroit. And while it's true that on the downtown Detroit rock scene there's music and there's industry, and rarely do the two overlap, his assessment of Detroit's spot on the industry starmap wasn't entirely true. But like the brother and sister gambit and the red and white color scheme, White knew that taking a stand against the music industry's scene-pillaging anti-ethos—even as he sensed that his band was about to get sucked up into that particular vortex—would simply make a more interesting story. In the context of the then-current boy-band pop shtick and nu-metal shite that the mainstream music biz was churning out, a statement like that drew a line in the sand on behalf of the independent music scene from which the White Stripes had sprung. But even in the heart of a depressed, postindustrial flyover country dump like Detroit—especially in Detroit, arguably—the music industry had long established A&R beachheads. In essence, Jack's rhetorical gambit was yet another little White lie.

After all, if there was no relationship between the music industry and Detroit's generally latent-from-a-business-perspective talent pool then Kid Rock & Eminem would still be Bob and Marshall. Moreover Gories and Dirtbombs mainman Mick Collins never would have had a (however short-lived) development deal with Warner Brothers. Dean Fertita of the Waxwings wouldn't have had a publishing agreement with Warner-Chappel. Warren DeFever's Livonia, Michigan-based band, His Name Is Alive wouldn't have put out a handful of critically adored and cult-worshipped albums for England's 4AD between 1988 and 2003. Hell, Goober & the Peas had people sniffing around their camp toward the end of their run. Around the same time, of course, post-grunge power-pop outfit Sponge released two consecutive hit records (1994's *Rotting Pinata* and 1995's *Wax Ecstatic*) that may not have had much of a ripple effect on other musicians' fortunes, but added a layer of rock celebrity to the local bar scene.

Jump-blues septet the Atomic Fireballs released a record on Atlantic's Lava imprint in 1997, and injected a momentary white-hot jolt of punk energy into the lame swing trend. Alabama-born musician Robert Bradley, a blind street busker who played acoustic blues and pop songs in Detroit's Eastern Market every Saturday released a trio of albums for major label RCA records between 1996 and 1999.

Even future Electric Six collaborators Mark Dundon and Chris Peters were signed to Sony's 550 imprint in the trip-hop/rock hybrid band Getaway Cruiser in 1997. The electric six had even had a disappointing flirtation with Hollywood records in '97.

By the time White gathered the bands that would comprise the lineup for the *Sympathetic Sounds of Detroit* compilation, many of them—like the Hentchmen, the Dirtbombs, Bantam Rooster—had already been working the indie rawk circuit for years and had achieved, if nothing else, acclaim among the audience that cared enough about the music to seek it out and embrace it. The White Stripes were on the receiving end of the labors of the bands that had come before them and there's no doubt Jack White would be the first to tell you that.

But as the old adage goes: Never ask a question to which you don't already know the answer. Whatever industry buzz had been generated in town in the late '90s had pretty much ignored or been ignored by the cloistered downtown garage rock scene. But here the White Stripes were, the little band that could, once again chugging on in the face of conventional wisdom and common sense.

And Jack was positioning himself as the ad hoc spokesman and poster boy for an entire scene. There certainly wasn't a more savvy, interesting, or media-genic candidate among the pasty-faced thirty-year-olds that were his contemporaries.

And better the compilation come from the heart and hands of someone who actually lived here than from an outside commercial force.

In hindsight, *Sounds of Detroit* was a prescient document of the bands to whom the White Stripes would look when they referred to "home" once they became common cultural currency for teenyboppers worldwide. But that perception's deceiving. Down the lineup, one by one, are bands—or at least the songwriters and performers—to whom the White Stripes were indebted in some form or another. To the Soledad Brothers Jack White owed his continuing, deepening exploration of the Delta blues. To Whirlwind Heat he owed a debt of screw-all-convention DIY courage. To the Dirtbombs and Bantam Rooster and the Detroit Cobras and the Hentchmen he owed a debt of community that could only be repaid by a leg-up once the means are in place. And that's exactly what White did with the *Sympathetic Sounds of Detroit* compilation.

And even though, there have been "Sympathetic Sounds of . . ." compilations created for London, Montreal, and other burgs, the Detroit compilation was, by most accounts, Jack's idea: Have a bunch of bands that represent a moment in time in a certain place record all together in the same "studio." It was really that deceptively simple.

Going Back to Memphis—White Blood Cells Recording

If Detroit has a doppelganger city—from its both storied and oddball musical lineage to the necessity to drive everywhere, its generally deserted vibe to the chintzy tourist districts that try desperately to lure well-to-do's downtown on weekend nights—it's Memphis, Tennessee.

The feeling of emptiness is jarring in Memphis—like Detroit. Jim Jarmusch's film *Mystery Train* is an eerily accurate portrayal and save for three seasons of snow in one of 'em, could have happened in either town. It's a pity there's not a highway that directly connects the two cities, as it would make the frequent travels between them by Detroit's and Memphis's respective musicians a couple hours easier. Then again, the relative isolation of the cities is part of what plays into their symmetry.

In 1990, the Gories became one of the first of the modern Detroit underground rock bands to travel to another city to record an album when no less than cult-hero and Big Star leader Alex Chilton invited the blues-punk trio down to the newly opened Easley Recordings to lay down tracks for their sophomore LP *I Know You Fine but How You Doin'?* Seems someone had slipped Chilton a tape of the band's first record and he became smitten not only with their modern primitivism, but also their drummer, Peg O'Neil.

Because sometimes it's good to get out of your hometown to really find your sound, *I Know You Fine. . .* is the Gories most accomplished, end-to-end great record.

Thus an underground exchange was established that would bear platinum fruit more than a decade later.

"I must admit the connection between the two cities is strong in my mind," says Memphian and Reigning Sound/Oblivians member Greg Cartwright.

"I think Detroit and Memphis are like two parallel roads that cross-intersect every twenty miles or so. My great-grandmother ran a boarding house in Detroit in the '30s. Lots of people (blacks and hillbillies) moved from the South to the more industrialized cities up north like Detroit and Chicago. Looking for work and taking their music and culture with them. This created a great cross-pollination that never really stopped. I think the other big similarity in the last three decades was financial depression. Kids coming up in Detroit and Memphis (still one of the lowest costs of living in the country) had to make their own fun."

Indeed, in Detroit it was joints like the 404 Willis and Finney's that got adopted by the rock crowd early and in Memphis, it was Barrister's, a divey joint with a back-alley entrance that hosted all manner of willing urban adventurers and Eric Freidl (né Oblivian)'s Goner Records. Detroit had Lafayette Coney Island, Memphis had Payne's Bar-B-Q. It's all relative. The kids are just looking for a thrill wherever they can find it because until someone tells you to stop, you're left to your own devices. This couldn't happen in bigger, better-managed cities like Chicago.

"When no one's looking, that's when great things happen. That's when you discover what's right there in your own backyard. Sun, Fortune, Stax, Motown, J-V-B. In the '70s and '80s this stuff could be had for pennies," reckons Cartwright.

"Spawning a whole generation of retro-armchair-musicologists and the rock scene their friends and themselves would create in the next two decades to follow. The only other cities that could boast the sheer number of record labels these two cities generated '50s and '60s was maybe Chicago or New Orleans, and a lot of the Chicago labels licensed their recordings from studios in Memphis or Detroit. That's a lot of music for a young mind to chew on."

And yet an entire generation of "armchair musicologists" in Detroit and Memphis were now aware of each others' existence.

In the early '90s, Easley Studios was a one-man operation—an analogue to Jim Diamond's Ghetto Recorders—run by Doug Easley at which bands like the Oblivians, '68 Comeback, the Compulsive Gamblers, Tav Falco's Panther Burns, and many others recorded eventually—Sonic Youth would be the first marquee name to draw a spotlight to Easley.

"Doug Easley's studio spoiled me at an early point in my career," remembers Cartwright.

"I went to their grand opening in '90 or '91. It was originally run out of a house in Doug Easley's backyard but they moved the whole operation out of his parents' yard in a gutsy move towards legitimacy."

The Gories were one of the first bands to record there.

Tucked away about ten minutes from the Memphis International Airport, the first non-home-based Easley was on the inner edge of an all-black neighborhood known as Orange Mound.

It was a "high crime area. Not the kind of place most rock bands would want to park a van full of gear. Right away this attracted the right kind of people. People looking for something a little out of the ordinary," says Cartwright.

The place had the kind of roots about which books are written and from which legends of haunted recordings are started. It was the one-time home to legendary soul instrumentalists the Barkays and at one time was occupied by well-known Memphian producer Chips Moman.

It was also according to both Easley and Cartwright one of the first buildings in Memphis built for the soul purpose of being a recording

studio. Before then, studios were housed in storefronts (Sun), old the-
atres (Stax), and other places that were already set up for acoustic performance.

"The best thing about Davis and Doug's studio," says Cartwright,
"aside from the free use of their finely tuned ears and intuitive engineering skills, was the feel of the place as soon as you hit the door. The
inside is like walking into a recording studio forty-five years ago. It's
amazing and totally disarming. You fix a pot of coffee and get to work.
You don't sit around thinking about how much money you're wasting
like if you were in a sterile new studio. Those places have so little character that you never feel at home. You just see yourself spending money.
Money someone else gave you. Someone else who expects a record in
the mail in a week. Who can make art under those kinds of conditions?
That's what Easley's has that no other studio has ever had for me. Now
I'm not saying there aren't some great studios out there. Jim Diamond's
Ghetto Recorders is great and pretty comfortable in its own way but in
Memphis it's Easley's or bust."

After being somewhat disappointed by the sound of *De Stijl*, this
was exactly what Jack White was looking for the band's next record.

The White Stripes had spent the last four years trying to nail down
that signature sound and the trial by fire that was their past year had
found them emerging in 2001 with that alchemy intact. Jack dove into
the Mississippi River, swam up the Hudson, and crossed the Atlantic to
pick up the sounds that he melded into what is best described as a cul-
mination of gathered musical heritage. When they arrived in Memphis,
they had their full trick bag in tow. The Reigning Sound's Cartwright
sums up the sound of the Stripes circa 2001 as "showtunes, country,
blues, gospel, rock, punk, folk, and even more modern urban stuff, too.
But you can't discount the importance of the British influence on Jack,"
he continues.

"Many of the aforementioned musical styles seem somewhat filtered
through his more European influences by the time they leave his lips.
The accent he affects is so weird. You can't put your finger on it (always
a good thing). Is it English (à a T. Rex), American (early East Coast

vaudeville), or the sound of a white man (that was funny!) earnestly in-
terpreting Blind Willie McTell's strange vocal patterns? Or falsetto
singing (definitely a Detroit staple from Nolan Strong, Smokey Robin-
son, and so on)? Whatever the case, it works."

They needed a fresh space with no baggage, no distractions, and a
new set of ears to get it right.

"We went down there sight unseen," said White upon his return to
Detroit in spring 2001 to Wilson. "We just heard the studio was nice.
We just wanted to get out of town and get a different sound for the new
record. And there's no blues, no slide, no cover songs, no extra musicians, no bass. It's nothing but *nos*."

Texas native Stewart Sikes was the head engineer at Easley when the
Stripes arrived in February of 2001. "They were friends with the guys
from the Oblivians and those guys recommended that they come down
and record there," remembers Sikes.

"I think that they wanted to get out of Detroit and do it and I think
that they trusted Jack (Yarber) and Greg (Cartwright) of the Oblivians
just because I'm sure that Jack (White) liked them quite a bit. And the
Gories came down and that was another main factor.

"He sent me the two records and I had talked to Jack Yarber and a
bunch of people I knew who liked them. So I sort of had a good idea
what they sounded like."

The Memphis crew came to lend their support, but they didn't
muck around in the studio and distract the hardworking Stripes from
their workday.

Jack, Meg, and Dave Swanson from the Whirlwind Heat (who had
traveled with the band to document the recording) stayed with Yarber
and Nick Ray from American Death Ray while they were in town. On
their few off hours, they all hung out and no doubt swapped many a tale.

While they were there, Yarber had shown White a cherry red Airline
guitar that White took a shining to.

"You know that red Airline Jack plays all the time? He bought it
from Jack Yarber. Jack's not very happy that he sold it," chuckles Sikes.
(The guitar, of course, died in 2003 only to be replaced by a generous

fan who found a mint vintage twin of the axe and presented it to White as a gift at a show in New York City in 2003.)

"I thought that their two other records as a whole were good. And I think Jack's a great songwriter and I think it all sort of came together on that record."

The days were straightforward studio days.

"It's not like they needed a whole bunch of mikes and stuff. They have a two-inch 24-track machine there and pretty much to save on tape costs, we used 12 tracks. I sort of split the tape in half. Tracks 1–12 I used that. And when that tape got filled up I used tracks 13–24 for other songs," says Sikes.

"Meg used the studio drums and they wanted a sort of big sound was how he described it. I just tried to reproduce what they were doing on their own."

An interesting thing happened when the Whites started playing in the expansive confines of Easley-McCain. They had originally set up Jack a bit away from Meg, but they gradually moved him closer to Meg to try to maintain the live dynamics. By the end of the session, they were recording exactly as they play live.

"He was pretty much right up on the drums while they were playing," remembers Sikes.

"That room's a really big room. Going from practicing at your house to playing twenty-five feet away from someone sometimes doesn't really work."

Jack's direction for the production was relatively simple. He told Sikes to make it sound good, but not too "studio." Sikes interpreted that to mean "don't flick it with piss, you know?"

Sikes remembers the band—at least Jack—being pretty confident in their ability to deliver.

"The confidence came through in the fact that they were so new, and Meg, I think she was a little uncomfortable just because she hadn't rehearsed them as much as she wanted to. But Jack had no worries about it not coming off as a good take or her not knowing the songs. I think that added to the whole feel of it."

Besides, when you play a song too many times, you lose the spontaneity of it and the White Stripes didn't let boredom set in.

"I don't think we did more than four takes. Six at the most I would say. So it just sounds like a band playing," says Sikes.

"That's sort of the way he works," says Sikes, who, following *White Blood Cells,* worked with Jack White on Loretta Lynn's record *Van Lear Rose.*

"I think it's a good way to work because with the age of computers records sound technically good, but there's no feel. I mean, listen to a Kinks record and you can tell the difference.

"When I say it was fast, it was like 'that one feels good, let's go to the next one.' We didn't sit around and talk about it. It was because we didn't have any time really. We cut almost all but one or two in two days. Vocals included," says Sikes. "And we only worked about twelve to thirteen hours a day. There wasn't any time really for fucking around.

"If a band is still being productive, I'll keep working. As long as they're not just wasting my time, it's pretty stupid to stop. Plus, they'd drove in from Detroit, so during that time they were probably pretty tired. They were sleeping on Jack's couch."

Sikes had a sure litmus test for when he figured a song was ready.

"One of the things that was interesting was making Meg happy. If Meg was happy with a song, we knew it was done. I think she probably liked recording in their house better than recording in the studio. I think Meg was just a little bit uncomfortable just because since the room is so big it can be intimidating.

"That was the fastest record I've ever seen a record come out. It was out within a month and a half after recording.

"My wife works at this restaurant and she said 'I heard that White Stripes record.' I was like 'how?!' she said, 'it's out!'" laughs Sikes.

"I was shocked. That's one way to foil the Internet."

Sikes, having become acclimated to recording dozens of bands for Estrus and other punk labels, didn't see the landslide of attention coming and figures no one but Jack was betting it would.

"To be totally honest obviously they had a huge hype behind them when that record came out," he says. "But I don't read the newspapers that much. I just sort of find out about music because people tell me about it. So I wasn't really aware of that."

The Stripes hit Austin, Texas, shortly after laying down tracks for *White Blood Cells* to play a show that would cement their buzz in the industry. Kaplan was asked by Sympathy head Long Gone John to book a label showcase at the annual Austin music industry shmoozefest South by Southwest (SXSW). The White Stripes, by dint of their road-ready approach to spreading their gospel had already garnered a loyal audience. Thus the duo were the star attraction on the bill on Saturday, March 17, at Room 710 which also included L.A. powerhouse the BellRays. White had figured out how to deliver the goods both rocking and ballad by this time and was using them as a one-two punch in the Stripes set. It's hard to argue with the power of their cover of "Jolene" when backed up against "Dead Leaves and the Dirty Ground" and other feedback-drenched headbangers, especially when White's singing the former gender-bending cover like Steven Tyler possessed by Norma Desmond. The show became one of those performances that the organizers of SXSW still refer to in their distinguished alumni advertising. But more importantly, in the audience that night was a music writer from the *NME* named Stevie Chick. Chick was sufficiently blown away by the Stripes performance that he returned to Britain all abuzz with news of his discovery whilst traversing the Colonies.

"Stevie Chick saw them at that festival South by Southwest and came back absolutely raving about them. As far as I can tell, he was the first British person to talk about the Stripes," says *Plan B* magazine's Everett True.

In June 2001, Jack and Meg pulled the audacious and creative move of scheduling three consecutive record release shows in Detroit at three separate venues. The first, on Thursday, June 6, was held at the Gold Dollar, which brought into sharp focus just how far the duo had come. You couldn't get near the place without a Taser and/or a tank.

"I was listening back to the tape of that show the other day," says Neil Yee, "and I realized that they played the album cover to cover in order that night. I didn't know it at the time, of course."

Friday night was at the Magic Bag in Ferndale, where the Whites' family was in prominent attendance cheering on their kids. Jack again took advantage of the Bag's working grand piano and tickled the ivories for a few of the numbers. As one of the band's few appearances in the suburbs, the folks around town who had heard the buzz but weren't bold enough to make the trip downtown to catch the Stripes in the past here lined up long before the doors opened. But perhaps the most moving part of the Magic Bag show was the film that aired just prior to the Whites taking the stage. It was a home video of a class of elementary school children from Kalamazoo, Michigan, whose teacher had gotten them all to sing the Stripes' *De Stijl* song "Apple Blossom." The Whites were visibly still moved by the film as they took the stage and there wasn't a cynical or half-drunk soul in the house who didn't let out at least a small *awww*.

Saturday night—the conclusion of the three release parties was at the Magic Stick. The joint sold out. The Magic Stick was the most raucous of the three release shows and came closest to the true spirit behind the shows: A going-away party of sorts for the band. A farewell tour to the sites that had let them play and hone and grow their sound over the past few years. It was only in retrospect that it was bittersweet for the scenesters who had come to take the White Stripes for granted. The baby band that only a few years ago would play anytime, anywhere, for anybody wouldn't return to Detroit for four months. And when they did, it would be in spectacular fashion and there would be nothing little about them.

The Last Gang in Town

Less than a month after they unleashed *White Blood Cells* on the Detroit faithful at the three-night, three-venue hometown stand, the Stripes buzz was officially on and so was the summer touring season. After filming their first two videos—for "Hotel Yorba" and "We Are Going to Be Friends"—in one marathon day, Jack and Meg gave themselves a day off to celebrate Independence Day at home. After the fourth of July fireworks and barbeques in Detroit, the duo loaded up their late-model Dodge Ram Van with the necessary red and white accoutrements, a Detroit flag, and a pile of CDs, and headed toward midtown to pick up their raiding party compatriots in the Von Bondies and the Waxwings—most of whom, luckily, lived within a stone's throw of one another.

White had expressed his interest in mounting an all-Detroit revue based on the bands that participated in the *Sympathetic Sounds of Detroit* compilation, but it proved too ambitious even for the workaholic White.

"I was hoping we could have done a tour of all these Detroit bands coming out. I mean, who wouldn't want to go see that?" White told Wilson. "But it's hard, man. Everybody's got some thing that we can't put it together—time off from work or whatnot. So this summer we'll be touring with the Waxwings and the Von Bondies as sort of a Detroit thing."

So it was that the three bands were set to play nine shows touring their way to L.A. where the White Stripes would tape their first national TV appearance on the Craig Kilborn show.

"What was great about it was the lack of pretense for how big it was," remembers Greg Siemasz, who, along with Ben Blackwell and tour manager John Baker numbered the civilians traveling with the posse.

"There's this band that a lot of people are going to see—and paying money to see, wherever they play they were selling out places, and they didn't care about that part of it as much as having a great time with their friends," says Siemasz.

"They already had a buzz. People knew who they were. All the places they were going to be playing had nice guarantees and were sold out."

Included on the tour itinerary were capacity shows at must-play joints like the Troubadour in L.A. (where the Stripes would make a reputation-solidifying two-night stand in front of a crowd packed with indie music glitterati, industry weasels, and rabid fans), Bimbo's in San Francisco (already an established White Stripes stronghold), and the legendary Crocodile Café in Seattle. It would be easy for any band to get a wee bit nervous about rocking this set of high-profile clubs head-lining a package tour that represented the best and brightest of their hometown. Indeed, ever since the *Sympathetic Sounds of Detroit* compilation came out, a Detroit package tour had been on the White Stripes' to-do list. And even though the logistics of mounting a full-scale traveling Detroit revue proved prohibitive, the Whites had the clout in the indie world to make sure that each venue on their itinerary made room for their pals' bands.

Even though the band's salad days were certainly behind them, it's easy to see how this tour could be looked upon as the last bastion of pre-fame innocence, a state of grace preceding the British music press hype that would light the signal flares which eventually led major labels to the White Stripes and vice versa. Not long after this tour, the community that the White Stripes, and Jack White in particular, had worked hard to build and maintain would start to find itself under increasing media scrutiny and begin to see some of their labors end up bearing some bitter fruit. But for now, it was summer, the vans were gassed up, and the dressing rooms were shared.

It was a perfect example of the kind of grace and generosity the White Stripes have made their hallmark when it comes to sharing their success.

"It wasn't so much about those shows as it was about going out on the road and going out to California with your friends and having a good time doing it," remembers Siemasz.

Of course, the bottom line is that the White Stripes were going to play shows and spread the word of their record release. They had danced around offers from larger indie labels and knew that something was afoot and certainly felt something more than the usual intense pressure that Jack himself put on the band to leave it all on the stage every night. Any pressure of expectations were firmly on their shoulders. But to hear Blackwell and Siemasz tell it, the focus wasn't on money or success or the high-stakes game of playing a good show as much as it was just fun. About sharing the most exciting elements of your bubbling-up musical community with the rest of the country. About casting the light of reflective acclaim on the folks who made everyday life more interesting when they were working and playing at home. Jack had shared the stage in "the Bricks" and in other informal pickup jam sessions with Waxwings members Kevin Peyok and Dean Fertita. Jack had just produced the Von Bondies' debut full-length, *Lack of Communication,* at Ghetto.

It might be expected that a tour like this—headlined by a band that was picking up media attention and had industry folks sniffing around their every move—would feature the White Stripes in big bold letters and the Waxwings and the Von Bondies in small print underneath "puppet show," but the Whites made sure the competition and egos stayed in check.

"I don't know if it was organized and it just turned out that way, or if it was a conscious effort for everyone to try to be on the same page, you know?" says Siemasz.

"There was never any kind of competition, but there was always support. Everyone sat around and watched each others' bands. It was back when people could do that," says Siemasz.

"You know, the Von Bondies were standing in the audience watching the show. It was when Jack would be in the audience watching the Von Bondies show. You'd get two or three people that would ask for an autograph, but for the most part it was still acceptable for him to be out there."

"We were playing four-hundred-person venues on our national tour with them, and they'd sell like $1,000 worth of merchandise. And we'd sell like $400 as an opening band," remembers Stollsteimer.

OK, maybe one person in this caravan of love was feeling a wee bit competitive. Far from a fly in White's ointment at this point, though, at this point Stollsteimer was more like the overeager acolyte.

In general, said both Siemasz and Blackwell, it was good vibes. "It was always really supportive, like 'you guys killed! It was awesome!' It was never 'We're going to out-do you!'" laughs Blackwell.

It helped that Jack had borrowed a large City of Detroit flag from his brother. They put it up at every stop along the way, no matter how little room there was for it on the smaller stages or how much of a pain in the butt it seemed to find the requisite adhesives and hangers to mount the thing. The White Stripes were literally flying the flag of their hometown and putting out a couple of the city's best-known acts under its gaze.

"The cool thing was that it was up for all three bands," concurs Siemasz. "And it applied to all three bands! So that whole trip had that kind of like the last gang in town vibe."

On the flag are written the words: *"Speramus meliora; resurget cineribus,"* which translates from the Latin as "We hope for better things. It shall rise from the ashes." Suffice it to say that Jack White has a flair for his town's history, the dramatic and an even greater proclivity for the kind of symbolism that makes rock fans really latch onto a band. So it was that over the course of the summer in which the White Stripes laid the foundation for their mainstream crossover, Jack and Meg became the unofficial ambassadors for the City of Detroit.

The first stop on the tour was Chicago's Empty Bottle, long one of the few Windy City strongholds for the Detroit brand of rock 'n' roll in a city predisposed to the fashions of native-indie-hero post-rock outfits like Tortoise and Shellac as well as bubbling over with displaced urban country music fanatics like the folks who ran the city's Bloodshot Records. But the Empty Bottle, a neighborhood joint on the city's rough-around-the-edges Polish-Mexican-Boho west side, felt like room temperature to bands who sprang from Hamtramck and Southwest Detroit and the Cass Corridor.

The Stripes had been to the Empty Bottle four months earlier, fresh off their buzz-building, star-crossed set at SXSW, and had wowed a packed house not prepared for the little band that could to do so. Hence the double-header. And the first show on this new generation Motown revue capitalized on that goodwill and buzz, with Jack leading the crowd through particularly energized versions of their electrified set list.

Chicago concertgoers have a reputation for being particularly stoic. The stereotypical Chicago indie fan is a twenty-eight-year-old overeducated grad student standing watching the band, arms crossed, occasionally stage-whispering remarks to whoever's accompanied him to the show. The White Stripes made that dude grin and jump around—or at least hoist an only semi-ironic devil horn "rock" sign.

Sufficiently charged up, the bands headed west on a two-day drive to Missoula, Montana—within striking distance of Seattle as the van drives. That the group took a leisurely pace instead of plowing ahead may seem incongruous to the Stripes' apparent breakneck working pace and ethic. But Ben Blackwell, who went on tour with the Stripes a number of times, was quick to note that at least on the pre–major label tours of America, Jack and Meg took in the scenery perhaps more than your average band drinking past bar closing time only to wake up mid-next-day and drive from Waffle House to Waffle House searching for the perfect hangover cure.

"The White Stripes were really just about playing music on tour. We never went to after-show parties, they rarely drank, I mean, we'd stop to look at buffalo in North Dakota and I spent my eighteenth birthday at the Mall of America," says Blackwell. "They never lost sight of the task at hand. They were out to play shows, and if time permitted, hit some record shops or thrift stores. It was more like a family vacation than all that cliché rock and roll bullshit."

So this trip out west was an extended family jaunt. Besides, all three vans had CB radios to keep them entertained, so the normal crushing boredom on the road was actually made fun.

"We'd be driving through the middle of nowhere and have all three CBs on and it'd be like 'csshhht. All right. Movie Trivia Time,'" laughs Blackwell. "I'll name people in the movie and the first person to get the name of the movie gets to move to the front of the line. OK, Gary Busey and Courtney Love. 'Sid & Nancy! It's Sid & Nancy!' All right Waxwings proceed ahead one space in line.

"But it just invariably turned into everyone making jokes about each other. It just descended into who could make who laugh," says Blackwell. "More than once we ended up on a truckers' channel and they'd get pissed."

Out of Missoula

The three bands rolled into cowboy country and Missoula, Montana, on July 9—Jack White's twenty-sixth birthday—to play a show at the Ritz. They felt like they were taking a chunk of Detroit with them on the road and, consequently, never felt like they were "not from around here" on this trip. Except in Missoula. For touring, as semi-successful indie rock acts go, the Ritz was pretty much the only game in town if that town is Missoula. Which, as it turned out for our heroes is really too bad, as they would soon find out.

"We showed up at the club and it was a really bad club. Not a cool fit for a good rock band. That night, the bar owner—who couldn't give a fuck and treated everyone that way—made it known he was running the soundboard, so you'd better not fuck with him," said Siemasz.

So the Von Bondies and the Waxwings took the stage, plied their wares and, all was good times in Big Sky Country. People were getting into the opening bands and the sold-out crowd was anticipating the White Stripes.

"But when the White Stripes got up and started playing, Jack started getting shocked by the microphone. The mike wasn't grounded and Jack had crappy '60s guitars that probably weren't grounded and neither was the amp, so you know, bad news," says Siemasz. "The best thing you can do is hope no one throws a beer on you. And Jack was getting shocked and they were trying *sooo* hard to play through it."

The Stripes continued to make a valiant effort, with Jack continuing to get shocked, but also knowing that even though it was Missoula, there were people there that had paid good money to see the band.

"So finally he got shocked, and he asked to have it fixed or a new mike or whatever," says Siemasz.

"The bar owner starts getting pissed and then Jack starts off asking politely to have the mike looked at: 'Can I have someone look at this mike or get a new mike because I'm getting shocked.'"

"Seriously, you could see it. He's like playing and his fingers went stiff. He'd put his mouth up to it and you could see his body just jerk," recalls Siemasz with a shudder of horror at the memory of his friend getting seriously zapped.

"So he started getting frustrated after the guy tried to 'fix it' and it was still doing it. So Jack started getting a little belligerent and of course, he made some smart-aleck remark about the soundguy/bar own-er. So they're playing a song and in the middle of it, the bar owner gets on the house PA—while they're playing!—and starts insulting Jack, like 'I'll show you who runs this fucking bar' and stuff like that and every-one's looking around like 'what's going on?!' And then finally Jack's like 'I need this mike to be fixed or we're not playing, 'cause I can't get shocked and keep playing.'

"So the genius bartender goes up there and he's already upset about getting off his perch and his solution to fixing the shocking problem was to put a dirty sock over the microphone. Nobody knows where the sock came from and Jack is looking at the guy when he's doing this like 'you gotta be fucking kidding me,'" says Siemasz.

So the White Stripes left the stage. Jack had had enough. As they ran off to the side of the stage, audience members were egging him on.

"They were like 'Oh, c'mon! play through it!' The audience was kinda weird," says Blackwell. "Jack said, 'Play through it?! You come up here and put your lips on the microphone and get shocked every twelve seconds and tell me how it feels.'"

The White Stripes tried to come back and play a few more songs during which the bar owner got on the PA and intoned in slow drawl, "Happy fuckin' birthday, Jack."

"So Jack said 'What's your problem, ass!' and the guy cuts power to the stage," recalls Blackwell.

"And as soon as Jack got off stage it was panic. It was like 'everyone grab your shit and get out of here.' It was pretty much total panic."

Usually when multiple bands share a stage while on tour, etiquette is to finish playing your set, stack your gear off to the side of the stage, wait until closing time, get paid by the owner, and, in an orderly fashion, load the van so as to maximize such things as sitting, sleeping, and storage room. There's a lot of crap involved with playing a show, and it's often a puzzle of the highest order to get everything to fit just right into the van. This was not the case that night in Missoula. Everyone randomly shoved whatever gear they could get their hands on, knowing that they'd sort it out later just so they could, says Siemasz, "get the fuck out of Dodge."

In the meantime, says Siemasz, "It was total chaos. All these people are running around getting in fights. Jack's getting hidden in the corner. Everyone else is loading gear, trying not to get beat up while doing it. One of the guys that was at the show jumps over the bar and starts pouring his own drinks."

The cops had to be called to settle everyone down and make sure that the bands got their money and after that, they couldn't get out of there fast enough.

But that still left them with the problem of being in the middle of nowhere, now that they didn't quite feel at home in Missoula.

Says Siemasz: "It was one of those 'OK, now what are we gonna do?' situations. We made the escape from the bar but we're in Missoula, Montana. The only option was to drive as fast as we could out of town and keep driving until we found something on the highway. We felt like we were being chased and everyone's looking back like 'are they following us?' and then someone came on the CB and said 'oh, shit, we're totally out of gas!' It totally happened. I swear to god. We were low on gas. We get out of the area of town where the bar was and pulled off in a gas station and I'm like 'why are we stopping?! This is going to be like Lone Justice or something?! We're three vans traveling together! We're in no-man's-land.'"

Turns out the lowlight of the tour was also the highlight, because, according to Blackwell and Siemasz, the group bonded even tighter "we were like the last gang in town or some shit," says Siemasz.

If Jack could survive severe repeated microphone shocks and the group could get out of a fire drill like that in Missoula, Montana, then members of the Waxwings and the Von Bondies certainly had no problem facing down five hundred to one thousand expectant White Stripes fans every night.

"It was kind of a defining moment for everyone," says Siemasz. "I think everyone felt the same way, that it wasn't the White Stripes taking everyone on tour, it was everyone on tour. No one felt the echelons until you got to the club the playing order took over. That was the easy part, though."

Luckily for the Waxwings and the Von Bondies, the White Stripes had already made a couple trips out west by that time and reestablished Detroit's good name among the Left Coast garage rock aficionados. California and Seattle were in particular primed for the Stripes and their gang of backward-looking, forward-rocking cohorts.

The West Coast was the first area of the country outside of Detroit where people bought into the mythology of the White Stripes and started turning up at shows with red and white on. Once the White Stripes started to get over, their fanbase made itself known by adopting the stage garb of the band, calling themselves Candy Cane Children, and diving deep into the quasi-mystical numerology and apocrypha. California—San Francisco in particular—has a history of adopting left-field artists from both the Bay Area and other environs and the White Stripes certainly fit the bill. San Francisco was also the birthplace of faux-Southern swamp rock revisionists Creedence Clearwater Revival and the artfully pretentious performance rock of the Residents. The Stripes made sense somewhere along the continuum between the two in that context. Of course, their coed, maritally ambiguous, and Goth-crush-worthy good looks didn't hurt them, either. In L.A.'s preservationist, collector-fetish culture, the White Stripes were like a couple of real-life Keane kids—wide-eyed innocents with a hint of dark macabre secrets painted into their background. No doubt, that's why L.A.-area-based Sympathy for the Record Industry took a shining to them, and that kitschy hook certainly worked to their advantage to get people in the door in LaLa Land. Fortunately, L.A. also has a huge crush on Detroit. From the Southern California car culture to the underground rock scene's adoption and subsequent sleazy morphing of Detroit's brand of

'60s muscular rock 'n' roll (MC5 and the Stooges in particular), there was already a history there.

"Garage rock is more established out there," remembers Siemasz, who toured to the West Coast as early as 1994 with the Hentchmen. "If you remember actual garage rock, that strange period of the early middle '90s' bands like [Bay Area garage punks] the Mummies and Supercharger were fun. It was about the music. It wasn't about making it," he says. "It's always been more acceptable on the West Coast. All the labels are out there, too—In the Red, Sympathy—so there were a lot of people out there that were aware of the music and the music's roots long before the White Stripes. That was the music that Jack heard even though he might not have owned the record, he hung out with Dave Buick and heard the Mighty Caesars. That whole Seattle scene adopted Billy Childish, too. So there's that kind of community that was already there to be exploited."

And of course, the Seattle area has a long history of exporting and enthusiastically supporting garage punk—from the early blasts of Tacoma raw instrumentalists the Wailers to their successors the Sonics (the band whose sound to which, in their heart of hearts, every garage rocker aspires) to latter-day blues-morphers Mudhoney.

Seattle was the next stop on the tour and the thirteen musicians gathered in the traveling vans couldn't be happier to get into some Crocodile rock. In attendance at the Seattle show were Andy Kotowicz and Jonathan Poneman—A&R representative and owner, respectively, of Sub Pop Records who had just released the White Stripes' Sub Pop Singles Club 45—two covers of Captain Beefheart Tunes "Party of Special Things To Do" and "China Pig/Ashtray Heart."

After that it was on to Portland, Oregon, where, if you polled the audience, according to Siemasz, you'd find that the Waxwings had connected with the crowd enough to break through the opening band stigma and emerge covered in buzz.

The morning after the first of their two-night stand at West Hollywood rock landmark the Troubadour (the Stripes' second such double-header there and an early indication of the Stripes' preference for meeting growing audience demand by playing two shows in front of smaller crowds rather than one in front of larger crowds), the band and their entourage readied themselves for their television bow. The preamble to the actual performance didn't go exactly smooth, though.

The White Stripes had recently brought their Kiwi champion John Baker on board as their tour manager/merch guy/keeper of the cell phone (which, remember, the White Stripes don't use). In typical White Stripes learn-as-you-go fashion, Baker hadn't run a full tour before and he certainly hadn't done one in the United States before. So when the caravan arrived in L.A., they had accumulated quite a large bag of cash from door and merch receipts.

"You've heard millions of stories about bands that get their bag of money ripped off. But that was totally the case," remembers Siemasz.

"It totally should have been put into traveler's checks and sent home. When all that stuff was going on with the Kilborn show, Ben and Baker had stayed in a hotel. I stayed out in the van that night and Baker somehow managed to get the money locked in the hotel safe and couldn't get it out. So there's all this drama going on about calling a locksmith and the locksmith wouldn't come because it was a hotel safe. In the meantime, we're going back and forth to Studio City [where the rehearsals were taking place]."

Blackwell stayed at his post at the hotel while all this was going on. Of course, Siemasz and Jack were goofing around checking out the *Price Is Right* stage.

"The cool thing about the Kilborn show," remembers Dan Miller, "was that they played 'Screwdriver' and it was so great that that was a song from a previous record and they were OK with it."

"I remember thinking how cool it was that they were on Craig Kilborn's show and how there was no way it was going to get any bigger than this," remember Buick. "It's national TV! C'mon!"

The Stripes made the most of it by picking a song that was special to them and in doing so, they set a precedent that would apply to just about all of their television appearances—they typically would never just go through the motions of playing their current single and giving a by-the-numbers performance. They never knew when they'd get the shot again and didn't seem to take any of it for granted. The Kilborn show was no exception.

"That was kind of one of those clutch situations that they've thrived in that makes them players instead of posers. It's like when they got the shot to open for Pavement, they didn't get up there and go 'Hi, we're the opening band. I'll look at my shoes,'" says Siemasz. "They got up, they did what they did. No apologies. Same thing, most people would be freaked out about TV, but they went there and it's one of those things where you can almost feel the stagehands glaring, because they don't get it. They're used to a certain kind of band. They didn't understand where their bass player was. Weren't you briefed on this? Don't you work here?" laughs Siemasz incredulously.

"You could definitely feel that the White Stripes were coming into someone else's house, but it never phased them.

"It was funny also that I think for Jack, the most exciting thing about that day was trying to sneak into the *Price Is Right* stage. Or at least getting to touch the Plinko wheel."

Meg White: Got No Secrets

Meg White is the not-so-secret powerhouse behind the White Stripes, the enigmatic yin to Jack's gregarious, garrulous, and outsize yang. Quiet is the "go to" adjective for the buxom, raven-haired drummer with the Mona Lisa smile. But if you ask some of the folks around Detroit who have known her for a while, you start to get a picture of an engaged observer with a wicked sense of humor who takes a lot of shit for being the less musically accomplished member of a world-famous two-piece with a remarkable amount of grace.

"I really like Meg. She's so quiet. She's one of those people that's kind of hard to get to know. She's so, so, I don't know what . . . ," said Brendan Benson. Meg was hanging out backstage with members of the

Datsuns during Benson's performance on August 24, 2003, at the Leeds Festival when he drafted her and her drum services for an encore of his tune "Jet Lag." "I just begged her to come out and do a song. It was our last show of that tour, for that record. After that we were done. And we were having such a blast doing all those festivals, so we were just trying to out-do every one. And Meg happened to be there, she wasn't playing, she wasn't doing anything so I just thought to have her come up and play on one of my songs, the drums are just so perfect for her. And it worked out so well, it was so fucking brilliant. 'Cause I didn't know. I prepared her moments before we went on. I was just like "the drums are doom-chick-doom-chick"—like that kind of prepared. And she was like *ah-hahuhhhh* . . . I don't know if she ever really agreed to it, they just kind of pushed her onstage. It was just such a perfect ending to that record."

Dave Buick of Italy Records, who has known Meg as long as he has known Jack, said, "Actually once you open up the gates she's not the most quiet person around. She can actually be the opposite. She's a sweet little lady. She can get very chatty. And it's not like she's quiet because she's insecure. It's not like she doesn't talk because she feels weird around people. It's just the way she is. It's not because she doesn't know what to say or feels bad, she just thinks 'when I feel like saying something I'll say something.' She's happy to just have her drink and not say anything unless he feels like talking or has something to say. And that's awesome."

Wendy Case, former Detroit journalist, said "what he [Jack] did was pare his band down to a very willing, very accommodating drummer, and the rest is up to him, and that was fine with her and him. For those of us who have played in bands, it's not just about getting out there and rocking, it's about character management and personal management and trying to create a situation where everyone gets along and it's a difficult thing to do when you're a songwriter and you care about what you do because it's your job to call the shots and everybody's gotta go along with that. Jack knew that in Meg he had a partner who was going to go along with it and who wasn't going to give him any shit or tell him the way his songs should be. She was going to do exactly what he asked.

Plus, she's a beautiful girl. She's a buxom, hot chick. She's very quiet and shy and she's not interested in the spotlight. The fact of the matter is, there couldn't be a better person sitting in that spot doing what they do because she makes it possible for Jack to do what it is that he needs to do. Don't you think Jack saw all this before anyone. Even Meg? For him, it's got to be a complete picture. I don't think it's any kind of happy mistake. She's the perfect person to fill a role that needed to be filled."

Dan Miller of Blanche said that "obviously with Meg learning drums and everything, Jack really embraced her lack of experience. Meg got it, too. Meg's a huge part of developing everything. Some of it was her limitations as a drummer, but some of it is—for someone as quiet as she is—that she really listens, and when she has an opinion, it's a strong one. And Jack is smart enough to listen. She's really smart, she has great taste and great instinct for music and she really helped push all that ahead."

As Tom Potter puts it, "Meg has always been the Stripes' not-so-secret weapon. I believe the whole White Stripes persona was/is really based around Meg's natural, magical being. Jack is a talented cat who can play guitar like a mofo, write a hell of a song, turn a mean phrase, etc., and he is very original and all, but he's that way because he's a worker (and a shrewd one at that). However, I've never really thought of him as 'childlike.' He's a charming guy, but I wouldn't say he's magical.

"Meg is just natural. She's the scene's 'lil' sister' for a reason. It's been fun to watch her grow and change, while still remaining that same person. Her once 'cutely simple, not quite always there' drumming style has gotten rock solid. She's still no Max Roach, she's just Meg . . . and it's great. She's a lil' sister, a helluva drinker, and a great person to talk to. She once busted into the DCC dressing room, at a gig in the UK, brandishing those giant talking Incredible Hulk boxing gloves and proceeded to pound me with 'em. That's Meg. She rules."

Greg Siemasz said that "she's not given enough credit in the band. It's lead singer syndrome for journalists. They give you a go for your money. They have the male and the female aspect of it and you can get into what you want. Rock journalists like guys. They know guys. I think that Meg really has the ability to just do her job and she's become more comfortable with her job and people really latch onto that and people go nuts when she sings 'Cold Cold Night' 'cause it's like 'wow, Meg has a voice!' I think that probably her silence is her strongest suit. Because if you had two loudmouths in the band, it wouldn't work. There's no mystery behind that. There is mystery with Jack and his cryptic belief system or when he's talking about being a gentleman. I think that Meg shutting up and playing is the most underrated thing. Just think about how the dynamic would change if she was someone who talked back or made some sort of effort to be funny or chatty. Her persona is that she plays drums and everyone loves her. That's her job in the band. She's very understated. She is more of a mystery. And I don't know if people consciously like that or not, but it's like 'Meg doesn't say much, so when she does say something it's worth more.'

"It's funny because there's nothing forced or fake about that. She'll sit back and listen and when you ask her a direct question, she'll answer you. But until then, she's content listening. And she's funny as hell, but not many people know that except for the people that go out with her.

"Everyone's aware of Jack and Meg's dynamic onstage, but they play up to it. They realize that probably 60 percent are there to see Jack and 40 percent are there to see Meg. They had buttons that said, 'I "heart" Jack' and 'I "heart" Meg' and I sold 'em. And so many people bought the Meg button. It was like a landslide.

"Anybody that goes to a Stripes show, they're going to be shaking their head saying no because they're torn between who they wanta watch. On one side you got Jack doing a solo and rocking with his cock and then you look over at Meg and she looks hot and you just start going 'I like rock 'n' roll! And I like girls! What do I do?!'"

1-2-3-4 Take the Elevator

It's one of the great paradoxes of the video age that when bands achieve the kind of success to allow them to really indulge in the rock 'n' roll night-owl lifestyle, they become beholden to a host of dusk-till-dawn schedule responsibilities. It's a wonder any successful rock artist even finds time for sex or drugs. Luckily, the White Stripes have from day one been that rare band that leads a disciplined lifestyle and keeps its partying well in bounds.

That discipline came in handy on the morning of July third when the band, actress/pal Tracee Miller, video codirectors Dan Miller and Anthony Garth, and photography director Kevin Carrico woke up at the crack of dawn with an ambitious schedule of DIY filmmaking on the docket.

The video for "Hotel Yorba" was the White Stripes' first. They hadn't yet been commissioned by their soon-to-be UK label XL records to make a video, but they were going ahead with it anyway, figuring it would be good to have a homemade clip in the can. Besides, they were going over to the British Isles in less than a month and they wanted to be prepared. And there couldn't have been a better visual primer for the authenticity-starved Brits than the shoot-from-the-hip, sepia-toned, urban rustic "Yorba" video.

The major themes were all there: a backwoods Americana setting, a scene in a grand cathedral, subtle suggestions of domination and subservience, a longing for a simpler time, a simpler life, an escapist fantasy rooted in dusty rural nostalgia. Like Jack sings in the song: "a little place down by a lake with a dirty old road leadin' up to the house where they never gotta worry about locking the door."

For a kid growing up in a rough neighborhood in a big, burned-out city, the song was the ultimate escape. So the most delicious irony of all is that the whole thing was filmed within a couple miles of where Jack and Meg grew up with the hotel in question a mere stone's throw from Jack's front door.

By all accounts the Yorba is, in reality, something of a dump. But it is classic White Stripes romanticism that the place has taken on a lore of its own. If you visit, with visions of Candy Cane Children dancing in your head, don't expect a warm greeting from the staff. They're a bit tired of fielding phone calls about their famous endorser.

And it came together as simply as the scenes it envisions.

"Dan called and said, 'Hey what are you doing tomorrow?'" recalls Carrico. "We're gonna do this little video for Jack and Meg. And I had nothing going on. It was fun because I was able to dust off my really old Airflex. They said 'we want it kinda grungy and urban and stuff.'"

So Carrico put the camera he used for professional shoots on behalf of Chrysler back on the shelf and pulled out his trusty forty-year-old Army camera that he had relied upon when he was a film student making guerilla clips.

"I had shown Dan some old films I'd done in college where you had to do everything yourself. I thought 'let's not make this like a Chrysler spot, let's do an organic approach to the lighting,'" says Carrico.

"So every decision we made technically seemed to fit with what Dan needed. I thought, 'We don't need twelve people on the crew, I can do everything myself.' And that approach certainly fit with the band.

"The night before I thought, 'If this is going to be guerilla filmmaking, like in college when I didn't know better and wasn't spoiled by the industry, I'd better try a different approach to lighting.' I ran to the Home Depot and got a bare bulb and wired it up in my living room," says Carrico.

"I kind of at that point did everything I could to not do professional filmmaking. It looks like everything we shot was completely available light. Not once did we go for 'oh, look how pretty we could make this.'"

With the White Stripes, their thought was, I think, 'you know those rules that you hear about? Let's break them.' And I was doing the same thing, but not obnoxiously. I still wanted to use some core disciplines where every shot you knew where to look real quickly because in music videos by the time you figure out where in frame you're supposed to look, the shot's over. At least if Jack or Meg are featured," Carrico figured, "they should be the focus of the shot."

The day began inauspiciously enough. Jack and Dan had arranged to get into the Hotel Yorba, but, says Carrico, those plans quickly fell through.

"While Dan and Jack were in the lobby trying to figure out if there was any way we could get in there, we had piled into Jack's van, and it happened to be the day that NPR (National Public Radio) was reviewing *White Blood Cells*," says Carrico.

"I remember sitting in the van watching Dan and Jack go back and forth into the lobby. And meanwhile there's a guy on NPR going on and on in a really dry voice about the record. There was this really strange contrast between what we were doing and what they were saying. Dan and Jack finally gave up and got back to the van in time to hear the end of the review. And the guy ended it by calling Jack a 'whiny little creep.' So we called him that all day," chuckles Carrico.

White and Miller had done their homework, of course, and had a backup hotel lined up—the Park Hotel behind the Fox Theatre just off Woodward Avenue downtown.

"It had the greatest look," remembers Carrico. "The rooms were a little bigger so we were actually able to fit our equipment in. Had we gone into the Hotel Yorba it would have been too small photographically. The other hotel had a great old-fashioned elevator that had all these great metallic tones."

Carrico shot the room scenes in which a red-dressed and black-tressed Meg jumps up and down on the bed while a T-shirt-bedecked Jack delivers the lyrics to the camera as through they were occupied by lifelong smokers.

"The one thing we kept joking about was that it should look nicotine stained," says Carrico. "I said, 'Dan can't you imagine everything with just that nicotine film that forms on the window of a room with a smoker?' And we went not just for the color, but the reason behind the color."

It couldn't have hurt that the Stripes were unapologetic smokers.

They filmed several exterior shots outside the Yorba before moving along to Belle Isle—a once-grand park island in the middle of the Detroit River that in recent years had fallen into disuse.

"The spots we used are off the beaten path a little bit, but if you're hiking around the park you can stumble upon them. Dan had looked at the sites so when we got there we would talk about whittling it down to what exactly it was we wanted to do, just unload our equipment, and shoot."

In the video, the wedding scene takes place in the lyric's "big cathedral" and Dan Miller stood in as the priest. In an appropriate bit of art honoring life, the church they shot in was Holy Redeemer, the church in which Jack had grown up and at which his father had worked.

"The idea was that we didn't venture more than a few miles from Jack's childhood neighborhood," says Carrico. "I think that's kind of personal and that's the idea of the song about him growing up and wondering what went on in [the Hotel Yorba]."

The crew didn't have time to linger long. It was shoot and move on as they had to finish the video in a day. They had to make decisions and make 'em quick, if not for art's sake, then at least to make sure they weren't going to run the risk of getting flagged by the city for filming without a permit.

"We had a pretty ambitious schedule," remembers Carrico. "While they were thinkin' 'OK, Jack will walk through this door and do that,' I could set up the shot.

"A lot of it, like the house we shot on the front porch scenes, we just walked up and said, you mind if we get some shots? And the people said, yeah sure. The whole day really had a spontaneity to it. And I think that really shows. When you overplan something, all your enthusiasm is gone, all the spontaneity is gone, and you end up going with the lowest common denominator. If you can paint a house any color and you get nine people painting it with different colors it'll invariably turn out horribly."

We Are Going to Be Friends

Adventures with the Hotel Yorba behind them, and with a day of filming in the can, the crew still had time to film one more, even-more-intimate video that day, the quiet clip for the lovely acoustic hush and strum of "We Are Going to Be Friends" (WAGTBF). This one was entirely Carrico's doing.

And a series of happy coincidences made it a signature White Stripes moment, a visual distillation of the innocence that struggles for order over chaos with Jack's inner guitar hero and raucous rocker.

"Sometimes when you shoot, you end up with some extra film," says Carrico. "I thought, I wonder if there's any way today when we have five or ten minutes we could just roll one take. When you do a one-take video, I think the audience really has a chance to hear the song as opposed to what their eyes are telling them to do. All day I kept wondering if we'd have a chance to do this," remembers Carrico.

"We got done around 11:30 or midnight and I was going to break off what they call the 'short end' when I noticed that we had about 200 feet of film left which is roughly four to five minutes of film. I thought 'We've got enough film for one run-through of a song!' I remember talking to them saying 'I wonder if you wouldn't mind setting up a shot.' Coincidentally, they had been throwing out this old couch and it was sitting on the curb and I was looking at it thinking, wouldn't it be cool if Jack sits here, Meg sits there, and Jack just plays the song. We rolled and what you see is what we got. One take, no editing, no rehearsal. I didn't really want to talk about it and lose the spontaneity. It was just in my head all day long. It was late. Meg actually fell asleep during the take and it was Jack's idea to look over to see how she responded. She had fallen asleep and he looks over and nudges her. I hate the filmmaking to get in the way of the film. To me it's always been about story."

It's interesting that the White Stripes would make the leap to MTV darlings on the strength of video work that is almost diametrically opposed to Carrico's above-cited axiom. And MTV found a place in its buzz rotation for the upbeat Gothic clip.

In any event, the sleepy couple resting on the discarded couch weren't long for DIY land. The director with whom the Stripes would collaborate in 2002, Michel Gondry, is as far from naturalistic as possible, with his mix of postmodern formalism and homemade experimental techniques. And yet, it's testimony to the scope of the White Stripes' music that there's a place for both directors to make content-appropriate films. The Hotel Yorba video is the last bastion of the White Stripes as indie phenomenon captured for posterity.

A couple days after the shoot, the Stripes would head out on a jaunt to the West Coast, make their first appearance on national television, and then, a week later, hop the Atlantic to meet White Stripes mania when they stepped on the tiny stage of the Dirty Water Club at London's Boston Arms pub. By the time they flew back stateside, their major label career would unfold in front of them.

For his part, though, Carrico would continue to collaborate with the Whites, including taking still photographs for an ill-fated Virgin Mobile–sponsored contest where winners would enjoy a Stripes concert aboard a Virgin Airline flight.

"We did some airplane still later on," laughs Carrico, remembering his subjects' arrival in flight garb. "Jack just shows up with a funny-looking scarf and strange pair of goggles. And he says 'Do you think this will work?'"

Stripes fans, of course, didn't get to see many of those photos as Virgin Mobile and the Stripes couldn't come to an agreement about the concert's execution and, judging by White's uncharacteristically profanity-laced rant against the corporate powers that be with which he was now working (the words *greedy*, *corporate*, and *pigs* were all used).

Revenge of the Hotel Yorba

White would return a few months later to the Hotel Yorba and successfully infiltrate its walls to record a live version of "Hotel Yorba" and Loretta Lynn's "Rated X" for a UK single.

Brendan Benson tagged along on Jack's neighborhood vision quest: "They weren't allowing us into the room. I can't remember what the deal was. So after an hour, we snuck up into the room with a four-track under our arm. The whole time I was just saying 'Jack, let's just go do this someplace else. You can just say we did it at the Hotel Yorba, it's no big deal, no one will know,'" laughs Benson. "And he's like 'no man, it's gotta be here.'"

"They had some rule where it was like you left your key there. So when Jack said 'give me the key to the room' there was no proof that he had the room, so they had to wait for the manager who wasn't in till six o'clock and it was like three o'clock. Some weird thing. But Jack got into a huge fight with the woman there. It was hilarious. It got ugly." Nevertheless, the group emerged with three songs recorded live at the Yorba.

The British Are Coming

It's been a cliché in Detroit ever since the "Belleville Three" first stated hearing reports back from the Continent about their techno tracks' impact on European dancefloors: Detroit acts can't catch a break in their hometown, but once the foreign press gets wind of 'em, look out. The hype starts-a-flyin'. Thing is, this was only partly the case with the White Stripes. The band had already made their flukish bow in Australia, to adoring crowds of at least hundreds of kids. They'd made a name for themselves on the domestic touring circuit, for three years playing weekenders in the kind of dives, dumps, and watering holes that occasionally lead a band toward larger glory, but—particularly in the Midwest from which the White Stripes sprung—typically continue to host the same mid-level-popular acts over and over again until those acts either give up or relegate themselves to also-ran status and just keep playing for the sheer love of it all. The White Stripes were to be neither.

When the White Stripes first found their way over to the UK to play a handful of concerts in July of 2001, they were about to discover the mythmaking power of the British gutter press combined with the star-making power of the hipster critical mass that was London's drama-starved hipster glitterati. When they boarded the plane for Blighty from Metro, Jack and Meg certainly weren't the first Detroit rock 'n' roll band

to make their way over to the island to see if there might just be an audience out there for primal rock 'n' roll besides the weekend warriors
that so many Detroit rockers had encountered on tour playing Pat's in
the Flats and Mac's Bar.

Bantam Rooster had already mounted a couple Crypt Records–
supported jaunts through the continent. The Dirtbombs had played the
reopening soiree for Club Vera, the almost pathologically intense Dutch
garage rock haven in the middling Netherlands burg of Groningen. The
Demolition Dollrods had recovered from jet lag and rocked France and
Germany. Hell, more than a year prior, the Hentchmen had already
been over to record several tracks at Liam Watson's already-legendary,
recently moved, and reopened Toe Rag studios—the same studio
whose name had over the previous ten years become synonymous with
some of the finest English garage punk recordings from bands like Thee
Headcoats (and Thee Headcoatees), the Buff Medways, the Armitage
Shanks, Holly Golightly, and a host of other eccentric Limey-punk lu-
minaries.

In the UK the White Stripes would find their most rabid audience.

Bruce Brand, the drummer from the Billy Childish–led punk outfit
the Headcoats, remembers hearing about the Stripes only once his band
had been traveling around the States. "When the Headcoats tour in
2000 got to California, we stayed with Long Gone John," remembers
Brand. "And he gave us the first album and a few singles. And I thought
they were pretty bloody good! I'm always given records and cassettes
and stuff and nine times out of ten, it's generic garage rock. The White
Stripes were the first time in ages that I heard something special," he
enthuses.

So what was it that made the Detroit duo jump out from the faceless
"Thee" copping masses.

"There was just a bit more underlying it. For a start, there was only
two of them and there was a girl on drums, and I thought, *hmmmm . . .*"
he recalls, ending with a faux lascivious tone. "But I was impressed with
their whole thing, the whole package, the whole concept," he says,
rather vaguely, before explaining, "They did [Leadbelly's] 'St. James In-

firmary Blues' and paid proper homage to the blues rather than playing heavy metal versions as so many garage rock bands do."

Brand's bandmate, DIY punk-rock elder statesman Billy Childish had a slightly less distinct first impression of the band.

"Long Gone John had told me about them," Childish remembers. "He was always going on about this group the White Stripes and he said that they were really good and that they'd tried to record one of my songs in Australia live to disc. Like, directly onto wax. And I thought, well, that's quite something," he half-chuckles.

There was a weird commonality among the rock folks who latched on to the White Stripes early in Britain, they all claimed to not be consumers of pop media. From Brand and Childish to rock journalist Everett True (né Jerry Thackray), all claim almost total ignorance of hype and buzz. This could very well be an indicator of the Stripes spreading their gospel among the grassroots underground where records are passed band to band and hand to hand. Of course, it could also be a conscious distancing from the White Hype post–platinum sales stigma.

Childish recounts his first real live musical encounter with the White Stripes with the casual air of someone who's made a lifelong trade of not giving a rat's ass about popular culture.

"The first I ever actually heard them—I don't actually listen to music or anything like that," he claims, "I was selling some records to someone—just popping in to his place, and he was playing a track of theirs. And I thought 'Well, that's not too bad.'"

Of course, one person who makes his living paying attention to such things is legendary BBC deejay and radio personality John Peel. As the White Stripes' star was beginning to catch a glimmer in 2000 following the release of *De Stijl,* Peel, typically, had his feelers out and came across an interesting record in, of all places, Groningen, where Detroit acts like the Gories, Bantam Rooster, the Sights, and the Dirtbombs had made a major impression on the passionate rock 'n' roll evangelists that make up that city's fertile music scene.

Every year the European music industry converges on the scenic north Netherlands town for a sort of hybrid between Austin's South by

Southwest festival and a beer-sponsored battle of the bands where every important radio jock on the continent is in attendance.

In this seemingly contradictory scene, Peel remembers exactly when he first encountered the White Stripes. "There are some excellent record stores in Groningen and one of them is called Platenworm," recalls the lifelong record collector. "Going there is one of the things I look forward to doing each year. I went there in 2000 and they had the first record.

"Obviously, after doing this for so many years, I develop a nose for these things, and the cover art was interesting and you do begin to buy things on spec and hope that they might be better than the artwork looks."

Suffice it to say that Peel thought the actual music was considerably better than the debut record's striking-but-straightforward cover art. In fact, the music harkened back to the same spirit that got Peel into rock 'n' roll as a teenager in England in the '60s.

He was struck enough, in fact, to seek out all the records with which Jack White had involved himself.

"I sought out their entire back catalog and I got loads of relatively obscure singles with Jack on them, Hentchmen records and whatnot."

Upon returning to the Isles, he began spinning the Stripes with the same kind of vigor that has gained him his deserved reputation as a tastemaker breaking hundreds of worthy artists.

So the White Stripes landed in the UK with some important underground boosters, but more importantly, they had a ride from the airport.

"Our U.S. tour agent contacted me saying the White Stripes were coming to England and would my group, open for them as well as let them use our drum kit, and put them up?" says Bruce Brand, drummer of the Headcoats and, at the time, the Masonics.

Brand, being a fan of the Stripes' first few records, said sure, but then didn't hear another word about them for a couple months save for picking up on "Hotel Yorba" being played on the radio every so often. *Hmm,* thought Brand.

One day he got a phone call at the print shop where he worked wondering if he could meet the Yanks at Gatwick airport. Anticipating shite traffic, he hopped the train to Gatwick figuring there was only two of 'em, how much gear could there be?

Wrong move as it turns out. "John Baker, their tour manager, was loaded down with merchandise, and they had a couple of hard guitar cases, a snare drum, and a cymbal case!"

They struggled with the gear for a while, sent a cab bolting from the prospect of loading four people and gear, and eventually borrowed a van from Brand's work and set about getting the band settled in London.

It was July 24, 2001. As it turned out, all of the shows the Stripes had booked were sold out and before they even had time to get settled properly, they had to pay a visit to a label that wanted to sign them and scout out a location for a secret show that Jack had been toying with playing at the end of their tour.

"The first thing they did was a John Peel session, which was my first encounter of them live," says Brand. "They set up in this little studio and played to an invited audience. I listened in the control room and it sounded amazing, I thought, 'Bloody hell, they really are good.' I was in awe of them every time. Apart from the energy and the style and the music, there's a weird telepathy thing between them that I can't quite pinpoint. Like when he did the guitar stabs and Meg was looking away with her eyes closed and hitting it every time. It was like they were meant to play together."

The first John Peel Session the White Stripes did on July 25 was, indeed, a thing of beauty. All nerves and spontaneity and rightful excitement over their opportunity, Jack and Meg did as they always did in clutch situations, stepped up with a set that included cuts from *White Blood Cells*, but that also dove into their catalog with the kind of live manic energy and seat-of-the-pants high-wire medley invention and improvisation that has become a regular occurrence in their sets.

"They did the live program and after a time we went for a Thai meal," recalls Peel. "And I was talking about the fact that I'd seen Gene Vincent and Eddie Cochran before Eddie Cochran had died in a car crash. And Jack came out and sang a Gene and Eddie song! That was remarkable. You wouldn't get Coldplay to do that. There's a thing about British bands that they don't acknowledge that they're aware of music pre-Oasis."

The Stripes got on well enough with Peel that they got invited to record their next Peel session at John Peel's house in the countryside. The session was mellow and casual with the Stripes setting up basically in the Peel house study.

"It's our house," says Peel. "It's not a recording studio. It's just a room where we keep our books with a desk in the corner. It looks like a rather vulgar and overstated home stereo setup. We had P. J. Harvey out here once, but she had too much equipment and we had to sit outside. It works really well with people like the White Stripes, though."

What appealed to Peel enough that he invited the Stripes back? "It's the same thing I heard in Howlin' Wolf or Lightning Hopkins," says Peel. "There's not necessarily enormous technical expertise or the ability to even play your instrument very well. There's a looseness, but at the same time it's intense. It's one of those things that's impossible to define. You could put on a Muse or Coldplay record and it's never going to be there. It's rooted in something that's impossible to put your finger on."

After the first Peel show, the UK press picked up on the notion that he had said the Stripes were the most exciting thing he'd heard since Jimi Hendrix. That notion was promptly adopted into the Stripes lore.

"That's really haunting me. I never said that at all. I never make those kind of comparisons. It's like saying Tuesday is better than a piece of string. What I said was that they're likely to find themselves having things said about them like 'the best thing since Hendrix.' To me that's a fatuous way of saying things. As a man who did gigs with Hendrix, I have some basis for comparison. You're not comparing like with like," says Peel.

When asked about his role in spearheading awareness of the Stripes, Peel is quick to defer: "I never claim credit for those sort of things. People try to attribute credit to you. I'm like the editor of a newspaper. You don't make the news. I don't like it when people say 'if it weren't for you.'"

It wasn't long before the *Sun* was running such probing items as "Ten Things You Didn't Know about the White Stripes" and wondering aloud whether the Stripes were family or exs.

Indeed, Peel's BBC cohorts had as much to do with quickly spreading the Stripes hype. "What made the massive difference in the UK wasn't the *NME* putting them on the front," says Everett True, music journalist and editor of *Plan B* magazine.

"It was the fact that they were a subject of a documentary on the BBC Radio Four—on Noises Coming from Other Directions. That made the rest of the media sit up and say 'Jesus Christ, what is this?'

"The other thing that [the British] absolutely loved—and you can't underestimate this—was that they were 'brother and sister'— and yet people were saying, 'well, they dated' or 'well, they were married' and 'is it incest?' the mystery of that. Then there was the colors—the red and white—and the fact that they were young and attractive. And the whole thing captured people's imagination," says True.

When the White Stripes began playing the six shows they had booked, Brand's suspicion that maybe he wasn't the only Briton who knew about the Stripes was confirmed.

"Every show was sold out to capacity. There was so much press, it was unbelievable and even the tabloids were running complete nonsense from anyone who had anything to say.

"I don't think they were expecting it to be so big, so fast—it was kind of like instant stardom," says Brand, who drove the band in a rented van to all of the shows that first tour.

With the rock torches burning across the UK, the Stripes played four shows in the north (or, as Brand puts it, "Oop the North") and two down south in London.

The first show was at the legendary jazz and rock joint the 100 Club. Brand's band the Masonics was opening and "someone came up to us and said, 'You were brilliant. Better than that lot,'" he laughs.

Well I Love That Dirty Water

The Dirty Water Club is a dingy little joint, but like any decent dingy little joint, it's been adopted by a bunch of creative folks and used for their purposes. In this case, the group of people was the Medways scene that centered around Billy Childish and whatever incarnation he was playing music with at the time. The punk raconteur/musician/painter/anti-celebrity played essentially every month in the nondescript hall attached to the Boston Arms Pub in London's Tufnel Park. It's little more than a glorified bingo parlor with a stage and a bar, but it was theirs. And when the White Stripes unexpectedly became the toast of Londontown that summer, it was the site of the band's legendary secret show. Pulp's Jarvis Cocker was there with a model in tow. It was a scene, baby.

"That was the night of a thousand celebrities," chuckles Brand.

"Jack had said that he wanted to tack on a secret gig at the end of the tour," says Brand. "That Friday, Billy's band was playing the Dirty Water Club, so we went round there. And they thought it might work better with Billy opening solo. Billy's solo thing was really raw and bluesy."

"We'd been playing the Dirty Water Club every month for the last fifteen years," says Childish. "So it was very strange to play that show at that club. They must have had fans but a lot of the people were models and TV people and it was all on the wave of the phenomenon because you can't hype something that isn't going to go and it was going regardless and I think Jack was completely mystified by it.

"Jack did sort of voice much the same thing to me and we did talk about the bullshit aspect of [the hype]," says Childish.

"Opening for them was very, very easy because the audience were very polite and clapped and were well behaved. They were a lot of people who hadn't been to a dirty rock 'n' roll gig before—or at least hadn't in a long time. There were a lot of trendy people from London, very much a fashionable crowd.

"I was just sitting on my own, and I'm thinking, 'I've got to play to this?' It would seem like it would be very difficult to play to this kind of crowd when you're sitting in a bar, with a 15-watt amp. But they were all right, very polite, it was like an English cricket match.

"At the Dirty Water Club show, they did some sort of covers that we'd done in the old days—like 'Death Letter' and the like—and Jack wanted to play on one with me but he's a bit too loud, isn't he? I was doing this solo blues thing and playing through 15 watts of power through this wee little amp and he was playing through a 100-watt amp.

"And we played them differently, too. He knew all the diddly parts and I said I don't know the widdles. I had been doing it on an old national. They were very friendly and they asked me if I'd go on American television with 'em and whether I'd do some recording with them and I never heard anything about that.

"Jack's always a gentleman and very polite and courteous with me and I respond to that," says Childish.

"Someone asked me whether I'd been asked to produce them. I hadn't and I would think it would be a pretty bad move. When they were recording at Toe Rag, Jack asked me if he could do some stuff on my half-track. And people are always saying about our records that they have such a "Toe Rag" sound. But we only record a quarter of our stuff at Toe Rag. But most is home recorded. I pointed out that if they did that, they'd be lucky to have a record in the top 100 of the independent chart," says Childish.

"I've directly asked him to record some of my songs. I told him that's what he should do because that would make me some money. I thought I'd try the direct approach [laughs]. I had the same thing going on with American bands like Beck and Nirvana, people saying that they like my music, but I've never made any money, you see. So with Jack I thought it appropriate to approach it directly. I sort of like the idea of getting on someone else's back.

"When we played in Guernsey, in the Channel Islands—it had even gotten there—they asked me why we weren't famous like the White Stripes were. I told 'em because I wouldn't drink champagne with

Richard Branson! I can't do that, but that's what needs to be done in that world sometimes. Branson is sort of like a dodgy character," says Childish.

"Really, what it boils down to is that he's a polite young kid who comes to see us play that happens to be far more famous and powerful than us," chuckles the mercurial Childish.

The last time Childish saw the Whites was in passing, in London on the heels of their appearance with Jeff Beck at the Royal Albert Hall in September 2002. "He come over and said hello through the van window. In our group I'm the roadie and the driver as well. We were heading off somewhere and Jack popped in and was wigging out with some hideous old dinosaurs of rock—and he's very open minded, he thinks it's all the same thing—the kind of people that I joined a group to destroy. It just shows how daft I am, how sensible he is.

"I always get it wrong, that's my specialty," says Childish.

Danger! High Voltage!

One of the strangest chapters in the wave of press and intrigue that helped spread the word of the Stripes far and wide in 2002 had very little to actually do with the band. Prior to the chart-topping success in May 2003 of "Seven Nation Army," the most popular song either of the White Stripes had been involved with was the Electric Six's campy disco-metal romp "Danger! High Voltage." The song is ridiculous: "Fire in the disco! Fire in the Taco Bell!" shouted over the kind of just-fucking-around disco riff that garage bands tend to do when they're waiting to play their next "real" song. It has one-hit wonder written in large letters across its forehead, and damned if it didn't lead to yet another chart-busting Electric Six when their equally retarded rock tune "Gay Bar" followed "Danger!" into the charts. Unlikely, yes. And yet it was another case of Jack White being in the right place at the right time. It's also a classic case of the age-old tale told around rock 'n' roll camp-fires about the song that almost never happened.

It was the year 2000.

And it was yet another hot June day in downtown Detroit and the Wildbunch was busy making time at Ghetto Recorders, blowing through what cash they could scrape together. They needed to get a handful of songs down for Ypsilanti punk label Flying Bomb to choose from for an upcoming single. Flying Bomb was run by the husband-and-wife team of Andy and Patti Claydon and was—alongside Dave Buick's Italy Records—the only game in town if a punk band wanted to put out a local 45. The Wildbunch, once a wildly popular area sextet that had only a couple years prior flirted with a deal on Hollywood Records, were still a couple years from becoming the Electric Six. They had just returned from a self-imposed "cryogenic hibernation" and had added a few disco licks to their '80s-loving, pocket-size arena rock repertoire.

"Before we had a record deal [with XL in the UK] we were really recording for ourselves," recalls Electric Six frontman Tyler Spencer, né Dick Valentine. "We would make $500 [playing a show] at the Magic Bag and then go to Jim's and record $500 worth of material. Certainly nobody ever regarded that song as 'wow, that's going to be the song.'"

In fact, the story goes that the rhythm section of Steve Nawara (a.k.a. Disco) and Corey Martin (a.k.a. M) were just goofing around with a disco vamp. As the other band members chimed in, the song gradually took its shape from the simple groove and Spencer penned a set of his patently ridiculous (and yet surreally moving) lyrics.

"Fire in the Disco! Fire in the Taco Bell!"—it doesn't get more succinct than that.

"The reason we had Jack come in was that Joe [Frezza, a.k.a. Surge Joebot] thought the way I sang 'Fire in the Taco Bell' sounded like the way Jack would sing. So Joe said we should get Jack to do it and within half an hour he was down at Jim's."

"Hold on, let me check with my attorney," says M, covering up the telephone speaker on the other end of the line. "OK, I have the all-clear—that was for dramatic effect. The deal was, we called Jack to see if he wanted to come in and he said, 'yeah, sure, I'm just watching the *Philadelphia Experiment* so I'm not really doing anything. I'll be right over' I can see where that part might be a little embarrassing because that's a really horrible movie."

"We wanted him really for the Taco Bell line, but he didn't want to 'endorse' Taco Bell," says Spencer. "So he agreed to sing the rest of it. I remember going over the words with him and he said, 'We'll do a call and response, then.' I didn't know what call and response was and I was impressed. I was working with a pro.

"Jim [Diamond] laid his million-dollar sax solo at some point," continues Spencer. "I remember Tom Potter came by and heard the mix and said, 'What's with the sax?' Joe explained that it was there to give the song a more urban feel. Tom reflected for a moment and said, 'Yeah . . . you're right . . . it definitely sounds urban.'"

Claydon recalls going in to Ghetto the next day to record with his punk band MHz (which, incidentally, featured Von Bondies skin pounder Don Blum on drums) and seeing the scrap of paper containing the lyrics on the floor of the studio.

"Jim told us how the Wildbunch had Jack in to sing them and he refused to sing 'Fire in the Taco Bell," recalls Claydon. "The Wildbunch were on the floor in the studio laughing at how serious he took it."

In that same session, the Wildbunch also recorded "Dance Commander," "She's Guatemalan," and "Neurocameraman." The latter two would get picked by Patti Claydon as the B-sides to the single and "Danger! High Voltage" was tapped as the A-side, much to the Wildbunch's surprise.

"We heard the new stuff and really liked it. The band hated 'She's Guatemalan' and we loved it. Since we knew they would never use it on anything else we thought we'd try to put it out," recalls Claydon. "Patti picked the songs and the order. She chose 'Danger' because it was a disco song and hilarious (we always appreciate humor in music) and something people wouldn't expect from our label; and Jack was on it and it would help get the Wildbunch exposure finally (how long had they been around and we were the only label putting anything out for them?)."

"They were very surprised at Patti's selection and Joe even asked 'why "Danger," why not "Dance Commander"?' Our response was 'Dance Commander' was too good for a 500-run EP save it for the album, besides Jack on a disco song is funny. Since they didn't think anyone would ever hear it, the record came out pretty quick—no typical Wildbunch obstructions."

"We didn't care that Jack didn't want his name on the record, it would only add to the buzz, and it did," says Claydon. "We held a guess the guest singer' contest on our Web site and gave everyone who guessed correctly a free mp3 of the song."

The pseudonym White chose, of course, was John S. O'Leary.

"I don't know the origin of that name," says Spencer. "But we knew the best way to go about it was to not have the song 'featuring Jack White' to keep it under the radar. I thing the main thing is that air of mystery. It is sort of fun to make something out of nothing. It gives you something to talk about.

"It's funny because when people ask us about coming up with these names as if it took us a big weeklong brainstorming session," laughs Spencer. "But how much thought goes into naming your bass player Disco?

"We made up a story about a guy from Cleveland who won a Wildbunch contest—he won first and second prize and got to win dinner with us," says Spencer. "Except the catch was that none of us had any money and we stuck him with the bill.

"I saw Jack on MTV after the song came out on XL and he was denying that he was involved—keep in mind that this was the guy who denied he was married to Meg."

The single came out in August of 2001 and quickly sold out of its 500-copy run. It was a hit on the late-night after-party circuit in Detroit, to be certain, but then a strange thing happened. The song became an international hit, and suddenly the stagnating Wildbunch had an instant career.

Around the fall of 2001 the Wildbunch started to hear reports of the song being used by the likes of John Peel on his BBC radio program and Jarvis Cocker and Erol Alkan at their London deejay sets. At some point, *Q* magazine does a feature on Cocker and in the photo, he is holding the single among others as his favorite music of the moment.

"Somewhere in this time period," says Spencer, "we also get the licensing request from [renowned and wildly popular dance mix DJ Crew] 2 Many DJs. We have never heard of them, nor have we heard of Belgium, the country they are from. They offer us $250 to put it on their compilation. We are elated . . . that's fifty dollars a man! The thing comes out and lo and behold, it's actually a really big deal. We are yet to receive the two-hundred fifty dollars as far as I know . . .

"The 2 Many DJs thing was a real happy accident for us. We had no idea what kind of an audience we'd reach that way. Everyone thought we were a funk band from the '70s from Luxembourg. People were shocked that we were a rock band from Detroit," says Spencer.

The combined exposure for the song pricks up the ears of White's UK label XL. "He may or may not have played it for people at XL," claims Spencer faux cryptically. White tips them off that they'll be hearing from the label. The band signs with XL in April of 2002, changes its name to the Electric Six—apparently some members of Massive Attack had been using the Wildbunch the whole time in the UK and, had the Detroiters had a chance to cross the pond earlier, there no doubt would have been fisticuffs, or at least shenanigans. That summer, producer Damien Mendis—who would go end up producing the Electic Six's debut full-length—remixes the record and it's radio ready. Just as importantly, the song gets a video budget of $100,000. The band make the most of it with the irresistible (in a gawker delay way) video of Spencer duetting with a woman at least thirty years his senior "singing" in the camp-drenched high-pitched rock wail of Jack White—who by then had a buzz all his own for the White Stripes "Fell in Love with a Girl" video.

"You gotta admit that the timing couldn't have been better for us," says Spencer. "When Jack came in and sang, they were kinda on their way but they were nowhere near what they would become. For all intents and purposes he was just a local singer."

In the first week of January 2003 "Danger!" debuts at number two in the midweek UK pop charts and there is a sizable gap between the

Electric Six and the number-three single. So they know they're at least going to be number 2. The number 1 single is "Sound of the Underground" by Girls Aloud, a five-piece singing and dancing group. And it doesn't look like "Danger! High Voltage" has a shot at knocking off the industry-anointed Girls Aloud.

Spencer picks up the story: "The rock illuminati are excited that an actual rock band has a chance to dethrone a 'manufactured pop act' from the top spot. Actual campaigns and pleas are sent forth for people to buy our single to end the tyranny of 'manufactured pop shit.' But lo and behold, our little grassroots campaign of a song that features Jack White, has a $100,000 video and countless remixes by well-known producers, just didn't have enough behind it to get it done. I feel like we gave it our best shot, though. . . ."

The "mystery" had a lingering effect, though. Even for the White Stripes as they were hitting their mainstream popularity stride upon the release of *Elephant* a couple months after "DHV" hit the charts.

"When they were on their month-long promo tour for *Elephant*," recalls Spencer, "they stopped by and visited us in England and Jack said every other question was about DHV and 'was it you?' It's unbelievable, but the press love that kind of thing."

I wouldn't have had the year that I had last year if it wasn't for the White Stripes. If you look at the two bands there's not a lot in common.

It was just another example of Jack White's occasionally accidental marketing genius. Let it never be said that the man doesn't know how to keep his band's name in the headlines when the buzz starts to quiet. But more than that, it's another example of White simply staying active, making the right instinctive business decisions (even if its something seemingly so small as recording vocals on a scratch track for a local band. He saw something. After all, says Spencer, "we were never close buds and our bands had never played shows together. Then again, when I had Bell's Palsy [a neurological disorder that leaves half the patient's face temporarily paralyzed], Jack was the first person to say, 'you know, two of my brothers had that' and he felt for me."

The E6 paid tribute to White in their own way in early 2003 when

they presented him with a shiny black Dacron Electric Six baseball
jacket with "John S O'Leary" stitched across the left breast. It was a
small gesture, to be sure, but White had become an honorary band
member (and constant unseen presence at gigs).

The White Stripes vs. Diego Rivera

In November of 2001, a couple days before they would leave for their
second tour of the UK and Europe, the White Stripes held court at the
Detroit Institute of Arts.

They packed 1,500 people into the spectacular echo chamber of
the Diego Rivera Court in the downtown Detroit art museum. The
Rivera Court is one of the great Mexican muralist's masterworks, de-
picting in all its sweaty gore and disfigurement on three forty-foot-
high walls the true labors of automobile workers in the 1930s. Henry
Ford is pictured as a near-alien figure presiding over his laborers. It
is an ever-moving protest against the inhumanity of the factory work
that the city was and is built upon. The crowd for this free show
couldn't all fit in the courtyard itself and forty-something museum pa-
trons were sipping chardonnay next to beer-guzzling, leather-clad rock
veterans while inside entire families with small children mounted
atop shoulders (the ones decked out in red and white were White's
nephews and nieces), hipsters, and hundreds of the curious had piled
in to witness Jack White take the stage triumphantly waving an oversize Detroit flag high above his head.

"I still get chills thinking about it now," recalls the Detroit Institute
of Arts' marketing manager Jim Boyle. "It was just one of those truly
moving moments. It was a really special night." Indeed, for when the
band slammed into "The Big Three Killed My Baby" it was as though
through sheer force of Rivera and the Whites' conviction, the people
would rise up and smash the industrial system. At least for three minutes. Seriously. Juxtaposed against White's passionate reading of Dolly

Parton's "Jolene" in which his own voice came bounding back off the concrete environs creating a reverberation most magical and it made for damn great theater.

One of the reasons the Stripes agreed to play the show, in fact, was out of their respect for the Cass Corridor abstract artist Gordon Newton, whose collected works were on display that night alongside an exhibit of works called "Artists Take on Detroit" featuring the works of many musicians-turned-artists and vice-versa. In honor of the event, White had had his amplifiers covered with reproductions of Newton's works. It was a collusion of theater, visual art, and raw, powerful music that the Whites must have envisioned when they set out the blueprint for the band.

It helped, of course, that the Stripes were hitting a heavy buzz period as well as really finding the kind of chemistry that would make them a viable musical commodity once the mainstream got wind of them. Jack White had bloomed into a bona fide rock star and so had Meg, who, recalls EWolf, "was really hitting her drums for the first time. It was the first time I remember thinking that she had become a really good drummer."

The Art of the Deal

No matter how much autonomy they retained, the White Stripes' signing with V2 Records, under Andy Gershon, in November of 2001 demanded that the band enter the high-stakes promotional game in earnest—videos, radio singles, New York Media Elite microscopes focused minutely on the pair. The up-front money deal was one thing (and though speculation had the duo living comfortably, the Stripes' lawyer/manager Ian Montone noted that they had turned down bigger money to ink a deal that better suited their overall needs). But the details of the deal as they were whispered about the industry left little doubt that the White Stripes were not mere milkfed Midwest innocents the media loved to coo about when it talked about two ambiguously re-lated kids from Detroit who mangled the blues to their own devices and made pop music that gave the thirtysomethings something to latch onto.

In fact, the particulars ensured the whispers would be of admiration at the duo's savvy. The records the White Stripes make for V2 are li-censed through Jack White's own Third Man label (over which he re-tains complete A&R autonomy). And they reportedly retained rights to their master recordings, to boot. That they retained rights to their mas-ters meant that V2 could only count on making its investment back from retail sales from new records alone. The label couldn't count on the Stripes' songs to be included in repackaging without Jack and Meg's ex-press permission and oversight.

Catalog sales are an extremely lucrative business for record com-panies. They've already made back a percentage of their initial cost in sales. Then they can turn around and sell the songs down the line—remasters, anniversary editions, greatest hits, box sets—all of these contribute to an artist's final tally in the eyes of the label that puts out their records. All of these are based on who owns the master record-ings. In the White Stripes case, they did.

"I definitely know they set their deal up so that they retained their masters. Then you can license it to someone else," says Jonathan Daniel of Crush Media Management. "It's hard to know because given the na-ture of the business, masters could be essentially worth nothing. It's a gamble when you own your own masters, but historically master record-ings are what sustain record labels' catalog sales.

"Instead of the record company repackaging it as 'Louis Arm-strong's Greatest Hits' seventeen times, you can do it yourself and re-tain control."

Further adding to the "strike while the iron's hot" atmosphere was the widely held belief that the Stripes' deal reportedly had them locked down for only two records (usually five record deals are bandied about by execs inking young bands). So to say that V2 had little time to get the Stripes up and running would be an understatement. In fact, the

Stripes' indie success and grassroots fan base was one of the things that no doubt made them so attractive to V2 in the first place. The label didn't have to invest a lot of time and effort building the band up. Jack and Meg had already done that all by themselves thankyouverymuch for the previous four years by virtue of their incessant and strategic/judicious touring during 2000 and 2001. They had positioned themselves perfectly for a takeover, er, to take the major-label leap.

"The White Stripes did exactly what they needed to do in terms of growing their audience," says Detroit deejay Willy Wilson. "They looked around and saw where their records were doing well and they focused their energies there."

It's a simple formula. Find out where your audience is, go play for them. Make nice with the college deejays and eventually the alternative jocks on mainstream radio will take notice. Play at radio station events. Shake hands. Repeat.

"When they realized that they had an audience in Boston, they went and played there," says Wilson matter-of-factly. The same happened with San Francisco. Then L.A. And on and on. It's not cynical, it's practical. The White Stripes, in fact, were doing the exact opposite of selling out. They were taking their music on their terms to fans who appreciated it and giving them their money's worth. Instead of driving the four-hour trip to Columbus because it was closer, the Stripes were going eight hours to Madison or twelve to Boston.

"They knew how hard they had to work to make it happen," says Wilson, "and they were willing to do that. And they deserve a lot of credit for that."

If nothing else is ever written about the White Stripes during the period in which they started to gain some momentum, it has to be said that they took a disciplined approach to doing the work necessary to reach a wider audience.

They were dancing around the edge of the mainstream in early 2001 when the indie labels started poking at their door, making offers that the White Stripes knew would do them precious little good in the long run. If you were a band after either long-term success or immediate capitalization on accumulated brand equity, you had to act fast. And the White Stripes did.

"Indies don't go to radio. They don't spend money marketing records. Indies start out as being very good word-of-mouth people and after a while they kind of coast on the word of mouth that they've set up for the band," says Daniel. "But majors aren't so good at word of mouth, they have the money to promote and market a record, to get videos made and played, to help an artist sell more than fifty thousand copies of a record."

The White Stripes seemed to sense intuitively that they weren't in need of another indie that may or may not be able to deliver them to a new audience (let alone get the record reliably into anything but mom 'n' pop record stores).

"Essentially, nobody was trying to sign the Stripes because they had a good demo. They wanted to sign them because they were selling three thousand records a week and had a ton of press in the UK. And they had ton of leverage with the labels," says Daniel.

"And it works for the labels, too. What the majors are good at is getting records in the stores and getting them on radio. Which V2 did for the Stripes. It wasn't necessary for them to be on a major for them to continue to sell enough records to make a living. The White Stripes did a really good job setting themselves up so they weren't dependent upon signing a record deal," says Daniel. "Period."

There is very little in the White Stripes world that isn't based on careful thought. The difference, of course, is that Jack and Meg do their thinking long before they act, deliberate though they are. Again and again, as you talk to people close to them, it becomes clear that Jack White is a disciplined practitioner of what self-help gurus call "visualization" and "self-actualization"—imagining all possible futures, imagining the optimum outcome, and further imagining as many outcomes as possible to account for chance and chaos. From his early days of posting motivational messages above his bed to his endless series of quasi-apprenticeships learning various facets of the creative life at the feet of folks like Brian Muldoon, Dan Miller, Jeff Meier, Dan Kroha, Brendan

Benson, John Szymanski, Johnny Walker, and anyone else with whom he chose to collaborate or who, in later years, he had contact with—iconoclasts such as Beck, Wayne Coyne, Loretta Lynn, and others. He knew what he wanted and he knew how to find out how to get it. As one Detroit scenester noted early in Jack's career: "Man, that dude's a sponge."

And that's not a cynical statement as both Jack and Meg seem to operate from an honest-to-goodness sense of curiosity and sense of discovery. (One is tempted to say "childlike" but one will refrain. Indeed, an armchair shrink would have him trying to better himself from the low expectations and anonymity of a depressed Detroit upbringing.)

So the Whites seemed to sense or know that the time was right to see how far they could take this little band. Or, as Jack presciently reflected in the lyrics to their song "Little Room" the "bigger room," which meant that, in their words, "you might have to think of how you got started sitting in your little room."

During the period of larger-indie-label courtship, the White Stripes had played the part of the blushing maiden who knows her good looks and youthful charm will keep the boys coming back with ever more extravagant gifts (and all the while, in the back of her head, she really wants a nice wedding ring, though she's embarrassed to admit it). They turned away Sub Pop and rumor in the girls' room had them rejecting suitors as varied as Chicago rawk label Touch and Go and Mississippi-based major-label vanity blues imprint Fat Possum. They were coy but demanding by all accounts, teasing Sub Pop with a "Singles Club" recording only to turn them down for a kiss goodnight when asked to sign with the label.

The Seattle boys weren't exactly what the Stripes were looking for, and no doubt, the fact that Sub Pop was tied up with the Go!—the only band that had ever asked Jack White to leave—had something to do with it.

But now, with their record sales peaking at around three thousand a month in America on the indie Sympathy for the Record Industry, by dint of that label's distribution and production constraints, the Stripes had a decision to make.

When an indie label experiences a flush of success, it can be both the best and worst of all possible worlds. For example, Bloodshot's Rob Miller explains the growing pains his label experienced in the wake of the success of Ryan Adams' album *Heartbreaker:* "It's scary, because all of a sudden you're getting a level of attention that you never had before. You're immediately suspicious of those people. Where will you be when this runs its course? On a nuts and bolts matter: we were much smaller than we are now, and our initial outlay for that record was five thousand copies. And we have to pay our manufacturer on thirty-day terms and we don't get paid by our distributor for ninety days. So it was an enormous freak show cashflow problem. It was like 'Jesus what if ninety thousand of these CDs come back?!' I'm going to have enough CDs to build an entire wing on the YMCA where I'll be sleeping. I was absolutely paralyzed with fear, and superstitious and twitchy."

It's night and day from the normal operations of an indie:

"When you're dealing with smaller records on a smaller label, you have a feeling that you know your audience and they get it. This was the first time I felt like I didn't know who these people were. Usually our return cards say people heard about our record from a cool record store and these are coming back saying [they heard about *Heartbreaker*] 'From Elton John'—are they just responding to Elton John's endorsement?! You lose sight of who the people you're dealing with are and the kind of industry sleazebags that come with them and you kind of look at them and go, eew, nice ponytail. Great, I'm really happy you helped break Billy Squier fifteen years ago."

There might have been some of this kind of thing going on on Long Gone John's end. In the end, judging by what White has said, it was a simple matter of the records not being in stores where the growing number of fans could find them.

"When the White Stripes started to happen, John tried to do the 'I'm gonna stick behind this band' thing," remembers the Detroit Cobras' Restrepo.

"The death of a small label is success. You're used to five to ten thousand, but now the demand to have thirty thousand by next week—

it doesn't happen. And you don't have time to do anything else. Long Gone wasn't set up to do any of that. He was a music collector. He has six hundred-plus releases!

"Jack, bless his heart he tried to do the right thing. Sympathy is a company that put out our first record and the same with Jack, it was hard to hate Long Gone," says Restrepo.

"Jack did the right thing, man. He said, if you did my last record, I'm going to go with you. Most of us, until someone does you wrong, you stick with them. Jack had a booking agent he got from Tom Potter, and he stuck with him. Jack moved up, the booking agent moved up. Everybody's going in the right way. He stuck with him when he didn't have to. When it came to Sympathy, he did what most of us would have thought was the right thing to do. On the Sympathy site, there was a thing from Long Gone bragging about how Jack had stayed with them. And it's like yeah, he did," said Restrepo, before noting that the White Stripes' growing popularity wasn't reflected in their monetary compensation. "It's like no good deed goes unpunished, marvels Restrepo.

Compound that with goofy stuff like the story that's told of when the White Stripes went on *David Letterman* and the show reportedly asked for fifty CDs and Long Gone told 'em to go buy them and you start to get the picture that the happy Sympathy family was a bit more dysfunctional than it let on.

They had finally reached the point where a band must choose between DIY for Life or Major Label Leap for Life (as the kids on the playground might have called it). The White Stripes simply didn't need another indie label. They had Sympathy and they had autonomy and they had built their own grassroots momentum. They needed a major if they were going to do anything differently than they already had.

So when Jack White was making earnest pronouncements about the virtues of an indie label out one side of his mouth while talking on someone else's cell phone about the cost/benefit analysis of signing to a major, he was being both a wily propagandist and totally honest at the same time. Surely his heart didn't want to leave the indie world behind, but his ambition for his band wasn't about to slow down because some dude in a bungalow in Long Beach refused to play by the rules of the major leagues. This is, after all, the artist who reportedly had one A&R representative following the band for two weeks on an East Coast tour, essentially begging for a meeting at every show only to get the cold shoulder. That A&R guy's boss gave him one job: Sign the White Stripes. Not so much.

It's only appropriate that the White Stripes would choose to take that leap from self-managed to pro-managed with Ian Montone, a lawyer who among people in the music industry has been described as both someone who drives a really hard bargain and someone who's a really nice guy. Sounds like a match made in rock 'n' roll heaven (or at least in the pews of the church of rock).

By the time the mainstream media descended upon Detroit at the invitation of the White Stripes (as measured by the fact that both *Time* magazine and the BBC had by then written stories and produced documentaries about the band) Jack and Meg had reluctantly hired a publicist (reluctantly not because it wasn't a career necessity, but because it was an expense that the frugal pair hadn't previously had to account for in their budget).

That was at the tail-end of *De Stijl*'s lifespan and just as *White Blood Cells* was rushed onto the shelves by Sympathy (and, not unimportantly, just around the time that Jack and Meg were feeling the pinch of having quit their day jobs). Sympathy for the Record Industry—with the famously reclusive Long Gone John as its only real employee—certainly wasn't prepared to deal with the hype that built around *White Blood Cells*. And despite his protestations in publications from the *Washington Post* to the *Orange County Weekly*, Long Gone had likely never experienced anything like the demands the Stripes were placing on his distribution system (which, let's remember, had the White Stripes making an emergency stop at their distributor Mordam's San Francisco warehouse to pick up enough records to last through a West Coast swing on an early tour).

So when, by conservative estimates, *White Blood Cells* was selling two thousand copies a week, it was straining both Long Gone and Jack

White for very different reasons. Something had to give and it wasn't going to be the strong-willed (stubborn if you will) White who had already glimpsed the bigger label fish available for the frying on the band's trips to the UK and in the wake of their signing with UK macro-indie XL Records.

But not everything smelled rosy to some of the people that had helped the Stripes out along the way. Case in point; Ypsilanti punk label Flying Bomb records. In 1998, the Stripes recorded the song "Candy Cane Children" for inclusion on the label's annual "Surprise X-Mas" 45, which over the course of its previous two years had included cuts from White Stripes peers the Wildbunch, Bantam Rooster, the Dirtys, the Dirtbombs, and several others. Over the course of four years, Flying Bomb had accumulated quite a few one-of-a-kind Christmas cuts from now-well-known Detroit bands, and proprietors Andy and Patti Claydon decided to compile all the songs and release them on a CD in time to hit shelves by Christmas 2002.

Flying Bomb had the tracks compiled and remastered for CD, they created new artwork and began the promotional process. They placed their order with their manufacturer and were anxiously awaiting what would likely be the most popular record they'd released to date. And it was all going fine, except for one slight detail. On the eve of the record's release, XL Records, the UK label home of compilation participants the White Stripes and the Electric Six (né Wildbunch), sent a cease-and-desist letter, thus forcing the Claydons to reissue the compilation minus the offending tracks and at great expense to the otherwise amicable and productive creative relationship that had existed between the Claydons and the White Stripes since the first Italy 45.

It's a cautionary tale, to be sure, about the perils of stardom as it relates to maintaining the community ties that helped get you there in the first place. Certainly one can't fault the Stripes for ambition. But doing right by those that raised you up is important, too. And the incident is seemingly in contradiction to the class and conscientiousness with which the Stripes seem to handle themselves in other circumstances. But, once they realized they were on to something after their first successful tours for the debut album and the growing interest that snow-balled seemingly with their every move, the Stripes seized opportunities that made sense to them.

Major-label survivor Brendan Benson chalks their success in that arena up to Jack's solid combination of instinct and intellect plus an ability to roll with the punches and see clearly even when events are transpiring more rapidly than most could handle: "Never once have I ever witnessed him put on the brakes at any point. I just witnessed him making great decisions. I remember thinking there were things that I thought I'd never do. He was passing on a big Coke thing or Pepsi thing and I remember thinking 'Oh my god, dude! Cash in now. Cash in your chips!,'" he laughs.

"You're losing out! God was I wrong. But it could have made him that flash in the pan. It could have fucked him in the end, really.

"And not just that, also, decisions about labels and switching labels. When he wanted off Sympathy I thought 'man, you got a good thing going, don't rock the boat.' He's got—it's not luck—it's savvy, whatever that means, about the business. He's got an instinct about it. He's just full of convictions, and luckily, what he believes has appeal to so many people. Like the red and white colors. I told him, 'Dude, lose the red and white thing. It belittles what you do. And he was really offended when I told him that, too. He didn't get it, he just said 'You don't understand, that is the White Stripes.' And of course, now he's selling a ton of merchandise. It's so easy for people to grasp. He's full of conceits. In that sense he's the most conceited person I know, in the true sense of the word and it's only served to propel him to stardom. That's what people want—some kind of mystique and mystery, something more than the music. It helps. And to think that to perpetuate that myth, that rock 'n' roll myth that makes him bigger than life."

Which brings us back to V2.

"There was a rumor that they signed to V2 after Richard Branson himself saw the band in action. That may be completely untrue. But it also may be completely true. "Either way it makes a good story," says Daniel.

So whether it was Virgin Records' billionaire maverick founder that rubberstamped the signing or the due diligence of Marjorie down in accounting or the massively enthusiastic boosterism of XL's A&R guy Leo Silverman or the well-timed machinations of Chloe Walsh, the Stripes' publicist at Girlie Action, or the backroom efforts of Montone or all of the preceding, the Stripes at last got someone to take the bait and ended up with what can only be called a sweet deal.

Hook, line, and sinker. The music industry doesn't talk about specifics to the public because the details are, generally, obscenely boring to the public. But when a band like the White Stripes signs, people in the industry start using phrases like "If they kept the rights to their masters," and "if, indeed, they only signed on for two records," and "if they signed for a good-size advance to boot" it's clear that some creative dealmaking is going on and that the band in question might just be the gull that warns of the sea change in the music industry from a period of label- and management-manufactured phenomena being pressed into action at the service of the bottom line to a period where A&R men and women actually earn their pay by seeking out bands that are legitimately connecting with an audience. (Of course, there's also the "vanity label" factor of the Stripes deal, Jack White's Third Man label, which thus far had only released an inorganically-hypd and thus underwhelming LP by his buddies in Whirlwind Heat).

That may or may not have been the case with the White Stripes. But what is certain—as mentioned before—is that V2 had no time to waste in capitalizing on the brand equity that Jack and Meg had worked so hard to establish. Jack and Meg, with their level of curiosity and experience, were no doubt aware that the only way to reach a new audience outside the magazine-reading and trend-chasing demographic was twofold: MTV and radio. And the primary reason for signing to V2 was to make sure that both happened and happened with the kind of financial and human resources that would assure they were top-shelf and occurred with the kind of control and oversight that Jack and Meg had come to expect during their do-it-yourself years.

The first part of the plan was, of course, MTV. Even as it lost its credibility as a music source in the '90s and early '00s, the old girl still is a tastemaker. Thanks to V2's patronage, the White Stripes were able to connect with a kindred spirit in French-born director Michel Gondry, who had already helmed buzz clips of Björk when V2 approached him to direct what would become, in essence, the White Stripes' star-making calling card—the gorgeously freaked-out animated Lego video for the Stripes' heartbreak-pop-punk anthem "Fell in Love with a Girl," the newly minted single off the recently rereleased-by-V2 *White Blood Cells*. Things were coming up roses.

Bonjour Michel

One of the first orders of business when the band signed to V2 was to get a video made for the proposed first single, "Fell in Love with a Girl." They found, in director Michel Gondry, not just a music video director, but a kindred creative spirit, someone looking for a new way out of old forms just as eagerly and studiously as the White Stripes were. The videos he had done for Björk were captivating, "Human Behavior" found the Icelandic singer in a lush, surreal forested otherworld that seemed to obey the logic of both dreams and tales from the Brothers Grimm. Gondry was bored with music videos and even more tired of cliché. In fact, he wasn't terribly fond of guitar music, either. So it's ironic that the band with which he's become so strongly associated is also a band wor-shipped by Guitar Center employees as standard-bearers of dinosaur rock. It speaks to the Stripes' malleability, classic pop sensibility, and gen-eral oddness that they can cross over between gear heads and Björk.

"I receive a lot of tapes and tracks and CDs and stuff," says Gondry. "And I was on holiday when I played them and I said to myself 'I have to do that song.'" The song was "Fell in Love with a Girl."

"I thought they were something really punk," says Gondry. "He had something like an urgency, like something primitive between like an early Cure and I can't think of what else, so I really wanted to do it."

It was those strange qualities of the song that made it stand above cliché, which Gondry was desperately trying to avoid.

Not to get too hung up on the Cure, but the idea for the FILWAG video was inspired by the gloomy post-punks' video for "Close to Me." "The one with the fridge, a lamp, and I think an ironing board," recalls Gondry. "I thought it was something really basic. And I thought the Lego blocks would do it justice and I always wanted to run away from the cliché of rock. Some of the bands that came in the same way as the White Stripes have too much of the past stuck to their butt.

"When I played their record and learned a little more about their history and their connection with the past, I understood them more. When I first heard it I thought they were just kids putting music out."

So it was that Gondry found himself meeting Jack and Meg and presenting them with a model of Jack's head he had made out of Legos.

"They really liked it."

What he liked about their music, too, was that "Meg was playing in a very simple way that gives enormous room for Jack to become enormous. It gives him a lot of space to exist."

The video—for which Gondry filmed the band running around the streets of London and in front of a blue screen—took fifteen animators six weeks to create. The clip found its way onto MTV moving rapidly from buzz bin to regular rotation. It was striking, the kind of video that keeps MTV at least in the periphery of hipsters' radar. It was also a nice visual analogue to the old-school Pong-style video game Stripe-out that had been developed by a fan around the same time and circulated around the web by rabid Stripeheads. Soon the Stripes found themselves walking through Central Park with Kurt Loder, playing free concerts in the Big Apple sponsored by Nissan (first song on the setlist? "The Big Three Killed My Baby," of course).

By the end of 2002, the White Stripes would be performing on the MTV Movie Awards with a three-tiered peppermint colored stage and a passel of lucky volunteers frugging to their hearts delight as the Stripes managed to what they do best—cram three songs into the time allotted for one. In this case, sure they rocked "Fell in Love with a Girl," but they segued into "Screwdriver," too, and "Death Letter," too. Welcome to the world of the White Stripes. The White Stripes took home two "moonmen" at that year's MTV Video Music Awards, too, most notably the "Breakthrough Artist" award. The FILWAG Lego concept has been subsequently copied for auto ads from both Volvo and Honda. Gondry was irrevocably tied to the Stripes and he seems genuinely appreciative of the opportunity.

"It's good luck for a director to catch a band on the way up and the bad luck is to catch an artist that needs fresh blood. You have to work with what you are given. Sometimes you get them going up or some-times you get them going down. I have been just lucky enough to have the main people that trained me doing music videos be the White Stripes and Björk."

In fact, Gondry talked to Björk about his work with the Stripes and she gave her approval ("but not in a 'big mama' kind of way," notes Gondry). "We both hate electric guitars and we want to destroy the gi-ant guitar, which is ridiculous as a symbol of musical freedom. But Björk said 'the White Stripes—they are the only band that has something sin-cere in his voice.' And she never gets it wrong.

"The White Stripes are more like art," Gondry says. "A comparison to like the Velvet Underground is not quite right, but they don't explain too much and they stick to their concept."

Since the FILWAG video, Gondry has created two more videos for the Stripes, for the *White Blood Cells* track "Dead Leaves and the Dirty Ground" and the second single from *Elephant*, "The Hardest Button to Button." By the time he made the video for "Dead Leaves" he said, the White Stripes had become much more camera savvy.

"Jack and Meg worked out totally how they wanted to be on camera. During the day, we had to shoot the same sequence not only three times, but many, many times, because we had to do some crosscutting," he recalls. "And during different takes, I noticed that Jack was changing his expression slightly and when we mixed the three performances, he had different attitudes. He seemed to know just what it was going to look like in the end. I say he became smarter than me about it. He became really smart about the camera."

Of course, even a hotshot director like Gondry has to take a backseat when Jim Jarmusch wants to direct a video for a band. And the indie auteur surely took his seat behind the camera for the hypnotic, futurist-looking video for "Seven Nation Army" shortly after the Whites were through collaborating on Jarmusch's *Coffee and Cigarettes* movie. Besides, at the time, Gondry was wrapped up in making the film *Eternal Sunshine of the Spotless Mind.*

Gondry was back in the saddle for the second single off *Elephant,* "The Hardest Button to Button." He created an elaborate stop-motion trip through New York City in which Jack and Meg never stop rocking even as an alarming number of drumsets and amps reproduce and disappear, weaving down staircases and into and out of subway cars and various locations around the city.

"Those were very long days," recalls Gondry. "It was a mathematical concept and the only way to make it work was to do the shoot in order and we had only two days. At each location we started with thirty-two drumkits and amplifiers and as we pulled them away by quad we'd construct the next setup. I had to pick locations that were next to each other. It was a very big puzzle and was very exciting to do. I worked very hard to make it happen."

And the icing on the cake was a cameo from Beck, a friend of the Stripes, who happened to be in town and who asked to be in the video. "I said yes, since he was being discreet so it's a proper cameo and he's doing something that reflects the lyrics, so it's OK," explains Gondry.

Since the White Stripes crossed over to the pop charts, one of the more notable achievements of the band, and Jack in particular, has been its ability to not just remain connected to the DIY rock 'n' roll community that birthed them, but to also introduce the bands from that world to the Stripes' new fans. White Stripes fan forums are chock-full of discussion about not just Detroit bands who have directly benefited from the Stripes profile, but also of bands like the Yeah Yeah Yeahs, the Kills, the Strokes, and other bands that hew to the punk ideal and attempt to forge their own new take on guitar rock from the old, tried tropes. Ofttimes, the association is direct, as in the case of the Yeah Yeah Yeahs, whom the White Stripes toured with just prior to the YYYs' major-label debut. When the Stripes made pals with the Strokes in 2002, both band names were often uttered in the same breath as standard-bearers of the "rock revival" even though their sounds and approach are as wildly disparate as can be. Part of that can be chalked up to the home-and-home sets the Stripes and the Strokes performed in each others' cities in August of 2002. The Stripes hosted the Strokes at shows at Clutch Cargo's—a converted church in the northern suburb of Pontiac—and at Chene Park, an outdoor pavilion on the banks of the Detroit River. The Strokes returned the favor with shows at the Roseland Ballroom and Radio City Music Hall—and at the latter show, Jack White joined the Strokes onstage to perform the encore of "New York City Cops." So if the bond was bandied about by a music press looking for an angle, the bands found enough common ground to rock out together, thus formally cementing their roles in each others' histories. The difference between the shows, points out Ko Shih (who attended each of the four), was that "in New York, you had to be on an exclusive guest list to go to the after-parties. But in Detroit, all you had to do was know where Dave Buick lived."

Building a Better Pachyderm (or I'm Bound to Pachyderm)

It's typically White Stripe-ian that even in the midst of the hypestorm that was making the White Stripes a bona fide British (and ever growing stateside) media phenomenon and sweeping *White Blood Cells* into the UK charts that the duo—well, at least Jack—was already thinking about the next record. By November, *White Blood Cells* had been out for five months—two months as a Sympathy for the Record Industry release and three with the additional attendant major label rush and push of XL records in the UK and V2 records worldwide—and Jack and Meg had been touring pretty much nonstop the whole time. In fact, as Jack stated, the riff that would eventually become "Seven Nation Army" had been born in a soundcheck whilst on that year's unending tour. And in point of fact, several of the songs that would appear on *Elephant* as had been the case with *White Blood Cells* had been works in progress for a couple years.

In any event, when 2001 rolled around, the White Stripes found themselves in the hot klieg lights of the UK media. And they had at least a few songs they were itching to lay down. They had already made records at Ghetto Recorders in Detroit when they were taking their first tentative steps as a band, at home when Jack had built up the confidence necessary to cast himself as both producer and artist, and in Memphis, a musical home-away-from home, a city with which they shared not just a musical heritage, but a fraternal bond with the city's DIY garage and blues-rock scene. It only made sense, then—in the complementary/apparently-contradictory White Stripes sense of the phrase—to make the next record in a place that was both the epicenter of their current popularity, at a studio in which some of the records that had inspired them had been made. Liam Watson's north London Toe Rag studio was the recording home of the so-called Medway scene as epitomized by the bands in which British iconoclast Billy Childish had participated. From the early recordings of bands like Thee Mighty Caesars and the Headcoats to such Childish-led outfits as the girl-vocal bands the Delmonas and Thee Headcoatees (which was the first outlet for garage-rawk godmother Holly Golightly), Watson's analog-only Toe Rag had become the go-to joint for getting that stripped-down sound.

"I met Liam at a party in 1990 when the Headcoats played with the Cramps. This guy had a big party for the Cramps after the show and it was a small scene so we all ended up there," recalls Bruce Brand, drummer for such Childish-led projects as the Milkshakes and the Headcoats, as well as the Masonics in which Toe Rag–head Watson played guitar. "I was chatting with him and he was talking about how he wanted to start a tube recording studio and he was asking stuff about how I tuned my drums and all this malarkey. And we talked for a while and he said 'I'll give you a shout once it's up and running.' And I thought 'well, that's the last I'll hear of that,'" recalls Brand with alight chuckle.

"And then about six months later, he did!

"So Toe Rag started about ten years ago in a crummy warehouse in Shoreditch," he says. The first place was a catch-as-catch-can affair that Watson shared with a handful of other artists who couldn't find a home anywhere else.

"He had this funny little mixing desk with radar knobs on it," says Brand. "And a friend of his had a sewing machine on the one side of the room and was making costumes. Another friend was making film props in another area."

In other words, a true DIY affair befitting a community of artists drawn to the punk-rock ethic of elevating what you're given to an art-form.

"Still, there was," says Brand, "a good deal of vintage gear in-house, and Watson certainly knew what he wanted to hear. That space lasted a few years until the crew were kicked out by a landlord looking to cash in on the real estate's growing property value. But by then, Watson had established himself as a producer with a decent ear and an undying enthusiasm for old-school rock 'n' roll as was practiced in the pre-digital era. Eventually, Watson found a new space and set about creating a new Toe Rag and collecting as much old gear as he could lay his hands on.

"When he found a warehouse," recalls Brand, "he purpose-built the studio. When we started, we were dead against modern recording technology," says Brand. It seemed an ideal match for the aesthetic ideals the White Stripes had established for themselves.

But the fateful aesthetic love connection might not have happened had it not been for the corrupting influence of their host and tourmate Bruce Brand.

"I talked them into forsaking some interview with a magazine to come and see Toe Rag studios," remembers Brand. "They protested of course. They said, 'we have to do an interview' but they really didn't want to do it, I think. It was for *Radar*. So I said, great, come 'round to Toe Rag. They had heard about the studio because the Hentchmen had recorded there. And I said, well, come and meet Liam and check out the studio. That's when they decided to record there."

Of course, that's not exactly how Watson remembers it. "I'd recorded a couple of guys from the Hentchmen who'd come over," recalls Watson of the time the Hentchmen visited his studio. They were visiting the UK as the backing band for '60s punk torchbearers the Lyres' frontman Jeff Monoman. "And they then went back to Detroit raving about the studio to Jack.

"Jack came in to have a look at he studio and he said, 'Oh, yeah we'd like to come and record here.'" But that was it. It was apparently that cryptic.

They spent half the day in Toe Rag, and half the day unsuccessfully searching for a someplace that sold pizza. "But we just ended up in some greasy spoon," sighs Brand.

"And then I didn't really hear much from him until the next tour of the UK a couple months later," recalls Watson.

Then, in November of 2001, he heard from the dynamic duo again. "I got a call out of the blue and it was Jack asking was I free? And he'd like to come over to try a song," says Watson.

Brand picks up the story: "They came back in November and booked a day in Toe Rag and Jack was staying at a hotel across the street from where I lived. So one night, I received a knock on my door and it was Jack and he said, 'I've written a song for me and Holly to sing. And he played it for me. I suppose I was looking at him aghast because after he was done he was like, 'You don't like it!'"

Not the case, insists Brand, he was just surprised by the earnestness of the young Yank. And so it was that the White Stripes made their first recording at Toe Rag.

"And Jack and Meg came over with Holly Golightly," says Watson. "And we recorded that song and it ended up on the record. There were a couple other things that we did that evening that didn't come out so good, so we scrapped it."

"I lent Jack my old beaten-up acoustic guitar that wouldn't stay in tune," recalls Brand, laughing. "And they all sat around in three chairs, sharing one microphone, recording and singing and playing acoustic guitar."

"There was a bit of piano overdub and percussion and then it was done," says Watson. "I got me marching orders to make the tea, which I dutifully did," boats Brand of the now-famous on-record request from Golighty: "How about a cup of tea then, Bruce, all roight?"

Little did Watson know that this wasn't just some casual pop-in. "When they were leaving, Jack said, 'Well, this has been a kind of test to see what it would be like working here. I really liked it.' I'd had no idea it was an audition or anything, but it worked out well."

And so Watson continued with his daily recording life until the next time the Stripes returned to the British Isles.

They came back in April of 2002, anxious to get the songs out of their heads that wouldn't see the light of day for nearly a full year. The White Stripes would take twice the time they normally took to record a record—they booked two full weeks in Toe Rag—and they still came out with a major-label record that cost a fraction of the usual deck.

"I think that they'd pretty much rehearsed for *Elephant*, they'd been done and arranged them before he came into the studio. And it was a case of going through them until we got good takes. I think he was finishing the lyrics off in the evening in the hotel," says Watson.

For what it's worth, the well-spread notion that none of the equipment at Toe Rag was made after 1962 is "a load of crap," according to Watson. It's a romantic notion, to be sure, and one that makes for good incidental copy, but it's not true. Watson scavenged most of the equipment when studios were switching over their equipment to digital in the '80s.

"Most of the stuff was from the '80s. The main mixing desk was from '81. That was something that I think that got out on a press release that said the studio was pre-1962. The press just gets a hold of it and it gets repeated and it becomes fact," says Watson.

"It's an analog studio and I haven't gone down the computer route because I find computers boring to use. Not that there's anything wrong with them sonically. I don't have a need to use them. The reason why I've stuck with doing it this way is that if I'm at home listening to records for pleasure, a lot of them are records done in a certain way. You don't need a great deal of stuff to make great records. So I haven't done much besides get a mixing desk or a tape machine. It doesn't bother me when something is from or whether it's digital or analog. As long as it sounds the same when I play it back, I'm not bothered."

From the get-go, Watson was making suggestions that would end up influencing the absolutely massive sound of *Elephant*.

"When we initially started recording, Jack wasn't too sure about the guitar sounds. I'd been thinking about this way of recording a guitar amp I'd wanted to try. So I said, tell you what, I'll do a bit of re-mike-ing that might be more up your street and then off we go. What I was trying to do was just get a really full up-front aggressive sound. He uses a Fender Twin Reverb and I had a Selma Zodiac so we had him split going through both amps, so I thought the combination of the two amps was really good. 'Cause I'm not too keen on Fender amps to be honest."

Because Watson mixes everything live to 8-track, the band had a lot of downtime waiting for him to choreograph his fader moves based on the songs. Watson explains: "There are four mikes involved in the recording of the basic guitar. Five mikes involved in recording the drums. If you were in a 24-track studio you'd have all those mikes going to the machine. But I had to do all that mixing right then and there. I was doing so many fader moves as they were playing. By the time I was ready and they came to the control room, they'd only be hearing the two tracks.

"I'd say, can you go through the chorus on a loop for me. They weren't actually aware of this because I didn't tell them. So when it came time to roll tape, I'd know exactly what I was doing.

"Sometimes they'd get to the end of it I'd say hey guys one more time because I didn't get a move. Sometimes you get musicians because they get bored, but they don't know what was going on in here. People don't realize that 8-track isn't eight microphones," explains Watson.

Which is a long way of saying that by the time it gets to your house, it really only comes out of two speakers, so the precondensing does a good job of getting closer to a powerful sound once you're camped out in front of your hi-fi. And that kind of power and volume was a priority for the Stripes during the *Elephant* recording.

"The thing is, with me," says Watson, "I'm not really that concerned. I think records that were done a long time ago are a lot bigger sounding than records that come out now. The Beatles were done on four-track and they're fucking mental. People would not be able to do that now. For one they're chicken. They don't know how to do it, technically. And three, they can't play it. It can work, but it doesn't happen often."

There were a couple happy accidents, too. "That bit during 'There's No Home for You Here' where it goes to feedback was something that came about by accident through muting something and I thought 'hey that sounds cool' and Jack was very good when something like that happened by accident, he was very good at listening to it. He wasn't being chicken!

"I'm not really into the myth of rock that a lot of people are into. What I like to call the bullshit side of it. It's more like 'OK, meet at the studio at noon, all right. Work an eight-hour day.' Luckily enough, it worked for them, too," says Watson.

"There's a whole new generation of people coming up in their teens and twenties who don't know where the White Stripes are coming from and that's good for them," says Watson.

"I must admit I was quite surprised at how big *Elephant* has been, I knew it would be a big record and I knew it was going to be the biggest record I'd ever done. That it was going to go in the charts for me was a novelty.

"Then it went to number one and then it stayed there. I knew it was a good record when we'd finished it and I was happy and satisfied. They'd done three records before. I thought if this record doesn't do well, who's going to get the blame, it's going to be me isn't it? But I got a Grammy for it," he chuckles.

The Whites tapped Brand to handle the design of the album under the name "Arthole." Brand had already done the cover art for the UK version of "Dead Leaves and the Dirty Ground," so the Stripes knew who they were working with.

Jack sent over Pat Pantano's photographs and gave Brand an example of an old blues CD he wanted it to look like—Walter Buddy Boy Hawkins, 1927–29 Complete Recordings.

"The layout is exactly the same as the back of the *Elephant* sleeve," says Brand. "I just basically slavishly copied it. If you want something done properly you might as well be pedantic," laughs Brand.

"Basically what happened was Jack asked me how the covers were going and I said all right. He said it sounds like you could use a new computer. Let's go and get you one. And this was over dinner. And then a couple days later there was a knock on the door with a new G4. I've never had that happen before, someone say they were going to do something and then following through in such a fashion."

After finishing up, White sent over the proofs to Brand. This was during the time when there was a controversial scatological art exhibit at the Brooklyn Museum.

"He said the paper the proofs were on was made with elephant dung. I thought, well, that's quite topical."

Later that summer, of course, the White Stripes played their UK rock 'n' roll coronation sets at the English summer festivals, most notably their festival-stealing set at Reading. These shows would cement their reputation in the hearts and minds of that year's crop of impressionable teens who spent their festival days camped out on the fest grounds creating their own Woodstock memories. The Stripes' blistering performance made sure that red and white were etched on the fans' brains.

The Elephant Drops

When the folks at V2 finally acquiesced to their own meticulously constructed buzz and released *Elephant* two weeks early, it was a foregone conclusion, of course, that the record would spike on the Billboard charts. It was like one of those friction cars that kids play with that you rev up by rubbing on the ground faster and faster. There comes a point where you can't get the poor little motor revving any higher and you gotta let the thing go. Between the specially packaged, vinyl-only review copies that were seeded out to influential press that winter (including bloggers and gushy uberfans, as well as the usual glossy rag tastemakers and industry-friendly hacks), the pre-release buzz about Jack's romantic, musical, and thespian enterprising on the set of the film *Cold Mountain,* poor Meg's broken wrist—the result of a slip and fall while on holiday in New York City, and the general late-winter/early-spring dearth of other news and cultural events of note, the media was just chomping at the damn bit for this thing.

Don't forget, *Elephant* was the first time the U.S. music press had a chance to make their own mark on the perception of the White Stripes after being caught, relatively speaking, asleep at the switch during the *White Blood Cells* wave that allowed the White Stripes to carry the summer 2001 and 2002 zeitgeist in the UK. (Of course, American media can't be entirely blamed for wanting/needing to focus its efforts on post–September 11 coverage in both tone and quantity.) The Stripes, though, had ruled the 2002 Reading festival roost with their coronation ceremony/mainstage set on August 23.

The White Stripes' publicity firm, NYC outfit Girlie Action did what they do best: build buzz for indie bands by working the indie media crowd's inherent tension between desperately needing approval and desperately needing to be the first kid on the block with the new toy. Major label resources like V2 behind the production and distribution, worldwide licensing, and all of the other icky affairs make bands millionaires, yet lose them that valued "cred." Up until this point, the White Stripes were nothing without their independent credibility. That's their whole story! Their very visible and voluble ruminations in the press about doing exactly what they want how they want to do it had only really gotten them a slap on the wrist from the indie-rock kangaroo court that had to pass judgment on them when they jumped from sentimental antiestablishment favorite Sympathy for the Record Industry.

And now that all signs appeared that the White Stripes were willingly diving headfirst into the mainstream, it was even more important that the launch of *Elephant* feel like a bona fide grassroots phenomenon.

Under the direction of Stripes publicist Chloe Walsh, it was and it did. Despite the easy bet of a top 20 chart entry, the music press, folks dwelling on the fringe of the industry, other indie bands eagerly watching the Stripes' every move and taking copious notes and, yes, even the fans were rooting—and rooting hard—for the toothsome duo. When the record debuted at number six on the Billboard album charts it was both a surreal and vindicating moment for the rock underground. One of their own had made it. But even then, none of the bands that were at the head of the "garage rock" class of 2002—the Strokes and the Yeah Yeah Yeahs chief among the most mentioned—have been able to capture the attention of the mainstream like the Stripes.

Chalk it up to a good choice of single. If the White Stripes' crucial second single to radio, "Seven Nation Army," (the first being "Fell in Love with a Girl") had stiffed, the band would never have moved 1.5 million records. Instead, as their pals the Strokes found out when the debut single for their sophomore effort "Room on Fire" arrived DOA at radio, the Stripes would have leveled off at a half million and there would be no reason this book would be read outside the city of Detroit. But "Seven Nation Army" was a great radio single. A big, fascinating chunk of classic rock that snuck the idea of a bass into the White Stripes mix just when they needed it most. The song is huge, simple, paranoid, brash, cocky, and—importantly—easy for kids who are taking guitar lessons to play competently after only a couple sessions.

The White Stripes bowed their new material live at the Masonic Temple in Detroit's Cass Corridor—just a few blocks from the Gold Dollar—an ornate '20s-era labyrinth of theaters, gathering halls, ceremonial rooms, secret passageways, and architectural wonders. The first night's show was in the tiny Scottish Rites Cathedral. The Stripes blasted through opener "Black Math," thus signaling the gathered hipsters, scenesters, English and U.S. journalists, and other gathered faithful that the ceremony had begun. The show was a tightwire act with the

Stripes working without a net. After a particularly hazardous run at a medley that included an absolute gutting of Son House's "Death Letter," as well as "Motherless Child" with Jack writhing around on the floor, barely rescuing the song's continuity as the energy raced in and out of him. Jack eventually made his way over to Meg's drum space, stage right, and wound his way behind the kit and found space on Meg's drum stool to sit so they were like two kids forced to ride together in the car for too long. And then he nuzzled into her, planted a quick peck on her cheek, and the song was done with a crash.

Jack sported the trademark Freddie Mercury–tight harlequin red-and-black pants and was working some nervous new dance moves that seemed inspired equally by James Brown and electroshock.

Before excusing themselves, Jack noted that they had to go, but that the crowd could come over for breakfast if they wanted to. There were a lot of old friends and family in attendance. It was sweet.

Backstage, where usually industry hacks and weasels would gather, the White Stripes were hosting a family reunion. Kids ran circles around the tree-trunk-like figure of mildly amused Stripes' bodyguard B. J. Jack, decked out in sharp pin-stripe suit and fedora, chatted amiably with his sisters, brothers, and cousins. Dan and Tracee Miller of opening band Blanche, still in their Sunday-best stage finery, brought some tunes. It was about as far from "rock" cliché as one can get while still in the presence of a bona fide rock star. And it pretty much sums up the White Stripes experience.

The following night, of course, was their public coronation in the sold-out four-thousand-seat Masonic Temple Theater, a Byzantine hall with echoing acoustics and a sprawling layout designed for Broadway-size events. That night, the Stripes were just that—huge, theatrical, with Jack entering the scene crawling on his hands and knees, an apple in his teeth, to the edge of the stage before spitting it into the audience that promptly frothed at the spectacle and clawed for a piece of the fruit. A film crew captured the whole thing. There was no longer much that was small about the White Stripes.

"I do not think there is any thrill that can go through the human heart like that felt by the inventor as he sees some creation of the brain unfolding to success. . . . Such emotions make a man forget food, sleep, friends, love, everything."—Nikola Tesla, inventor.

TV Party

Once the White Stripes broke the ice on their national television debut on the *Late Late Show* (a.k.a. the *Craig Kilborn Show*), all bets were off. As with most things White Stripes (record sales, merchandise sales, celebrity fans), Kilborn's show was just the beginning of an ever-escalating high profile. Especially after the Stripes caught the MTV buzz, they started working their word-of-mouth mojo in front of a de-cidedly mass media audience.

When they appeared on *Saturday Night Live* on October 19, 2002, with Arizona senator John McCain (who coincidentally is the father of Stripes' V2 publicist Sid McCain), the Stripes made sure they stuck to their no-compromise rule. When the show pushed them to play their breakthrough single "Fell in Love with a Girl," the band balked. They said they'd play "Dead Leaves and the Dirty Ground," but not "Fell in Love with a Girl," a song they never really liked playing live. Instead, they proposed their second song be "We Are Going to Be Friends." The producers weren't crazy about the idea. But Jack and Meg stuck to their guns.

"*SNL* wanted them to play "Fell in Love with a Girl" because that had been their big song," remembers Dan Miller, who went to the show with the band along with Dave Swanson, Ko Shih, and Jack's mom, Ter-essa, among others.

"And [the Stripes] wanted to do "Dead Leaves," 'cause that was their current single. And Jack had talked about seeing George Harrison on *SNL* just sitting down and doing "Here Comes the Sun." And he said 'God, it'd be cool to do something like that where Meg was sitting on the ground with a tambourine and I was playing an acoustic guitar.'

"The *SNL* folks, said, Well, if you do "We Are Going to Be Friends,"
it'll get cut." But it was such a great performance that they couldn't cut it.

Indeed, the instant-best-of-moment performance had at least Shih
weeping. "I cried the whole song," she says without apology.

"But it was down to the last second whether *SNL* was going to let
them do it," says Shih.

But it wasn't all weeping and drama. "I watched it from backstage,"
recalls Shih. "We were there for like three hours before the show and
during taping and we kept having all these running bets, like 'I bet you
won't do this or that.' Dave Swanson from Whirlwind Heat went running out onto the soundstage—the cameras were all running, but you
never know if anyone is paying attention—and he went out and did his
Mick Jagger impersonation for like fifteen seconds or something. He got
a good fifty dollars out of that!"

"I do remember Jack's mom meeting [*Jackass* star] Johnny Knoxville
who had asked to come back and talk to Jack and Meg and she said to
him 'I don't like your show.' And he said, 'You know, I don't know if my
mom likes my show, either.' I think everyone at *SNL* ended up liking her
more than all of us. We had to go to Columbus the next day because the
Stripes were playing with the Stones. And Jack's mom was like what's
wrong with you guys?! Let's go out."

Strangely, in this context we the Stripes' growing success a few show
opening for the Rolling Stones seemed far forths course.

Conan O'Brien, who was a big fan of the band, wandered down with
some of his staff to watch rehearsals that day, too.

He introduced himself to Jack. "Jack said, 'Hey, we went bowling together once before,'" recalls the *Conan O'Brien Show*'s music producer
Jim Pitt.

O'Brien had made a promotional visit to Detroit in 2000 and White
and O'Brien had hung out at the Garden Bowl and spent a little time
knocking around town. Conan told the Stripes, "Anything you wanna
do. Any time. Just let us know." When they renewed their acquaintance
at *SNL*.

So when it came time for *Elephant* to come out, the Stripes' publicist Walsh called Pitt and said that Jack was proposing that they do a full week on Conan, and what did they think? "We thought to ourselves, wow a week, that's a lot of one band," says Pitt.

"But then it took thirty seconds for everyone to realize that this wouldn't work for many acts, but for them, the timing was just perfect," says Pitt. "It benefited both of us. Having them for four nights was great, but what made it better for us was that they really didn't do any other shows after that—they didn't do *SNL*, Letterman, or Leno. They didn't really do anything until the Grammys. So, it really was an exclusive thing.

"It's funny, when we were deciding, in those thirty seconds, I knew what the future would hold for me from a booking perspective. I knew that I'd start to get a ton of phone calls for bands who wanted to do multiple nights, which has certainly been the case. But no situations have come up since the White Stripes where there was such anticipation for the album and the right mix of things happening all at once to make it seem like the right thing to do. And, really, Conan was the first one to say that the White Stripes one really seems like a good idea."

O'Brien and the Stripes were a natural match. The host "got" the Stripes and they "got" him, meaning that they shared a sense of humor. And, according to Siemasz, who traveled to the show with the Stripes, "Everything that they could possibly do right, they did. Conan really involved the White Stripes in the show," he recalls. "Not only were they playing the show all week, Conan and his staff totally latched onto the whole sensibility of the White Stripes."

Which, in turn, made Jack more receptive to ideas for comedy bits featuring him and Meg. "Anybody who saw the show had to crap their pants as Meg explained how the economy fluctuates by stating 'sometimes it's up and sometimes it's down' on the set of NBC News. It was pretty amazing seeing how the writing staff just threw out ideas and rewrote them and put forth a great effort for White Stripes jokes."

The White Stripes also brought B.J. to the set. Here was a 300-plus-pound black man who was a L.A. cop, jammed with Rick James, was an amateur wrestling champ, and got attacked by a shark. He became the unsung hero of the week of shows with his impeccable timing and silent demeanor. Jack's mom even got in on the act, making self-effacing jokes about Jack and Meg's relationship.

"You could tell that the White Stripes were starting to embrace what they had become—or at least how they are perceived by the general public," says Siemasz. "They knew that Conan was sincerely on their side. It wouldn't have happened on any other show."

"I just think about the enduring qualities of a musician, it's so hard for musicians today to keep a little bit of mystery about them," says Miller.

"You know with the Internet and everything being under a microscope. I think there are people that have tried to stay mysterious like Will Oldham, and that's fine, but with Jack and Meg both, they are really funny people with a great sense of humor and that's why it was so great that they did that on Conan.

"I can see somebody saying 'Oh, we're not going to degrade ourselves by getting involved with the skit thing.' But it was so fun. The music's good enough where something like that's not going to take away anything. It just showed so much of how serious they are about their music, but they don't get overly serious about themselves. Sometimes people who are really successful have a difficult time enjoying themselves and that's the case with Jack and Meg sometimes, but they do take time to do things and enjoy things."

Cruel Summer

The year 2003 was a cruel summer for Jack White. On the night of his birthday, coming home from a celebration, he was driving in Detroit with Renee Zellwegger in the passenger seat when apparently another driver reportedly made an improper turn and White couldn't avoid a crash. He busted his middle finger in five places, effectively ending the

White Stripes highly anticipated summer tour season. As he noted on the band's Web site in a message to the "Candy Cane Children," he escaped the much mythologized "year of rock 'n' roll death" with only a warning. At first, he had an overly ambitious prognosis that had him playing guitar a little bit too soon and White eventually ended up getting a couple pins stuck in the finger. In typical White Stripes fashion, Jack (an avowed fan of medical TV programs) posted footage of his surgery on whitestripes.com. The film showed a grinning White in hospital garb with "Seven Nation Army" playing in the background plus actual footage of his surgery.

"He may have thought it was funny," figures Dave Buick. "I think that he genuinely felt bad about having to cancel shows, and people cancel shows for reasons all the time, and I think he wanted to really give an actual real explanation. And then he probably wanted to do it as a rare present to the fans. On another level, he probably thought it was like something Letterman would do, you know? I don't think it was just to get them more press or anything—though it did get them more press [laughs]—I think his intentions were genuine and true."

Indeed, thanks to the notoriety of White's passenger in the crash, the White Stripes were never far from the headlines, even when the band was idling. Zellwegger made her first appearance in Detroit gossip columns that spring, shopping at a riverfront grocery store with her no-name boyfriend. Eventually the *Free Press*—ever the tongue-waggling fishwrap—figured out that her boyfriend was a rock star and that the rock star actually lived there. But the great thing about Detroit is that besides the office workers sipping their coffee and bored housewives, nobody really seems to give a shit about celebrity culture. So Zellwegger was allowed to roam free in the music dives and hair salons of Detroit.

Buick sums up the general attitude nicely: "I guess if there's gonna be headlines, it should be about the quality of their music and their shows," he says. "It shouldn't be about the fact that Jack's going out with Renee. So big fucking deal. Renee's a cool lady and a nice lady and it's doesn't seem that weird that Jack's going out with her or that she's going out with him because the same goes for Jack. He's a nice guy and a cool guy. Or that Meg's on a yacht somewhere in Australia with Beck or something. So big deal. They're both nice people.

"Shouldn't the headlines, at least in Detroit, be 'Local Musician Makes Good'?" he laughs.

Jack was pent up at home when his inner businessman knew damn well that he should be out there on the road touring the hell out of the White Stripes already-platinum-selling record.

The weird thing was, even as the Stripes were sidelined, other rock bands were doing the promotional work for them. The Stripes had become a cause célèbre among the major-label rock set. Little brother and sister to both the well-fed stadium rock crowd like Audioslave and inspiration to the hipster elite like Beck and the Flaming Lips. Both in the United States and abroad, "Seven Nation Army" had been a hit on alternative radio for a couple of months in the late spring. And by the time White's finger had been operated on, bands like Audioslave were tackling the cut in rock sheds across the United States during their Lollapalooza sets. The Flaming Lips had tweaked the song to their own psychedelic needs and performed it at UK summer festivals that the White Stripes had wowed the previous year. And Wayne Coyne had penned a cut called "Thank You Jack White for the Plastic Jesus That You Gave Me," a song about, you guessed it, a plastic Jesus that Jack White had given him. The duo were very much present in their absence, with magazines like the *NME* and fansites like whitestripes.net mounting "get well soon" e-cards for Jack. And a sixteen-year-old British soul singer named Joss Stone had turned in a slow-burn, funky neo-soul take on the Stripes' "Fell in Love with a Girl," as "Fell in Love with a Boy." It was pretty horrible, but it was a hit and the Stripes even took to playing their own song in a slower, funkier style in the wake of Stone's track.

The White Stripes eventually made their way back onto the road, making up for lost time by packing in as many shows as possible. That old Catholic work ethic was flaring up again with a vengeance. Jack and Meg rung out the new year by packing the family into the van and taking a trip to Chicago. Except in this case, the van was a stylish tour bus and the family was the members of Blanche and their spouses. They were headed for the Aragon Ballroom where the Stripes would co-headline a show with their newfound pals, the Flaming Lips. Blanche opened the show.

The last the general public would see of the White Stripes until the summer festival season commenced once again was their white-hot performance on the Grammy Awards show on CBS television February 8. The duo provided a stark counterpoint to the bloated music industry parade when, stern-faced and with nothing but their instruments to decorate them, launched into their hit single "Seven Nation Army," only to segue into a blazing version of Son House's "Death Letter" during which they were illuminated so brightly that the television screen simply went white and unsuspecting Grammy watchers used to meted out pabulum of Celine Dion or waiting for Beyoncé's elaborate set piece got an earful of raw guitar squall and primal drum bashery. It was, simply, great television. If Jack seemed a wee bit nervous as the song kicked off, by the end, he was in full guitar flail. And it was trademark White Stripes—get an opportunity, seize it, make it your own. The White Stripes left L.A.'s Staples Center that night with a Grammy in hand for the clunkily titled Best Alternative Music Album. Pity they didn't get to give an acceptance speech. Though the Whites hobnobbed with MC5 guitarist Wayne Kramer and other admirers backstage, they were noticably absent from the red carpet tomfoolery, an encounter with a roving fashion critic apparently one step over the line from humor into insulting.

Later that month, Jack announced that the tour for *Elephant* was over and that the band was headed back home to work on new material for the next record. Cut to May 2004. In the three months since they announced the end of touring for *Elephant*, their downtime consisted of the Grammy performance; Jack going to court and pleading guilty to misdemeanor assault and battery; partaking in the promotion of Loretta Lynn's *Van Lear Rose* which he produced and on which he and members of the Greenhornes and Blanche played (and including prominent appearances on national television in which he wore neither red nor white clothing); and celebrating the opening of Jim Jarmusch's *Coffee and Cigarettes* film (in which the duo enact a scene over smokes and java in which they, typically, discuss a Tesla coil.).

The most exciting moment of their downtime—and likely one of the most exciting moments of White's life—if that's not too bold a projection—came on March 18, 2004. White's idol, Bob Dylan, was making a three-night stand at Detroit's State Theatre as part of his "Never Ending Tour." On the third night of the stand, the band had worked through an energetic set and had already played one encore. But the crowd wasn't letting them go anywhere. It was clear that the band was going to come back out, but also waiting in the wings was a familiar silhouette, a tall shadow with neck-length stringy hair strapping on a guitar. Jack White emerged from the wings and joined Dylan (who was playing organ on this tour) on lead guitar and sharing vocals with Dylan on the White Stripes' "Ball and Biscuit."

"Jack he played the solo in the song," remembers longtime WDET-FM Detroit deejay Martin Bandyke, who also happens to be Jack's cousin.

"I've seen Dylan somewhere in the teens and it's rare for any outside guest to join him. I've never seen anyone out of the immediate Dylan circle on stage. The crowd was nuts. The vast majority of the people knew Jack White and reacted very, very strongly. And Dylan, who is not one to tip his hat emotionally, to smile, or anything, you can go through a whole concert and he won't change his expression, he was looking at Jack and grinning broadly. There was almost the sense of 'here's the young man carrying it on, not one, but even two generations younger, and he's a guy who understands roots music and is going to carry it on in a respectful way.'"

After they finished the song, Bob Dylan and Jack White walked off the stage with their hands around each others' shoulder. "It was really an emotional experience," says Bandyke. "Just to see Bob kind of glowing as he's watching Jack do the song."

If all of that action sounds like downtime, you're a masochist.

"For some reason," notes Dan Miller, "Jack's always had this thing where it's almost like he's gonna die tomorrow. Especially for the music he likes doing, it's important to just work toward the goal. You can always perfect everything, but it takes all the soul out of it."

White's breakneck work schedule certainly doesn't leave a lot of time for such childish pursuits as playing pinball or bowling or goofing around with your buddy's band let alone writing music that, presumably, will make its debut at the slate of summer festivals at which your "little band" is scheduled to headline. So it was that the White Stripes took a break from all media. Catch their breath. Figure out what happens next. If they've taught us anything over the course of their career, it's that only *they* know for sure what happens next. The rest of us have to wait to be surprised yet again.

Paycheck Postscript

On a slushy February Wednesday night—a few days before the White Stripes took home their multiple Grammy Awards and rubbed elbows with the music illuminati—Paycheck's owner Johnny Paycheck is holding court with a half-dozen lifers. He's speaking in alternating tongues of Polish and Bar English. When I tell him I'm writing a book about the White Stripes, he flies off the handle.

"I'll tell you what about that fuckeeng band! That night, I was standing out on the corner. There were a ton of people in here and all of a sudden"—he throws his hands in the air—"whoosh!"

He points at the sprinklers over the bar's ten-foot ceilings. I'm not sure exactly what he's talking about.

"They didn't tell me nothing! And all of a sudden those fucking fireworks go off and I tell you what, they hit the ceiling tiles and they're dripping from heat. If those fucking fireworks had hit the wood, whooo, I don't know what. I feel sorry for all those people who died, but that fucking band didn't tell me anything. Not a word. If they tell me, I have a couple fire extinguishers ready, I tell the soundman, you know? But nothing."

It is possible, after all, that at least in some parts of the world, Great White are still as recognizable a rock commodity as the White Stripes.

Discography

SONGS:
You're Pretty Good Looking
Hello Operator
Little Bird
Apple Blossom
I'm Bound to Pack It Up
Death Letter
Sister, Do You Know My Name?
Truth Doesn't Make a Noise
A Boy's Best Friend
Let's Build a Home
Jumble, Jumble
Why Can't You Be Nicer to Me?
Your Southern Can Is Mine

White Blood Cells LP/CD Sympathy For The Record Industry 2001
White Blood Cells LP/CD XL Recordings, 2001
White Blood Cells CD V2 Recordings, 2002
White Blood Cells LP V2 Recordings, 2003

SONGS:
Dead Leaves and the Dirty Ground
Hotel Yorba
I'm Finding It Harder to Be a Gentleman
Fell in Love with a Girl
Expecting
Little Room
The Union Forever
The Same Boy You've Always Known
We're Going to Be Friends
Offend in Every Way
I Think I Smell a Rat
Aluminum
I Can't Wait
Now Mary

I Can Learn
This Protector

Elephant LP/CD XL Recordings, 2003
Elephant LP/CD V2 Records, 2003

SONGS:
Seven Nation Army
Black Math
There's No Home for You Here
I Just Don't Know What to Do with Myself
Cold, Cold Night
I Want to Be with the Boy
You've Got Her in Your Pocket
Ball and Biscuit
The Hardest Button to Button
Little Acorns
Hypnotize
The Air Near My Fingers
Girl, You Have No Faith in Medicine
It's True That We Love One Another

SINGLES:
Let's Shake Hands 7" Italy Records, 1997 (re-pressed, 2002)
Let's Shake Hands w/Look Me Over Closely

Lafayette Blues 7" Italy Records, 1998 (re-pressed 2001)
Lafayette Blues w/Sugar Never Tasted So Good

The Big Three Killed My Baby 7" Sympathy for the Record Industry 1999
The Big Three Killed My Baby w/Red Bowling Ball Ruth

Hello Operator 7" Sympathy for the Record Industry, 2000
Hello Operator w/Jolene

Lord, Send Me an Angel 7" Sympathy for the Record Industry, 2000
Lord, Send Me an Angel w/You're Pretty Good Looking (Trendy American Remix)

Party of Special Things to Do 7" SubPop, 2001
Party of Special Things to Do w/China Pig/Ashtray Heart

Hotel Yorba 7"/CDS XL Recordings UK/Third Man Recordings USA, 2001
Hotel Yorba Hotel Yorba (live at the Hotel Yorba) w/Rated X (live at the Hotel Yorba) & Hotel Yorba Video

Fell in Love with a Girl 7" XL Recordings UK/Third Man Recordings USA, 2002
Fell in Love with a Girl w/I Just Don't Know What to Do with Myself

Fell in Love with a Girl CDEP XL Recordings UK/Third Man Recordings USA, 2002
Fell in Love with a Girl w/Let's Shake Hands and Lafayette Blues

Fell in Love with a Girl #2 CDEP XL Recordings UK/Third Man Recordings USA, 2002
Fell in Love with a Girl w/Love Sick (live at The Forum), I Just Don't Know What to Do with Myself and Fell in Love with a Girl Video

White Blood Cells Bonus Tracks PROMO CDEP V2 Records, 2002
Jolene w/Hand Springs, Hotel Yorba (live) & Love Sick (live)

Dead Leaves and the Dirty Ground 7" XL Recordings UK/Third Man Recordings USA, 2002
Dead Leaves and the Dirty Ground w/Suzy Lee (Radio 1 Session) and Stop Breaking Down (Radio 1 Session)

Dead Leaves and the Dirty Ground CDS V2/Third Man Records, 2002 promo CD
Dead Leaves and the Dirty Ground

We're Going to Be Friends CDS V2/Third Man Records, 2002 promo CD
We're Going to Be Friends

Red Death at 6:14 7" Mojo Magazine, 2002 Mojo Magazine giveaway
Red Death at 6:14

Merry Christmas From . . . The White Stripes 7" V2 Records, 2002
Candy Cane Children w/The Reading of the Story of the Magi and The
   Singing of Silent Night

Merry Christmas From . . . The White Stripes 7" XL Recordings, 2002
Candy Cane Children w/Story of the Magi and The Singing of Silent Night

Seven Nation Army 7" XL Recordings, 2003 Promo
Seven Nation Army w/ Cold Cold Night

7 Nation Army 7"/CD Single XL Recordings, 2003
7 Nation Army w/Good to Me and Black Jack Davey (CD Only)

I Just Don't Know What to Do with Myself 7"/CD Single XL Recordings, 2003
I Just Don't Know What to Do with Myself w/Who's to Say . . . and I'm
   Finding it Harder to be a Gentleman (Peel Session, CD Only)

The Hardest Button to Button 7"/CD Single XL Recordings, 2003
The Hardest Button to Button w/St. Ides of March and The Hardest Button to
   Button Video (CD Only)

There's No Home for You Here 7" XL Recordings, 2004
There's No Home for You Here w/I Fought Piranhas and Let's Build a Home
   (Live At Electric Lady Studios)

split 7" with The Dirtbombs Extra Ball Records, 2000 with Multiball
   Magazine #19
Handsprings

various (Compilations, etc.)
X-Mas Surprise Package Volume 2 7" Flying Bomb Records, 1998
Candy Cane Children

Hot Pinball Rock Vol. 1 CD Extra Ball Records, 2000
Handsprings

Sympathetic Sounds of Detroit LP/CD Sympathy for the Record Industry,
   2001
Compilation produced and recorded by Jack White
Red Death at 6:14

It Takes Two, Baby 7" Sympathy for the Record Industry, 2001
Fell in Love with a Girl